a river never sleeps

by *RODERICK L. HAIG-BROWN*

Illustrated by Louis Darling

Introduction by Steve Raymond

D1601478

LYONS & BURFORD, PUBLISHERS

DOUGLAS & McINTYRE
Vancouver/Toronto

PRINTED AND BOUND IN THE UNITED STATES OF AMERICA

DOUGLAS & MCINTYRE LTD.
1615 Venables Street
Vancouver, British Columbia V5L 2H1.
10 9 8 7 6 5 4 3 2 1

Library of Congress Cataloging in Publication Data

Haig-Brown, Roderick Langmere, 1908-1976.
    A river never sleeps.

    (A Nick Lyons book)
    1. Fishing. 2. Fishing—British Columbia. 3. Steel-
head fishing. I. Title.
SH441.H15   1983   799.1'2'09711   83-3552
ISBN 1-55821-116-0

Canadian Cataloguing in Publication Data

Haig-Brown, Roderick L., 1908-1976.
    A river never sleeps.

    ISBN 0-88894-724-0
    1. Fishing. 2. Fishing–British Columbia.
I. Title.
SH441.H34   1991   799.1'2'09711   091-091164-9

CONTENTS

Contents

INTRODUCTION TO THE 1991 EDITION

You are about to read one of the greatest books about fishing ever written. If you are among the many who have read it before and are about to return to it again, as many do, often, then there is no need for me to tell you that; but if you are about to read it for the first time—well, then I can say only that I envy you the pleasure you have in store.

A River Never Sleeps was one of the first books I read about fishing. I was young then and it was a good time in my life to come upon such a book because it did much to shape my views on the philosophy and ethics and wonderment of angling; but there is never really a bad time to read a book such as this, and over the years I have returned to it again and again, finding each time in its pages a quiet serenity of thought and profound observation that is as much a balm for anxious days as is the act of going fishing itself.

I grew up among a generation of anglers for whom Roderick Haig-Brown was a giant, and his angling and literary exploits were well known to us all. But now we are witnessing the rise of a new generation of eager young anglers, more numerous than ever, who are just beginning to explore for themselves the mysteries and delights of angling literature, and perhaps for their benefit it is appropriate to try to place Haig-Brown in proper perspective, both as an angler and a writer.

Roderick Langmere Haig-Brown was born in Sussex, England, in 1908. His formal education was at Charterhouse School, of which his grandfather had for many years been headmaster, but he enjoyed a scarcely less formal education in the arts of fly fishing and wing shooting on the chalkstreams and downs of southern England. At the age of seventeen he traveled to the Pacific Northwest to work as a scaler and survey crew member in logging camps, first in Washington State and later on Vancouver Island, and quickly applied his fishing knowledge to the new species and new waters he found there. In 1929 he returned to England briefly to begin his writing career, but the lure of the Pacific Northwest summoned him back to

Vancouver Island where he eventually settled. By the time he reached full manhood he had thus been exposed to the varied angling cultures and opportunities of two continents, from the well-ordered deliberate fishing tempo of the English chalkstreams to the wild, disordered salmon and steelhead rivers of the Northwest. It was an enviable background for an angler or a writer, and much of that diversity of rich experience is on display in these pages.

Haig-Brown's first published work was a children's book, *Silver*, the life story of an Atlantic salmon, which appeared in 1931, and although it was the work of a young writer still in search of his own literary style, it nevertheless revealed talent of great promise. It was followed a year later by *Pool and Rapid*, now long out of print and the least favorite work of its author, and then in 1939 by the beautiful two-volume Derrydale Press edition of *The Western Angler*. The latter was a landmark work for its time, the most definitive treatise on Northwest angling yet published, and though its prose was smooth and seamless it was notable more for its depth of research and for what it said then for how it said it. But it marked the beginning of Haig-Brown's stature as an angling writer.

In 1941 came *Return to the River*, a fictional work based on the life cycle of the Columbia River Chinook salmon, and while not an exceptional book in terms of plotting or characterization, it revealed Haig-Brown's remarkable prose style in full literary stride for the first time, with some of the finest, richest lyrical writing ever lavished on any subject. Having set such a standard for himself, Haig-Brown maintained it with unwavering consistency in the book you have before you, first published in 1946, and later in his famous "season" series, *Fisherman's Winter, Fisherman's Spring, Fisherman's Summer, and Fisherman's Fall*, which are to angling literature as Vivaldi's *Four Seasons* are to classical music, and in his other fishing books, *A Primer of Fly Fishing, The Salmon, The Master and His Fish*, and *Bright Waters, Bright Fish*, the latter both published after his death in 1976.

So to say that this is the best of all Haig-Brown's fishing books is to say a great deal, for almost any other angling writer would give his eye teeth to have any one of Haig-Brown's titles to his credit. In fact, many other writers have tried to emulate his style, most of them badly and none of them as well, and if, as the saying goes, imitation is the sincerest form of flattery, then the frequency with which other writers have tried to imitate Haig-Brown is a good measure of the regard they hold for his work.

Haig-Brown's great talent was in his sensitivity to all things going on around him and his ability to describe those things in the most vivid terms. Yet there was more to his writing than just natural talent; there was also discipline and method, just as there was in his fishing, and he seems to have understood—either consciously or intuitively—the close relationship between writing and music; his writing flows always with the natural rhythm and precision of a Bach fugue or a Beethoven symphony. He also was a student of the technique of alliteration, which he used wisely and well, and he never was content to describe a thing with only a single adjective or adverb when two or more would do the job more vividly. So he portrays his forebears not just as men, but as "small, spare, wiry men"; a trout not just as a trout but as "a clean, pale, round-bodied fish"; storm clouds not just as clouds but as "heavy, dull, vicious and blue," and a mountain sunset not just as colorful but as "flushed and glowing with the reflection of clean, bright flame." His great genius was in stringing together ordinary words in such a way as to evoke extraordinary images that became vibrant and alive in the eye of the beholder.

Thus his technique, which is on display in all his later books, though never any better than in this one. What makes this one unique is that Haig-Brown reveals more of himself in it than in any of his other fishing books. It is the closest thing to an angling autobiography that he ever wrote, and from it we learn much about his family history, his early childhood fishing exploits, his adventures in the northwest logging camps, his maturity and marriage and family, and from all this he emerges not just as the narrator of another angling tale, but as a fine, sensitive man whom it becomes our delight to know. So it is Haig-Brown's own living presence in these pages that makes *A River Never Sleeps* the best of all his great works.

It is also a work that has endured well despite its age, now going on forty-five years. During that time the tackle has changed, the tactics have changed, the environment most certainly has changed, and goodness knows there are now many more fishermen and a lot fewer fish than there were in the days when Haig-Brown was setting words to paper. But the things that fishermen feel deep in their souls do not change, ever, and it is these thoughts and emotions, these vivid impressions, keen disappointments, and great moments of fulfillment, that Haig-Brown has somehow captured in the pages of *A River Never Sleeps*.

And now they are ours forever.

—STEVE RAYMOND
March 1990

FOREWORD

The fishing is not what it used to be. Of course not. How could it be in an age of dams and pollution, of outboards and automobiles, of population growth and affluence, of massive machines that build roads everywhere and strip timber from the steepest mountain slopes? This book was written nearly thirty years ago and some of the fishing was fifty years ago. Yet I am not at all sure that there is less for the fisherman today than there was then. In some ways he may be able to do better, even in the same places.

It is true that I thought some of the south of England rivers less well-cared-for than I remembered when I revisited them a couple of years ago, and a few have less water than they used to have. In some places, I understand, their courses have been changed by road building. But the trout are still there and the mayflies still hatch, and pollution, I suspect, has often been reduced. Atlantic salmon, for instance, now run through to the upper reaches of the Frome; in my boyhood they were stopped by the pollution below Dorchester.

The Nimpkish River still has its runs of all five Pacific salmons, summer and winter steelhead, and cutthroat trout. You will find the big fall chinooks as I found them, over the flats of the river's mouth and all the way up to the last tidal pool. The chum salmon run has declined from its immense abundance, but is recovering rapidly under proper management; the sockeyes, too, are better managed and protected. The lower river is little changed and surprisingly little used, although the highway bridge now crosses just above the blue clay. If I were nineteen again, willing to climb up and down the steep banks and wade chest-deep in blue jeans and caulked boots, I am sure I would find the big cutthroats and rainbows there as I did more than forty years ago.

The upper reaches of the watershed are now nearly all accessible by road. Lakes and pools that meant two or three days of woods travel are now within easy reach. True, most of the big timber has been cut away, but there is much re-growth. There are no dams on the watershed and only the limited pollution of logging operations.

A friend who visited Theimar Lake recently tells me that the fishing is still good and sent pictures that clearly showed the clean water and healthy re-growth, even the water grasses in the shallows. The lake is more remote than ever, but more worth finding than ever.

The fisherman of today has two very substantial advantages: easy access to a great deal more water, and ready-made local knowledge. I had to find out a great deal for myself, which is a fascinating process but a slow one. Now it is nearly always possible to find someone who knows the water, the trails and shortcuts, the timing of the runs, and what the fish will take.

In the interior of British Columbia the Kamloops trout is as abundant as ever. New lakes have been stocked and many of the old lakes are holding up well. Fishermen have increased, of course, and some lakes are excessively crowded, but many are not and there is room for everyone.

The coho salmon of the Strait of Georgia and Johnstone Strait have declined, but are still caught in tens of thousands and the sport fisherman's range has been increased enormously by the fast modern boats. Much of the decline is due to logging operations that have stripped the timber away from stream banks and hillsides and it should be temporary. Trees and other ground cover grow back rapidly on the coast; more accurate management of the commercial fishery, with restoration and improvement of the highly productive smaller streams, can work miracles, with or without some modest and intelligent use of hatcheries, if such a thing is possible.

I enjoyed the past and I like the prospects for the future. We have a resolution today, in spite of adverse pressures, to treat our land and waters better than in the past. We know much more about fish and their needs, especially the anadromous trouts and salmons, and we understand their values better. We can build them back and even increase their greatest natural abundance. Nothing is quite as it was two generations ago, nor ever was. It can be better, for it is time now to move into an era of constructive conservation that nourishes the natural world and all its creatures instead of destroying them.

Roderick Haig-Brown
20 May 1974

JANUARY

It is easy to forget about the river in winter, particularly if you are a trout fisherman and live in town. Even when you live in the country, close beside it, a river seems to hold you off a little in winter, closing itself into the murky opacity of freshet or slipping past ice-fringed banks in shrunken, silent flow. The weather and the season have their effect on the observer too, closing him into himself, allowing him to glance only quickly with a careless, almost hostile, eye at the runs and pools that give summer delight. And probably his eyes are on the sky for flight of ducks or geese or turned landward on the work of his dogs. Unless he is a winter fisherman, he is not likely to feel the intimate, probing, summer concern with what is happening below the surface.

In the south of England our school holidays might have been planned to emphasize this break in interests. The Easter and summer holidays were times when the duns and sedges hatched and trout rose in every favorite holt of the quiet chalk streams. The Christmas holidays left us free for a full two thirds of each January, but trout rods were stored away and we hoped that tact and good behavior might win us permission to go out with shotguns. Fortunately—it seems now—the center of things, the pheasant-stocked coverts on the downs, the windy stubbles and root fields where partridges were wild and wise as geese, was kept for our elders and betters; the easiest-won permission was for a day in the water meadows after snipe and ducks, with the exciting chance of an old cock pheasant in any one of a dozen cropped and tended willow beds. They were good for many things, those winter days in the frost-browned water meadows. Plentiful game never yet made a good hunter, and we walked all day to spend a dozen shells. We learned where to look for snipe, how to walk them, and how to drive them. We learned where the ducks fed and when, how to test the wind and stalk them cautiously, how to hide ourselves along a line of flight at dusk or dawn. And we learned in sharp surprise that the duns hatched and the trout rose even in midwinter, even in the January frosts that brought the snipe south to us.

Perhaps the knowledge was profitless to us—certainly we could not turn back to the trout rods then, for trout were always left free to attend to their own affairs between October and April in those good waters. But the upright float of pale-winged flies on the winter-dark water and the heavy suck of a rising trout spreading on an overfast run were somehow even more thrilling and enticing to the mind than they were in summer. In the happy misery of cold and wet—for we were often cold and nearly always wet—under the gray skies and leafless trees of soaking or frost-brown meadows, one felt an affinity with the rising fish, a bond of hardihood that permitted one a share in this secret off-season life of his. In spring or summer he rose expectedly, and other fishermen watching there might see him and know his ways; probably they would be able to see, not merely the circle of his rise but his long, thick body also, poised close to the surface and waiting the float of the duns. In this winter water he was unseen, of a size only to be judged from the manner of his rise to an unknown hatch; but you judged him big, bigger perhaps than any fish you had ever seen in the river, a winter wanderer from the dark depths of some deep weir hole half a mile farther down. And you wondered about him: Did the roiled water seem good to him? Had he spawned and was he now growing back to condition for April? Did he feel the rain and the heavy sky as you did? Would he wander farther or find a summer holt near where you had seen his rise?

On those snipe-shooting days I marked down many good trout that I found later on fishing days, and it was borne in upon me that the life of the river is only slightly less full through the winter months. Inevitably this suggested winter fishing. But our Dorset river, unlike most south of England chalk streams, had no pike or grayling in it where we fished—a virtue that I regretted at the enthusiastic age of twelve or thirteen, though it probably made for better trout fishing. Pike, certainly, are a menace to a trout stream, and they seldom grow large enough in such water to make really interesting fishing; but grayling are another matter altogether. True, they

compete with trout for the available food and so presumably
reduce the river's yield of trout and the average size, but they
are noble fish themselves and really test a fly-fisherman. Further, their competition is limited by somewhat different feeding habits, so it is likely that the total yield of the stream is
increased, even though its yield of trout may be reduced. If
you admire and respect grayling and if you want late fly-fishing when the trout have turned to spawning, you are better off
with them in the stream; if you want only trout, presumably
you are worse off, except that all the finest south-country trout
streams have them. Anyhow, I was sorry that we had no grayling, and I still am because I am quite sure I should have
learned a lot by fishing for them.

Apart from trout, the best fish we had in our river were the
dace. Dace are little fish, seldom as large as a pound, never
larger than a pound and a half, but they are bright, cheerful,
quick little fish—the name is from the Old English dare or dart
—and they spawn in April, so they were in prime condition
during the Christmas holidays. And to make matters better still,
we acquired merit by catching them because grandfather
reckoned them as evil as other trout-stream owners reckon the
grayling.

Most of our dace spent their days feeding over a long reach
of shallow water between a big pool we called the Hatch Hole
and a lesser pool known as the Trough Bridge for a wooden
trough that crossed it to carry water to the meadows. They
did not school as closely as I believe dace do in the Thames
and other rivers but scattered out over the gravel and worked
a slow way upstream, not independently, but in spaced formations of seldom more than five or six individuals. Each forma-
tion had its favorite beat of ten or fifteen yards and would
work slowly up it, feeding steadily, then swim back down and
start again.

Dace like worms and grubs and bottom feed of all kinds,

and probably I should have done well with them had I been expert with such baits. But they also rose to surface flies, not steadily and regularly as trout do, but often enough, so I stayed with what I knew, and there were several winter days when I caught six or eight of them on a small dry fly. They are pretty fish with their big tight scales, bright silver on belly and lower sides, faintly olive or lemon gold on their backs, and they fought well when they were hooked. Fishing for them I learned many things. They would take a dragged fly that would have scared the wits out of a sensible trout, yet they were fussy risers, often coming up in important, satisfying dimples that left the fly to float away untouched. A strike to such a rise did not send them scurrying away in instant flight; the effect was far more irritating and educational. The little group that a moment before had seemed so friendly, accommodating and unsuspicious suddenly became aloof and contemptuous; it fed on in its own way, perhaps rising to surface flies less often, certainly disregarding anything I could offer.

Under the Trough Bridge one winter day I caught a dace that weighed fifteen ounces. That was the largest, though I suspect there may have been larger ones there. Sometimes as I fished for them in January, a good trout rose within reach and the temptation was too great; occasionally I made an honest mistake and covered a trout where I thought there was only a dace. Faithfully and always I turned such fish back, but they taught me that some of the trout whose rises we saw on snipe shooting days were clean and bright and hard in winter as they ever were in summer.

The dace introduced me to winter fishing and confirmed me as a winter fisherman. From them I learned that fishing is pleasant and the river worth knowing even when water from the line forms ice in the rings of the rod; and the lesson made me look for other winter fishing. In *The Fishing Gazette* I read often of the great Scottish salmon rivers where twenty- and thirty-pounders run in January and strong men go out in breast waders to catch them on huge flies thrown by sixteen- or eighteen-foot rods. I dreamed of those fish and that fishing and should still like my chance at it one day. It is difficult to imagine a stronger fishing experience than that of handling a big rod against the drive of wind and snow and hooking a thirty-pounder on the fly amid the fierce tumble of a great January river. But Scotland was far away, and I knew of no one who would ask me to fish such a river, so I thought again of pike and grayling.

To hear the owners of trout and salmon rivers talk of pike and grayling, you might well suppose that they would turn out the butler and a couple of footmen and welcome with open arms anyone who expressed a desire to catch either of those fish in their waters. This isn't exactly what happens, but one can usually get permission in the end through an introduction or a distant connection or something of that sort. Sometimes the permission is given very graciously, sometimes suspiciously; usually in my case it was given suspiciously, because a teen-age boy is not unreasonably expected to be about as dangerous as a good-sized pike on a closely preserved trout water. I think that for this reason I never had a really good winter grayling day—I was always limited to some minor stretch of water or to times that did not give me a real chance. The pike fishing was better, and I have had January days in private lakes and in the slow, heavy water of salmon rivers that I should hesitate to trade for anything short of a really fine chance of salmon.

It was January when I came with a rod to my first river in North America—the Pilchuck near Snohomish in Washington. My good friend Ed Dunn took me there, and we caught nothing, at least partly because neither of us knew very much about the fish we were after; but I cannot forget the day, because it was the first day and it started me thinking of steelhead—a habit I haven't grown out of yet. Two or three days later we went to the Stillaguamish, and I remember that day too, though the river was roaring down in tawny flood and I suppose we hadn't a chance of a fish even if we had known all there was to know. But there were dead salmon along the banks, and I saw and loved a fine Pacific coast river, so that day also is remembered.

And now, if all goes well and the Campbell, on whose bank I live, does not rise in full freshet, I know January for the best of all winter steelhead months. The fish have come in in good numbers by that time, but they are still fresh and silver and clean. There may be snow on the ground, two feet of it or more; and if so, the river will be flowing darkly and slowly, the running water below freezing but not ice, just flowing more slowly, as though it meant to thicken into ice—which it never does. Steelhead fishing can be good then, and there is a strange satisfaction in the life of the river flowing through the quiet, dead world. On the bank the maples and alders are stark and bare, drawn into themselves against the cold. The swamp robin moves among them, tame and almost bold for once, and perhaps an arctic owl hunts through them in heavy flight whose softness presses the air until the ear almost feels it. On the open water of the river are mergansers and mallards, bluebills, butterballs, perhaps even geese and teal. Under it and under the gravel, the eggs of the salmon are eyed now; the earliest of the cutthroat trout are beginning their spawning, and the lives of a thousand other creatures—May flies, stone flies, deer flies, dragonflies, sedges, gnats, water snails and all the myriad forms of plankton—are slowly stirring and growing and multiplying. But the steelhead, with the brightness of the sea still on him, is livest of all the river's life. When you have made your cast for him, you are no longer a careless observer. As you mend the cast and work your fly well down to him through the cold water, your whole mind is with it, picturing its drift, guiding its swing, holding it where you know he will be. And when the shock of his take jars through to your fore-arms and you lift the rod to its bend, you know that in a moment the strength of his leaping body will shatter the water to brilliance, however dark the day.

ABOUT STEELHEAD

I CANNOT remember now what I expected of steelhead before I ever saw one. The name almost certainly gave me a mental picture of a fish whose back was a polished blue-gray like steel and whose strength was all that steel implies. One could do a lot worse than that. Cobb says the name probably comes from the hardness of the steel-head's skull, which forces the net fishermen to use several blows of a club to kill him when they bring him into the boat; and a steelhead fresh from the sea has a blued-steel back whose color is deepened by a brightness of silver below the lateral line. Matching his skull, all the bones of a steelhead are thicker and harder and stronger than the bones of Pacific salmon, and perhaps his strength is greater for that.

I do remember very well that I had preconceived ideas about fishing for steelhead. All I had heard of them suggested that their habits and life history were almost exactly those of Atlantic salmon—yet, I was told, only salmon eggs would catch them. I didn't know how to use salmon eggs and had the strongest of prejudices against using them, so I easily persuaded myself that ordinary methods of fishing for Atlantic salmon should be successful for steelhead. Perhaps not the fly, I told myself; that would be expecting too much, but certainly min-now or prawn or spoon.

Those two first days on the Pilchuck and the Stillaguamish did nothing to prove my theory, but they did nothing to disprove it either, because I didn't see the salmon eggs catching anything and I had fished out plenty of blank days for Atlantic salmon with minnow or prawn. Soon after that I went up to work at a logging camp near Mount Vernon in Washington, first as a scaler and then as a member of the survey crew. There was plenty of good fishing near camp—for cutthroat trout and largemouthed bass in Lake Cavanaugh—and plenty of steelhead talk. But the steelhead talk was distant; the fish ran in June and July, which were six months away, to Deer Creek, a good many miles away through the woods. The steelhead talk was mixed in with hunting talk of bears and cougars, much of it designed to impress rather than to enlighten. I led with a chin that asked incessant questions about fishing and hunting and got less than I deserved. I am still amazed at the kindness of those men to an immigrant greenhorn—Red Wayne, the scaler who broke me in, Ed Phipps, the timekeeper, Jim Curtis, the bull bucker, Jack Murray, the bridge foreman, Frank Breslich and Johnny O'Leary of the survey crew and a dozen others. Americans generally seem much kinder and more friendly toward an immigrant than my Canadian brothers and sisters, and I think it must be because they are more sure of themselves in their country and yet at the same time more conscious of being themselves immigrants or of immigrant stock. When I had been in camp only a week or two, a little old Irishman whom we called Frank Skagway showed me the strength and passion with which America grips her immigrants. In the bunkhouse one evening a few of us were talking of Europe and America and the differences in the life of the two continents. Probably I said my say for Old England—I don't remember now—but being only two or three months away from her, I must have. Frank had been listening without offering a word, but suddenly he looked over at me, his lined and long-jawed Irish face serious as I had never seen it.

"Lad," he asked, "do you know what country this is?"

"No," I said doubtfully.

"It's the land of the free and the home of the brave."

Frank's voice was steady and calm and sure and kind. He wasn't boasting, he wasn't correcting me; he was simply stating a solemn, unshakable fact. Nobody laughed, even though there was white moonshine in the bunkhouse.

The cougar and bear and steelhead stories were kind and gentle as Frank's fine statement of his belief. You can string a greenhorn along and make him pretty miserable if you want—it's an easy sport and not without its attractions I suppose—but no one ever tried to do that to me. The evening after I came down from Camp 10 to Camp 7 to start work with the survey crew, Jack Murray told me, "You'd better watch how you go out to that new bridge tomorrow."

"Why's that?" I asked him.

"They brought in a windfall bucker from up there tonight. Badly scratched up he was—by a cougar. If his partner hadn't been there with an ax, he'd 'a' been killed, likely."

I believed him and wanted to see the windfall bucker, which made Jack happy. I could have gone on believing such stories for weeks and making everyone very happy if Jack hadn't suggested snipe hunting a few nights later.

"Ever been snipe hunting?" he asked.

"Sure, lots of times."

That wasn't the expected answer, and one of the boys had to help Jack out a little.

"He means with a gun," he explained. "Not the way we do it here, Jack."

I had to admit that was true, and Jack gave the rest of the explanation.

"Snipe won't fly at night," he said. "So all we do is get one guy to stand at the lower end of a gully with an open gunny sack and have the rest of the bunch walk down toward him. We'll let you take the sack, seeing its your first time, but you'll have to stand awful still and quiet."

I had seen snipe fly at night many times in the Dorset water meadows; but even so, this was a new country and probably a different kind of snipe, and for a moment I wasn't sure. Then I was sure, quite sure, and I thought, "If I'm at the foot of the gully, they'll have to go up at least a little way, and I can be back in camp ahead of them and say I took the snipe to the cookhouse." So I said sure I'd go. But no one could find a sack and the show was off. Jack told me afterward that they had realized I knew the score.

That made me suspicious of the hunting stories, but the steelhead stories all seemed to have the silk thread of the genuine article and many of them were firsthand. Ed Phipps told me he had gone into Deer Creek the previous July, hooked a steelhead and lost rod, reel and line before he had time to think of moving. It was easy to believe that when he showed me the counterpart of the lost outfit—a hollow steel telescope rod, a tiny multiplying reel and less than fifty yards of heavy cuttyhunk. Someone else, crossing a Deer Creek log jam, had seen a group of yard-long gray shapes lying under it. Someone else again knew of a party of sportsmen who had gone in to the creek and come out with a fabulous catch of big fish. Most of the stories had the same moral—they'll take you for everything you've got; you just can't hold them. I felt I could hold them but wondered if I could hook them and if I'd get the chance to try.

The chance came at last in June. The survey crew—Johnny and Ray and Frank and myself—had gone out to camp about four miles from Deer Creek. Johnny and Frank were both quite newly married and liked to get back to Camp 7, the main camp, over each week end; Ray generally went with them. That left me free to get away for Deer Creek sometime on Saturday afternoon and stay there until almost dark on Sunday night.

The first of those week ends was in many ways the best of them all, partly because the whole experience was new to me and partly because of the bears. Our camp, like Deer Creek itself, was some twelve or thirteen hundred feet above sea level, but the country immediately around it was a big flat which the bears seemed to like. We saw signs of them all the time along the preliminary line on which we were working. On the way out to the creek that Saturday afternoon I met a female bear and a cub along the trail about a mile from camp. I stopped, looking for a second cub, and she seemed to watch me with solemn unfrightened eyes for a long time. Then the cub moved as if to pass her and come on toward me. The old bear swept one forepaw sideways and knocked the cub rolling into the salal brush. He picked himself up with a frightened, half-angry squeal and ran. She followed him. I ran ahead in the hope of seeing them again; then I began to think once more of the second cub. I don't know what persuaded me that there was a second cub, but I was persuaded and Jack Murray's stories began to do their work. I decided I was probably somewhere between the female and this theoretical second cub, and for the next mile or so along the trail I was constantly turning back to make sure that she wasn't after me.

I came to Deer Creek at a fine pool above a log jam. Upstream the river swung over to the foot of a round timber-covered hill about two thousand feet high; downstream, below the jam, it twisted its way between heavy green timber on the left and a slope of alders on the right. The river was a lot bigger than the word "creek" had led me to expect, and it was beautiful, clear and bright and fast, tumbled on rocks and gravel bars. I was standing on a wide gravel bar which gave me every chance to cast and fish as I wished, and my heart beat hard and my fingers trembled as I dumped my pack and began to put my rod up—they do that even today when I come to the bank of a river I have not fished before and find the reality of it better than anything I had dared hope.

I had brought in with me a nine-foot casting rod, a silex reel and a boxful of the spoons and devon minnows and phantoms we had used for salmon on the Dorsetshire Frome. As soon as the rod was up and the line was threaded, I went up to the head of the pool and began to fish. I made cast after cast across the swift water, working down a step or two at each cast, swinging the minnow across as slow and deep as I could. The pool became slower and deeper, and I really began to expect a fish. The minnow touched bottom several times among the big round rocks, and I knew I was deep enough. I made a cast whose swing carried the minnow almost under the log jam and felt a sharp, heavy strike. This was it, I told myself, a steelhead at last. The fish ran almost instantly from the strike, and I held hard to turn him from the log jam. It was a strong run, clear across the river; then he came back a little, and I began to think of the stories. In spite of anything I could do, he would run again under the log jam and break me there. He ought to jump soon; all the stories said they jumped like mad things. I began to walk him upstream, away from the jam, and at first he came quietly enough. Then he seemed to decide that he wanted to go that way anyhow, and he ran steadily and smoothly right up to the head of the pool. Still there was no jumping and no sign of the fierce strength of a good fish that raps the handle of the reel against your knuckles and makes you think you really have lost control this time.

I put pressure on him, and he came into the shallow water at the foot of the gravel bar steadily and quietly. I walked close and lifted him to the surface; he struggled and bored away once, came back and was finished, quiet on his side on top of the water. I ran him up on the beach without difficulty and stooped down to look him over. He was a fish of about four pounds, silver gray all over, very little darker on the back than on the belly; he was thick and fat, and along his sides there were pale lemon-colored spots.

I didn't think he was a steelhead. I almost hoped he wasn't, because he was so far from what I had looked forward to, in strength, size, fighting quality, beauty, everything. Yet no one had warned me to expect any other fish but steelhead in Deer Creek, and it was hard to believe that such a good-sized, handsome fish as this certainly was could be overlooked. Doubtfully I went back to my fishing.

I caught three more fish that evening, all almost exactly like the first one. Not one of them had jumped; but all had fought well enough for their size, and at least they made something to take back to camp. I went up from the creek a little before dark and made camp beside a small stream that ran down to it. About fifty feet below my camp the stream ran shallow under a big log, and I threw the fish down there, thinking it was cool and shaded and they would keep well through the heat of the next day. Then I made supper and rolled happily into my single blanket, tired, thoroughly contented, in love with Deer Creek and fully determined that it should show me a steelhead the next day.

I woke in the quiet dim light before sunrise. For once I didn't want to go on sleeping. There was a whole day of Deer Creek ahead, and I sat straight up in my blanket. Below me, near the log where my fish were, I saw a movement. It was a bear, a fine, handsome black bear who hadn't the slightest idea I was within a hundred miles of him. For a moment I was more pleased than scared; then I realized he was eating my good fish. I yelled in fury. He looked up at me, and I thought he looked calm and contented, as he very well may have. I reached for my boots and yelled again, and he turned round then, lifting his forepaws from the ground in that lovely liquid movement bears have. I drew back a boot to throw at him—a logger's calked boot at fifty feet is something of a weapon—but he didn't wait for that. I pulled on my boots and went down to look at the wreck of my fish. His meal had not really been disturbed; my first yell had come merely as a grace at the end of it.

I was a little worried when I got down to the creek after

breakfast. The bear story was a honey, but I should never dare to tell it unless I had fish to take back with me, or the boys would write it up as the record fisherman's alibi of all time. The first cast reassured me; another lemon-spotted three- or four-pounder took hold and came in to the beach.

During the morning I worked a long way up the river and caught three more Dolly Vardens, for that was what, months later, I found they were. Then I rested for a long while on a gravel bar in the warm sun and wondered what to do next. The river seemed to have an endless succession of pools, nearly every one of them good for at least a strike. I decided at last to fish down over the same water, because the steelhead could be there as well as anywhere else and possibly I had fished through most of it too fast. Several more Dollies took hold as I worked down, but I gave them slack line; or if that wasn't enough to free them, I turned them loose when they were played out. I came to a pool near the foot of the round mountain just as the sun was going down. It was a good pool, with the deep water on my side and a long sloping beach of pale gravel on the far bank. I had worked about halfway down it when a fish took, out in midstream, right on the swing of the minnow. There was no question of striking; he was away before I had the rod point up, taking line with a speed that made the ratchet of the reel echo back from the timber. Then he jumped three times, going away, and the sunset was gold on his side each time. He turned after the third jump and started back across the pool, and suddenly I knew I was reeling in a slack line with only a devon at the end of it.

I caught my first steelhead in Deer Creek two or three weeks later—a fish of seven pounds. A summer fish, of course, caught in June, not in January. Probably I shouldn't have written of this Deer Creek fishing at all under a January heading, but it has always seemed to me that I started fishing for that June steelhead back in January on the Pilchuck and the Stillaguamish.

All this was in 1927. In 1928 I caught a real January steelhead in the Kla-anch River on Vancouver Island. The Kla-anch, which is sometimes called the Upper Nimpkish, is the largest stream flowing into Nimpkish Lake and is a hard river to know for several reasons. It is a very long river, with scattered pools that are not often easy to approach; it comes into heavy freshet rather quickly and easily, and it is an isolated river in a totally unsettled area, so that few people have fished it and anyone who goes there to fish must gather his own local knowledge as he goes along. But I think it is almost certainly a very fine winter steelhead river, and I know that very large fish run to it. One day the road will reach in there, and then fishermen will learn the river and name the pools.

By January, 1929, I had found my way to the real Nimpkish, a seven-mile stretch of big river that runs from Nimpkish Lake to the sea. Like the Kla-anch, the Nimpkish is little known to steelhead fishermen, and I had to build my own local knowledge there. I had learned my way about the river in two summers of trout and salmon fishing, but I do not, even to this day, know its steelhead lies properly; I am not even sure to what extent steelhead do lie there in preference to running straight on through to the lake. The Nimpkish is a fairly difficult river to travel and, except at low water, a very difficult one to wade. It is further complicated by two long, slow, deep pools, either one of which can only be searched thoroughly by the better part of a day's fishing; and if you fish them through and find them blank, you still have learned little, because you can always tell yourself that the water was perhaps too high or too low for the fish to be holding in them, or that the fish were not taking that day, or that you may have missed the best lie in the place or failed to bring your bait properly across it. That's the way steelhead fishing is; a great number of variable factors enter into it, and sure knowledge comes only from the hooking and killing of a fish and decently close observation of the place and conditions of the catch.

But one pool of the Nimpkish, at least partly because it was more accessible to me than most of the others, gave me results in January, 1929, that let me feel I had grown into something of a veteran winter steelhead fisher. This was the Canyon Pool, the first pool above tidewater, a long, straight, very deep reach between high, steep banks. The river enters it from a sharp rapid through a narrow throat choked by a great pinnacle of rock that thrusts up from the bottom. The heavy water, surging against this solid obstruction, breaks into a complication of currents and eddies and whirls that I never could fish properly, and I am still not sure whether steelhead lie in that upper part of the pool. A hundred feet or so below the rock, the pool widens, and on fairly low river the currents sort themselves out into some sort of order. Steelhead kelts lie there on the edge of the eddy, but so far as I know fresh fish do not. All the fresh fish I caught were lying near the tail of the pool, where the river divides to pass round a large island.

January, 1929, was a cold month on Vancouver Island, and my partners and I were busy with a series of trap lines. Since there was the perfectly legitimate argument that we needed fresh fish for trap bait, I took a day out every once in a while to work the river. One cold, windy Sunday I took the skiff and poled up into the Canyon Pool. We knew steelhead were running to the river because we had found them trapped by the falling tide in the pool behind the Indian Island, but I was not feeling optimistic. Snow began drifting in coldly from the north, and the line kept freezing in the rings of the rod. After half an hour of it my fingers were so cold and stiff that I could hardly turn the reel to bring the bait in. I thought of going home but made another cast instead and hunched down into my mackinaw to watch the swing of the ice-hung line as the rod top followed the bait around. The fish took with a jolt that snapped the ice fragments yards away. He ran straight upstream, deep down, jumped as he was opposite me and fell back on his tail. My stiff fingers fumbled wildly to recover line and failed miserably—only the drag of the current on the belly of the line kept a strain on him. A moment later I was trying as frantically to find the drum of the reel and check his heavy run to the tail of the pool. I had the feeling that a big fish in his first runs should give one—a feeling of temporary helplessness, of being a little late for every move he makes, dependent on a break of luck to reduce his strength until it is evenly matched to the strength of the tackle. This fish seemed determined to run right on out of the pool and down the rapid, and my only hope was to follow him in the skiff. I began to run and stumble toward it over the difficult, icy footing. Then he jumped again, just above the rapid. Without help from me he turned and held almost still in five or six feet of heavy water. I tightened on him gently and began to walk slowly backward to where I had hooked him. He came, slowly and quietly, and from then on I had a measure of control.

He kept me busy for ten or fifteen minutes after that. I filled my boots with ice water, stumbled after him, checked his rushes, watched his jumps and at last brought him close enough to set the gaff. He was clean and beautiful, so strongly marked with deep-water colors that he might have been caught in salt water. And he weighed twenty-two pounds, the only steelhead of over twenty pounds that I have yet caught.

One thing that had given me some hope when I first came to the pool that day was the sight of two seals up near the big rock. For some reason the seals run right through Nimpkish River to the lake and spend a great deal of their time in fresh water when fish are running; it is the only river I know where they do that. In January only steelhead could be running. I saw the seals again after I had killed the big fish and partly for that reason went on fishing. For a long while nothing moved to my minnow, and I almost decided to go home and get out of the misery of my wet boots. But I had a brand-new artificial prawn and I wanted to try it. I did and hooked a fish almost at once, the only one I have ever hooked on an artificial prawn. It wasn't a big fish and seemed to be coming nicely under control; then something jolted it into the wildest, fastest run of its life. It crossed the pool without a check in spite of the strongest pressure my cold fingers could put on the reel. Close under the far bank the run ended in a tremendous flurry of silver, of round, gleaming bronze and black and of broken water. Then my line was cutting the water behind something heavy and strong that fled with a rhythm of movement subtly different from anything I had felt before. I looked down at the reel and saw the gleam of its metal drum under the few remaining thin turns of line. I pressed my fingers tight on it and for a moment thought that the run would turn. Then everything broke at once—the rod at the first ferrule and the top joint, the line somewhere out in the water. I stood in frozen, horrified amazement and watched what I had seen before only in the broken water of a rapid, never against the still surface of a pool—a seal jumping, head, flippers, body and tail free from the water, several clear feet above the surface of it. I could see his thick body suspended there in the falling snow long after it had slipped back into the water again; but I did not see—perhaps at that distance I could not have seen—the scarlet artificial prawn that must have hooked itself somewhere into his tough hide.

A FISH FOR FIRMIN

Firmin wrote that he would like to come up and try for steelhead around February seventh. Firmin has to come some three hundred miles by car and boat and he is a busy man. He is also a very good and keen fisherman, and I was in his debt by reason of a fine day on the Green River down in Washington the previous summer. So I wanted to be able to write back: "Come along. The river is in good shape and there are lots of fish. We'll look for you about dinner time on the sixth."

But when his letter came, there had been no fish at all and the river was high. I watched as it fell through a few fine days, and on January twenty-seventh it seemed just low enough to get out to the Island Pools. January twenty-eighth was perfect, warm, brightly sunny and with a light breeze from the west, such a winter's fishing day as seldom comes when the water is right. I packed up and started out.

The Island Pools are fishermen's water in a way that the rest of the river is not. The Canyon Pool and the Sandy Pool are all right; they are big, deep, heavy-water pools that hold steelhead well. But much of the Sandy Pool fishes best from a boat; and unless you can cross to the far side you must fish the Canyon Pool from one single point of rock, by shorter and longer casts at varying angles. The Island Pools are swift water, sparkling and broken, seldom deep, and you can wade down them and fish the day through without more than covering them properly.

I always like to start out for the Island Pools. They seem remote from everywhere, and few people go up to them, but forty minutes of good walking from my house takes me there, and I know that I shall see nothing all day long except bright water and heavy green timber, eagles, mergansers, mallards, perhaps water ousels and almost certainly fish. In the winter, particularly, it is good, and on this day, because it was the first time of the season and because the sun was on the alder trunks and on the wet dead leaves under them, it had the quality of rich and full experience.

I passed the Sandy Pool with scarcely a glance at the water. It had been fished heavily for several days, ever since the water came to fair fishing height, and had not given a fish. No part of the river had yet given a fish, nor even a good solid strike from a fish, though it was six or eight weeks past the time when the first of the run should have come in. That it had not come I was pretty sure; I had tried hard for a fish early in January, in the only other short period when the water was low enough. And the General had written a few days before to say that the rivers down on his part of the Island had missed their usual January run. No theory seemed to account for it, but they had to come sooner or later. The return of salmon and steelhead is inevitable as the spring of grass or the fall of leaves; it may be delayed a little, reduced from year to year, affected in many ways, but it cannot suddenly and mysteriously fail altogether.

So I came past the Sandy Pool and past the stretch of rapid above it to the mouth of the Quinsam, that swift, considerable tributary of the Campbell, oversensitive to rain in the hills and always an uncertain quantity when you start for the Island Pools in winter. If you are lucky, you can wade it just above the mouth; if you are unlucky, you will have to plow half a mile upstream through the brush to the crossing log, then half a mile back again to the main river.

This was one of the doubtful days. It looked just possible, but an error in judgment means a day of wet feet, and I hesitated. I thought of the trip up to the log, then of the Island Pools and how much I wanted to be up there and fishing them. I found a heavy stick for a wading staff and started into the water; it surged about two inches from my boot tops on the upstream side, where the current piled against them. It would be all right if the high water hadn't washed the center channel deeper and if I could keep my footing. I worked across, well up on the toes of my felt-soled sandals, weight on the staff as much as possible. It went well—no more than a quart of water in the left boot as I edged over the deepest place. I let the current take my staff and made the last few easy steps to the far bank.

A little water in one boot, even at the start of a winter's day, doesn't mean much if you have a pair of dry socks in your bag.

But don't put them on at once. I took off the wet boot and emptied it, then wrung out the wet socks, shook them and put them on again; then the boot. While I walked up to my pools, the damp wool socks would keep me warm enough and would soak up the last of the water in the boot—you can never drain it all. Then there would be dry socks to go into a dry boot before I started fishing.

Coming up to the Islands on a fine day is beautiful. As you come opposite the downstream end of the Lower Island your troubles with brush and hard going are over. You can wade across to the island quite easily and walk up the center of it, on freshet-swept gravel and grass among tall spruces and distorted crab-apple trees. At the head of the island you come suddenly round a great log jam and upon the pools.

The upstream end of the Lower Island tapers away in round rocks and willow clumps to the water's edge and slants on under the water in a shallow bar three or four hundred yards to the downstream end of the Upper Island. This bar, with its broken water, big rocks and hard, fast runs, is at once the head and one slanting side of the Upper Pool. The pool itself is a broad stretch of water that nurses the leaping waves of the rock-broken current to a smoothness of strong deep flow, then collects the full force of the river and hurls it over a narrow tumble of rocks into the Lower Pool. The current runs strongly through the Lower Pool, against a cut bank on the far side, but spreading and slowing behind the protecting shoulder of the island. And there, not far from the head of the pool and only a little toward the island from the edge of the current, is where the fish lie.

I had a big fly rod with me and a short bait-casting rod as well. This was a day in search of fish, not merely fishing, and unless I could find fish, I should have to write Firmin not to come. I felt in my bones that he had picked a good time, that the river would be fishable then and would have fish in it. But if today was blank, what could I say? Not a fish caught this year; come on up; I'm sure it will be good? You couldn't say that to a man who had to pick his fishing holidays carefully. I wanted fish.

So I changed to the dry socks and almost regretfully put up the casting rod. It was a beautiful day for the fly, warm air, clear water and a fair, full flow to work it over the best lying places. But the devon minnow was the right thing to start with; one knows that it gets well down to them, gives them a real chance to take hold.

I treat the Lower Island Pool with respect and fish it carefully, every inch of water right down from the head. The record rod-caught steelhead for the whole of British Columbia came from there a few years ago—a fish of twenty-four pounds, dressed weight—and there always seems to be the outside chance that it may happen again. My minnow curved out in the sun, halfway out over the heavy water and a little upstream of straight across. It swung round, came deep into the easy water behind the shoulder of the island, and I brought it slowly back to me. Two steps; another cast. Half a dozen more, moving down, and I was coming into the best of the water. It isn't much, that best part of the pool; three casts cover it fully, though one always tries more than that. I made the first cast and brought the minnow back, slow and deep. Then the second, and as it swung smoothly across the easy water, something struck at it. It was a gentle touch, almost certainly a small trout I told myself. But it had come in the best spot in the whole pool, the surest steelhead lie in the river. I sent the minnow over once again, then fished on down the pool to give him a rest.

When the pool was fished out, I came back and ate my lunch near the head of it. So far there was nothing to put in a letter, and I wondered what to do. A smaller minnow perhaps and a lighter lead to let it fish slower? But if that, why not the fly? I put up the big thirteen-foot rod and threaded the heavy fly line through the rings. Three yards of good gut, well soaked, and what fly? It stared up at me from the first box I opened, Preston Jennings's Lord Iris, on a long, slim hook, silver bodied and very handsome with the orange hackle and the built wing of blue, green, yellow, red, the furnace hackle laid along and jungle-cock cheeks. I knew how it would look in the water, slender and full of life, with the orange showing up well and the dark streak of the furnace hackle along the side. The minnow had had its chance. There could be no magic in it that the Iris had not also.

I started down the pool happily, rolling the fly out into the tumbled water, mending the line upstream to give it a chance to sink well down. A little more line and a little more, until I was covering the water at the angle I wanted to. The fly came over the loaded place, and I held it there in the quiet water at full stretch of the line with the long rod pointing straight downstream. I recovered line slowly, two yards, four yards, moved my two steps down, cast again. Again it swung into the quiet water, and I held it there, knowing how it hung, how it looked, how the water plucked at it and gave it life. I moved my left hand up to recover line, and the pull came, heavy and solid, then slack in the same moment. A great swirl boiled up to the surface below the fly. I brought the line in slowly and moved back from the water. The fly was all right. He was just a lucky fish, not even a short riser, but lucky to take the fly so that it came freely away from him.

The only thing was to rest him and leave the last few yards of the pool until later. I knew now that he was a really good fish and I knew also that the fly was all right, so I left the casting rod behind and went on to the Upper Pool.

The river was too high, and it was a fight to get up against the current along the bar. The big run in the middle of the bar was too deep and too heavy to cross, so the best part of the pool was unfishable. I cast a long line across the run, well upstream, and fished with the rod held high. In this way the fly covered some of the good water before the heavy flow caught the line and dragged it out, but nothing moved to it. I worked on down, slowly and carefully, and once again there was a good pull, strong and straight below me. The reel ran and the fish came out twice, bright and clean in the sunshine; five pounds, perhaps a little more, perhaps less—less, I thought as I saw him, more I was sure when I felt him taking the line out and across. The pressure turned him, and he came back up the pool, swimming slowly against the current. Still fifteen yards below me, he turned and ran again, but the big rod stopped that quickly and humored him up again. Not five pounds, I knew now. Over that weight they don't humor so easily. I held hard, lifting his head and drawing him up on his side along the surface. He came within reach, and I got a good hold of the shank of the fly; a steelhead, all right, probably just under four pounds. I twisted the fly out, and he turned and swam off with the current; the game laws protect fish under five pounds until after March 1.

Fishing on down the pool I hooked and freed four others of about the same size. Each time the heavy pull, the strong run, then the revealing leap, and I knew there was little chance of a sizable fish in that part of the water. The small ones were early, but that is where they always lie when they are in. The big fish prefer the deeper water beyond the main run in the center of the bar.

I came out of the water and went down to the Lower Pool again. It had been satisfying to fish the big pool through like that, with a long line out and the quick, heavy rises straight below. It would be something to tell Firmin. But what of the big fish, the real January run? Perhaps the fish of the heavy pull and the big boiling rise in the Lower Pool was just another five-pounder. The time was short now, and the chances of the day were almost gone. I started in only a little above where he had come to me and fished each cast slowly and carefully, with only a step between them. The fourth cast came round into the easy water, and I left the fly there, straight downstream, with no movement from rod or line. The fish came suddenly, and the big rod was suddenly bent in its long curve against the sunny sky, the reel ratcheting out, the heavy line taut and flinging fine spray from it. He ran out for the heavy water and jumped far clear, flung over by the drag of the line. A thick, deep fish; the sun made a rainbow along his side, but only the palest of rainbows, so that one knew he was fresh and would be beautiful out of the water. The first run was very strong, and I slipped my fingers round onto the drum of the reel to increase the pressure. I felt the backing come up, and he was still in the strongest water, traveling, really traveling, down the pool. Briefly there was the feeling of helplessness and frailty that a really big, strong fish can give one. I thought of the gut, heavy, but three seasons old, and of the light iron and small barb of the fly hook. Then he jumped twice again, but not with the strength of that first jump. He turned, and I began to work him up the pool.

He came well up, and there was fly line back on the reel before he turned and ran again. I checked the second run short and felt I had him. He came up very easily but still in the strong water, tiring himself that way, but in good shape to turn and run again as far as the first time. He did run again, but this time came over into the easy water at the end of it. He was still strong, and I brought him up gently. He swam past me, fifteen feet away and near the surface so that I saw him clearly and knew that he was real fish, long as well as deep and thick, fifteen pounds anyway. Now that he was upstream of me and tired, I had only to pull him over, off balance, and lead him back past me to the gaff. A fish for Firmin, I said, the first of the season and a good one. I looked down to free the gaff and get it into my hand. Then the rod sprang straight and the fly was trailing its orange across the surface of the water. The fish turned very slowly out into the fast water.

I sat down on a rock and swore, picked up the fly, saw that barb and point were perfect and swore again. "Dear Firmin, I lost a good fish yesterday. Saw him clearly, a really good one, so I know the winter run is in the river all right." Well, it might do, but it wasn't right. I cut off the fly and knotted it to the gut again. That hold had had all the strain it should be asked to take.

The rest of the pool was worth a dozen more casts and a prayer. It wasn't so very late, but by the time I got down to the pool above the Quinsam or the Sandy Pool it would be, and neither pool really offered a better chance than those twelve more casts in the Lower Island Pool. I waded in, worked a short line over where the fifteen-pounder had taken, lengthened it and was into a fish. A crazy fish this time. He ran straight upstream in the heaviest part of the run and made three jumps, one below me, one dead opposite, one above me almost in the white water just below the Upper Pool. There was no strain on him except the drag of the drowned line, and I recovered as fast as I could, hand-lining through the rings of the rod. The line came tight between fish and rod, and a foot of gut showed v.ith the fast water cutting against it. I moved out a little, took the loose line onto the reel, then lifted on the rod and tumbled him back down. He let me pull him into the quiet water behind the shoulder of the island, and I kept him there, drew him past me, set the gaff and carried him ashore. Not more than two or three days from the sea, a little fish— perhaps eight pounds—but perfect of his sort, with the sharp- cut line of three years' deepwater life along his side between the polished steel of back and brilliant silver of belly.

I loosed the gut from the line and coiled it away, then took down the rods and started for home. "Dear Firmin," I wrote in my mind, "had a really good day yesterday. Only hooked two big fish and only killed one of them, but both were on the fly. The weather is fine and the river is going down nicely. By the time you get here, it should be about perfect."

FEBRUARY

Febrary, like January, is a
fine steelhead month, in some ways the better month of the
two. January can be cold and dry, but it can also be a very
wet month, a month of heavy rain or quick thaw and freshet-
guarded rivers. February is more dependable, at least on the

Campbell. And February is likely to have splendid days of
bright sun after frost, with the first faint feeling of spring in
them, for the sap is rising in the maples again and the willow
shoots are scarlet with it and the alders and fruit trees budded
with it. By the middle of February some of the December and
January fish may have lost the perfection of their ocean loveliness, but it is not likely that you will catch a really ugly fish,
and fresh fish are still running steadily. This is February's great
advantage over March, for in March—certainly after the fifteenth—you stand a very good chance of hooking fish that have
actually started to spawn, and these fish have no beauty of
shape or color left in them. Even when you return them safely
and see them swim away almost strongly, you feel that you
have done an unnecessary thing, an evil thing—which you
probably have. I like almost everything about fishing, but I
hate to catch an ugly fish, particularly a trout or a salmon that
has lost even the ferocious beauty of spawning time and become a miserable thing with health and color and nearly all of
life itself gone out of him.

February is a good month too because Washington was
born on the twenty-second, and that means that my brother-
in-law Buck Elmore will probably be able to take time out and
come up to try for a fish. Buckie is not a polished fisherman—
he won't mind my saying that because he hasn't been long at
the business and he doesn't get much time for it—but he is as
enthusiastic and determined as any fisherman I have ever
known and likes to look at new water just as well as he likes
to catch fish. In the war year of 1942, Washington's Birthday
got Buckie two free days from an otherwise unbroken succession of seventy-hour weeks, and he used them to come up to
us. On the first day we caught a fish or two in the Islands Pools,
and I mentioned a theory that an exceptionally long period of
high water had drawn the fish up the Quinsam, a large tributary of the Campbell, more quickly than usual. You can fish
the Quinsam, but it is a little river with the pools far apart and

small when you get to them; the banks are thick with alder and crab apple and salmonberry and logging debris along all the miles of it that I had worked. I told Buckie this and that I thought the fish might have traveled on through the lower pools to the falls.

"Where're the falls?" Buckie asked.

I didn't know exactly. I had never been in there, and no one I knew seemed able to tell me much about them. They weren't big falls and fish did get over them. I knew that because I had seen steelhead farther up the stream.

"There's a new forestry road that goes somewhere around where they're supposed to be," I said. "I've been meaning to try it out for nearly a year now."

"May as well do that," Buckie said.

We did, and we had one of the best days we've ever had. It blew from the north and tried to snow. We climbed a hill and tried to judge where the falls would be, picked out the rocky forestry road from among half a dozen abandoned logging roads and found that it took us to within a hundred yards of the falls. From the falls we fished down a reach of broken water without a touch, then a swift pool under a high cut bank which also held nothing, then a long, quiet, deep reach that seemed a certain place for fish but turned out to be as empty as the rest of the river. We were both happy enough, but I began to think we should have turned up from the falls instead of down. They were very little falls, certainly no obstacle to fish except in the lowest of low water, and there had been nothing of that sort for months.

Below the quiet stretch there was a huge log jam, a mountainous pile of charred and battered tree trunks that had been building itself for two or three hundred years, if the bleached and rock-hard bones of dead trees at the lower end were evidence. Below the log jam the river split to pass over an alder flat where the beaver were working. And below the flat, where the streams joined again, was a pool that made the day one of useful as well as pleasant discovery. It was a long pool, eighty or a hundred yards of even flow and even depth to a right-angle bend against a rock face and from there thirty or forty yards of deep, slow flow to the draw of the little rapid at the tail.

We began to fish it with enthusiasm, but we had to admit that we wished we were fishing a summer evening instead of a February afternoon, working up with the dry fly instead of down with minnow and wet fly. That first eighty yards was almost like a stretch of fine chalk stream, with rushes on the far side and the smooth surface creased here and there by the thrust of boulders from the bottom. Even in February one could imagine a score of big trout scattered through it, rising steadily to a good hatch of flies. But it held no steelhead, and perhaps it is a little shallow for them. We fished the deep water at the bend more carefully, and once a fish of some kind took the minnow firmly but did not hold on to it.

It was getting late, but the next pool down looked good (as the next pool always does), so we had to try it. As we walked across the shallow breakoff from the big pool, a steelhead tried to swim up between us, turned in a surge of water and went back down the rapid. We tried for him, and while we were doing so, another steelhead jumped in the big pool near where the fish had touched the minnow. It was almost dark then, and we had to cross two miles of logging slash to get back to the car.

"One thing," Buckie said, "we'll know where to start in next time."

"I'm coming back before next steelhead season," I told him. "I want to see a good trout rising along by the rushes and put a brown sedge over him."

That is a promise I still have to keep, now in this coming summer of 1946. The war years lasted a long time and the Quinsam and all its pools have been far out of reach for me ever since that day.

February

The times with Buckie are always a little bit different from other fishing times. Two or three years ago he came, not on Washington's Birthday, but on March first. I had been up the river a few days earlier and found few steelhead but plenty of cutthroats, so I told him we'd make a day of starting the trout season and not bother much about steelhead. We came to the Lower Island Pool, and I said, "Start in there, Buckie. You might pick up a couple, and then we'll go on to the Upper Pool and really make a killing."

Buckie started in with a trout fly and a 2X leader, and when I looked up again he was fast in a ten-pound steelhead, which broke him in short order.

The next season it was Washington's Birthday and the steelhead were in. We came to the Lower Island Pool again, and I put up the minnow rod.

"Take a few practice swings, Buck," I said, "up here at the head of the pool. There's never a fish here; they always lie half a dozen casts farther down."

The practice swings didn't work out quite right, so I took the rod to see if I could adjust the reel a little for him. I made one cast, right into the broken, shallow water, and a bright steelhead came from nowhere and took the minnow almost as it fell. Buckie fished the rest of the pool and I fished it, and there wasn't another fish anywhere.

But that day ended well. We crossed the river at the Upper Pool—a nice achievement at the best of times and a matter for wholehearted applause if your boots have plain rubber soles as Buckie's had—and went on from there to the Canyon Pool. On fairly low river the Canyon Pool can be a winter fisherman's hell. With the water at a good height the fish lie well up in the pool, and you can reach them from the rock ledges. But on low water they lie at the tail, and you can only reach the tail properly from a bar about fifteen yards out. To get to the bar, you have to wade over the tops of thigh boots, and even

when you get there, the least wavelet slops in—though that
doesn't really matter much perhaps. Buckie went out there
while I built a fire to dry him off. In half a dozen casts he
hooked a twelve-pounder that took his line round a rock and
traveled on down the rapid. We took the gaff to him instead
of bringing him to the gaff, so that was all right. But Buckie
said, "That's not going to happen again."

I started back toward the fire, and Buckie hooked another
fish, a five- or six-pounder this time. It happened to be one of
those fish that swim right up to you before making up their
minds where they really want to go. Those might have been
pretty fair tactics if Buckie had been in another mood. Un-
luckily for the five-pounder, Buck was remembering what he
had said as the first fish was gaffed. He reached down quickly,
grabbed the leader short and hung on to his fish.

"Get his gills, Buckie," I shouted, "or he'll break the hooks
out."

Buckie made a grim, solid effort, got his fingers in the fish's
gills and sat down in three feet of water. Twice more on the
way in toward the bank the slippery boots let him down, but
when he came ashore the fish was still with him. We got part-
way dry in front of the fire and laughed till we were warm
clear through. That's why I like fishing with Buckie. I hope
he'll be here again when Washington's Birthday comes round.

ABOUT PIKE

To create a legend, time is
needed. There must be time for stories to grow and men's
minds to work upon them and build them larger yet, time for
eyes and minds made receptive by tales already told to collect and magnify new fragments of evidence, time for par-

tisans of the growing myth to raise about its essential points
a hedge of protecting dogma. So a fish, to make a good subject
for a legend, must belong to one of those species that stay
put,—migratory fish, such as salmon, haunting a single locality
at most for the brief span of a season, have little chance to become legendary.

Brown trout are excellent subjects of minor legend. Almost
any village public house in the British Isles has its monstrous,
hog-backed hero who is seen from time to time through the
dark depths of a great pool or under the dim center arch
of the nearest road bridge. Carp, because they are long-lived
and cautious fish, are favorites of some storytellers. But no fish
has inspired such legends as the pike. He has every necessary
quality—size, strength, ferocity, a cruel cold eye, a wicked
head and a love of dark, still waters.

Because, as I have said, it takes time to cultivate good stories,
it is natural that the oldest ones should be the best. In 1497 the
famous Mannheim pike was caught, a neat little fish nineteen
feet long and 267 years old. The age was readily ascertained
from a brass ring in its gills, which was inscribed as follows:
"I am the first fish that was placed in this pond by the hand of
Frederick II, Governor of the World, on the 5th October,
1230." The skeleton of the fish and the ring were preserved in
Mannheim Cathedral for many years in clearest proof of the
tale. True, some busybody checked the skeleton and found
that it had been lengthened by the addition of a number of
vertebrae, but the Mannheim pike has found its way into more
printed records than most fish, and the debunker's name is
quite lost.

Sir John Hawkins slipped a fine pike story into several of
his editions of *The Compleat Angler*. This fish, which weighed
170 pounds, was taken from a pool near Newport that had
been drained, and a contemporary newspaper report has the
following note:

Some time ago the clerk of the parish was trolling in the above pool, when his bait was seized by this furious creature, which by a sudden jerk pulled him in, and doubtless would have devoured him also, had he not by wonderful agility and dexterous swimming escaped the dreadful jaws of this voracious animal.

The fishing writers tell that one without a single debunking note, but it is a long drop down to the next monster—the Kenmure pike, of seventy-two or sixty-one pounds, depending on who is telling the tale. From examination of the measurements of the skull, Tate Regan believes the fish really may have weighed that much.

Irish pike stories are innumerable and for a long while they were regarded with the greatest suspicion by all the authorities. Then the late R. B. Marston, editor of *The Fishing Gazette*, offered a prize of ten pounds for any properly authenticated Irish pike of fifty pounds or over. This was probably the best-spent ten pounds on record and the kindest service ever done for pike fishers throughout the British Isles, because in 1923 John Garvin caught a pike of fifty-two pounds in Lough Conn and received the reward. This gives substance to all the records and reports of Irish thirty- and forty-pounders and makes the ninety-six-pound fish from Killaloe and the sixty-pounder from the Ballina Lakes well worth thinking about.

Nearly all these big fish have fine tales built around them; but the fish are unnecessarily big, for a twenty-pounder, under the right circumstances, can do just as well. There is so much about a pike for the imagination to work on—the lean swift body, the love of dark, deep places, the flat head and long jaws filled with sharp teeth, the cold, upward-staring eyes, even the mottled green and olive brown of his sides and back which allow him to melt into invisibility against an underwater background of reeds and rushes. A pike lurks—that is the perfect word—in wait for his prey. When it moves close enough to him, he springs forward or upward upon it. He seizes it crosswise in his huge jaws and sometimes shakes it. When he is ready to do so, he turns it and swallows it. He has a boldness in pursuit that leads him to reach for ducks and grebes on the surface of the water, for a swimming rat and perhaps for other and larger creatures that come within reach. In Svend Fleuron's book about a great pike, his heroine (Grim is her name) graduates into legend through a splendid series of crimes. One unfortunate angler falls from his boat in the excitement of reaching to gaff her and is drowned as she tangles the line about his legs. Another, who unwisely chooses to go swimming when sport is slow, almost loses a leg to the slash of her great teeth. Later she drags down a roe deer fawn that has come to drink at the edge of the lake and after that a swimming dog. She learns to lie in wait at the drinking holes of the cattle and to seize and tear the noses of steers and horses. As her fame spreads through the villages, she becomes a serpent, a dragon, a crocodile. A milkmaid saw her as she shot up out of the deep water and shook herself. The jingling of the scales in her mane was clearly to be heard. Ole, the wheelwright, saw her too. "Such a head! As big as a calf's! And the skin round the corners of its mouth all in great thick folds!"

This is the very stuff of good pike legend: crocodile, serpent, dragon; lurking, lying in wait, dangerous, mysterious; of the swampy marges and the blackest depths; seen only in breathtaking, terrorizing glimpses. There must, I think, be American and Canadian pike legends. I have found a trace of one in a book by William Senior, the famous "Red Spinner" of the angling periodicals: "Captain Campbell of the Lake Ontario Beaver Line informs me that he once brought over in a whiskey cask the head of a muskinlonge from the St. Lawrence that was said to weigh one hundred and forty pounds." There are the bare bones of a fine story, and it would seem that there should be others to be found in lands which have not only the common pike but the pickerel and the muskellunge as well. After all, the muskie commonly attains weights that are the outside limit for ordinary pike. Or perhaps a country that breeds the gator and the catamount, to say nothing of Paul Bunyan and Mike Fink and Daniel Boone and sidehill gougers, need not concern itself with mere fish.

Though I have listened faithfully to all pike stories, I have never yet come close enough to one of these fabled monsters to go out after it myself. I have many times fished waters where every cast gave me a chance of a salmon of forty or fifty pounds, and probably I have never shown a bait to a pike much larger than twenty pounds. But pike fishing has always given me a strange excitement. It is a different excitement, musty as folklore, yet with some of the radiance of mythology, built on curiosity and a sense of vague possibilities rather than on the expectation of a great fish and an uncontrollable fight.

Once I built my own myth. It was only a little myth and all my own, but it was very satisfying and there was room for doubt in the end of it, as there should be in all good myths. It started in a south of England railroad train which stopped, unaccountably, between stations. I saw that my carriage was on a steel bridge over a slow, dark river and stood up to look out of the window. The guard came along as I did so and I asked him, "How long?"

"About ten minutes," he said.

"Can I get out? I'd like to take a look at the river."

He hesitated a moment, then said, "All right. Don't be long. Not more than five minutes."

I climbed out and went to the side of the bridge to look down. The river was big and deep as it passed under the bridge, and I realized that I should not be able to see what I had vaguely hoped to see—a big spring salmon passing upstream. Then the long curve of a backwater caught my eye, and I thought of pike. It was a perfect place, stirring in tiny whirlpools where the easy current swung round against the river's flow, its surface hidden under a raft of little dead sticks and leaves and rushes near the bank. I saw the pike as the guard called me back to the train. A long, still shape, four or five feet down in the water, wide-backed, bronze against the darkness beneath him. I turned away and ran for the train. All the way to London I thought about that pike, and perhaps, as good pike do, he began to grow. Anyhow, I mentally weighed him at twenty-five pounds as I waited for a taxi at Waterloo.

It took me over a year to get back to the backwater under the railroad bridge. The river, as I had known all along, was closely preserved salmon water. But there was a hotel in a nearby town where one could stay and get day tickets on the water to fish for pike and coarse fish of all kinds. A bad case of mumps earned me a February holiday, and I persuaded Mother to spend it with me at this hotel. In the hotel lobby a great pike looked down from a glass case. I began to ask about the fishing. Pike like that were a thing of the past, I was told; the river wasn't what it used to be. I might get something around five or six pounds, but not much more than that.

To reach the main river, we had to cross the millstream at the mill. I stopped to fish through the milltail, and the miller came out to watch me. He was a pale but cheerful man, with flour-whitened clothes and a stoop from lifting heavy sacks. He watched my fishing intently, his head a little on one side as though sizing up what I could do. I asked him about pike, and he gave depressing answers. After a little he said, "There's zalmon up t' river now." His voice was suddenly much softer than it had been.

"I haven't got a salmon ticket," I said. "Only pike."

"If so be 'ee should get one on, 'ee wouldn't think to turn un loose, would 'ee?"

I made another cast. "What else could I do?"

"There's sacks to the mill. There wouldn't be no one the poorer if 'ee was to send t' lady back after one."

I laughed then, because I didn't think I'd hook a salmon. But the miller was too friendly and his conspiracy too flattering for me to turn him down.

"I'll remember that," I said, "if I hook one."

He went back into the mill, and in a little while Mother and I started across the wet meadows toward the main river. I was not in a hurry to try for my big pike, but I began at once to look for the black steel bridge under which he had been lying. We were about half a mile above the railroad, and there were two bridges, one over the millstream, the other over the main river. I realized that I wasn't sure which was the right one. We decided to fish down the main river, then cut back along the railroad to the bridge over the millstream. I told Mother I was sure I could recognize the place as soon as I saw the water.

The big river was a disappointment. Not that it wasn't a fine river—it was, broad and strong and deep in wide, flat meadows that climbed almost sharply into low timbered hills a mile or so away on either side. But it was in flood, not in heavy flood, but full to the height of its low banks and soaking back into the meadows so that one could only approach it properly where there was a slight rise in the flat ground. I plowed in with knee boots and got wet almost at once. After making a few casts I had to circle back into the meadow to move on; then I could make a few more casts and circle another wet place. So it went, and Mother said, "Why don't you leave it and go back to the millstream? It's just right there."

I thought I knew better. The big river looked like big fish, and in spite of the high water there were beautiful places for pike to lie. I was using a big bait too, something new, the first pike plug I had ever owned. With a one-ounce lead and my silex reel I could get it well across the river and search some of the likely places, but I was not fishing as I had been taught to, moving down only a step or two between casts and working the bait so that it covered the whole river from side to side in slow, careful arcs. The wet places that forced me back from the bank prevented this and made me uneasy and uncomfortable.

When we came to the bridge, I had caught only a single

pike, a little fish of about four pounds, which is the same as nothing at all if you are used to such rivers as the Frome and the Dorsetshire Stour, and this was a river at least as famous as either of them. I looked hopefully at the water just above the bridge and tried to see in it the place I had looked down on from the railroad bridge. Mother asked me, "Is this it?"

"No," I said. "I'm sure it isn't. Lord, I hope we find it."

"It must be on the millstream, then," Mother said sensibly. "And that's lucky because you'll be able to get to it without any trouble."

So we crossed to the millstream, and that was it and I could fish it. The wide eddy was under the far bank, almost as I had seen it a year before, with the same scum of little sticks and broken reeds on the surface and the same little whirls where the current turned back. I can never look at such a place in any river without thinking of pike and now I found that my fingers were shaking as I held the plug in my hands and looked carefully at the hooks.

"Do you think he's still there?" Mother said. "I do hope he is."

I nodded. "He's still there—or another one just as big. It's too good a place for them to give a little fish a chance."

I made the first cast carefully and accurately into the up-stream tip of the eddy. The plug sidled down into the black water, and I could feel the gentle throb as it worked, suddenly stronger as it came out of the eddy into the current. I fished the eddy for an hour and I don't think I made a bad cast the whole time. I tried every different angle, worked different depths, brought the bait to me at different speeds. I changed the plug to a big rubber wagtail, blue and silver; from that to a brown and gold phantom; from that to a little silver reflex minnow. Nothing touched any of them and at last I had to give up. Mother takes it hard when I don't get what I want. "What a shame!" she said. "He must have moved, or else somebody has caught him."

"Nobody's caught him," I said quickly. That idea hurt. "He's still there. If he wasn't, we'd have caught a little fish like the one we've got. It's too good a place to be empty."

We went back to the mill and ate our lunch of blue vinny cheese with thick, crusty white bread, yellow butter and Dorset beer for a Dorset cheese. The miller came out to us and I offered him the little pike. He accepted it gratefully.

"And 'ee haven't zee'd no zalmon?" He shook his head and clicked his tongue. "Must be that 'ere bait's too durn big for un."

I tried to say again that we were fishing for pike, not salmon. Then he looked at my rod and saw the little silver devon on it, and his face lighted in a great smile. He winked one eye solemnly as he turned away. "Don't 'ee forget where to come fer t' zack, will 'ee?"

After lunch we went up above the mill and began fishing where the stream split to pass a reedy island. In spite of the miller's confidence in me, I changed the minnow for a wagtail, which has always been my favorite pike bait. The millstream was big, almost as big as the main river itself, but the banks were dry, and I could drop the bait comfortably across it to within six inches of the rushes of the island. To be fishing properly was satisfying in itself, and I was scarcely thinking of fish as I cast across to the mouth of the lesser stream at the lower end of the island. A good fish took the wagtail before it had traveled six feet from the bank. He ran well, and Mother asked, "Is it a salmon?"

"No," I said. "But it's a bigger pike than they said we'd get at the hotel."

"You must get him, my dear. It may be your only chance."

But I didn't feel that when he was on the bank, a fine thick fish of thirteen pounds.

"That's just a beginning for us," I said confidently. "This river grows fish big enough to make a meal of him."

Mother looked at the big, flat head and sharp, backward-

44

pointing teeth as I cut the hooks out. She was used to Frome trout.

"I call him an ugly brute," she said. "I don't think I'd like to see one very much bigger."

For some reason, perhaps because the wagtail was battered and twisted, I changed back to the plug again. For half a dozen casts nothing moved to it; then there was a broad silver flash close behind it under the far bank. I felt nothing and did not strike, but I knew what it was and moved down half a dozen paces before I cast again. I asked Mother if she had seen anything.

"No," she said. "What was it?"

"The miller's salmon," I said. "The bait's too big for him and he only showed at it, but we'll try him again in a minute with something smaller."

"We shouldn't really," Mother said. But it was only a formal protest.

I felt salmon excitement strong in me, and it was hard to keep on and fish out the rest of the pool before going back to him; but I knew he should be rested, and it was easier to keep fishing than to stand quietly on the bank and wait out the time. Then a four-pound chub took the plug at the end of the pool and filled in more time. When he was safely on the bank, I changed to the two-inch silver reflex again, and I was as shaky as I had been when we found the eddy by the bridge. The river was famous for big pike, all right, but it was famous for even bigger salmon.

I had the place exactly marked, but I started a few casts above it and worked down. The minnow was easier and pleasanter to cast than the plug, and it began to spin the moment it hit the water, so that one could work it down deep and slow even under the far bank. The salmon took it there, deep down, with a heavy, solid pull, and started straight out on a run that made the reel talk its loudest.

"I've got him," I said triumphantly.

"Oh, no, my dear," Mother said. "What are we going to do?"

Then the fish broke water, twice and splendidly. He was big and silver and beautiful. Mother started down the river toward the mill.

"We must tell the miller," she said. "We promised him we would."

For another five minutes the fish played me, then I began to feel on top of the fight. Guiltily I looked behind me across the broad meadows. There was a man in the distance coming down toward me. I saw Mother disappear into the mill. The salmon ran again, jumped again, then let me bring him slowly back. The unknown was closer now, and I felt sure he was a keeper or a water bailiff. Mother came out of the mill, and the miller was with her. The salmon was directly below me, lying almost quietly, but not on his side. I knelt on the bank where I could see him very clearly and knew he was nearer thirty pounds than twenty. It might be a chance to tail him; by getting him out that way I should still be free to slip him back if the unknown man upstream of me was too close. I reached down, just touched him and sent him away on another fine run.

He had run against the stream and against heavy pressure and out at the end he rolled over, obviously tiring. He came slowly back, making short downward rushes whenever he felt the surface of the water too close. I looked downstream, then up, and knew that Mother would reach me with the miller and his incriminating sack at almost exactly the same time as the unknown man. The salmon was at my feet again now, really played out, and there seemed only one thing to do. I reached into a pocket for my pliers and knelt down once more. The minnow had been blown up the trace and jammed on the lead, and there was only a single small hook in the side of the salmon's jaw. I gripped it in the pliers, twisted sharply, and he was free. But he lay there quietly under the bank, just moving his great tail. Twice he opened his mouth and forced water out through his gills. Then he began to swim slowly down and away in the dark water. I looked upstream: the unknown man had turned off toward the main river. The miller came up panting, a hundred yards ahead of Mother.

" 'Ee didn't lose un, did 'ee? I came as fast as I could."

"No," I said. "Turned him loose. I had to. That fellow up there," and I pointed to the unknown man out in the middle of the meadow now, "was coming straight down at me. What is he? The keeper?"

The miller snorted in disgust. "Yon's nowt but Jim Ford, going over to look at t' hatches. How big was t' zalmon?"

"Twenty-five pounds," I said. "Perhaps more."

The miller clicked his tongue. "A fi' pun note," he said. "A fi' pun note. That's what 'ee throwed away."

I pointed to the pike on the bank. "How's that one?"

"Yon's big," the miller said. "For what they do be 'ere nowadays. But her beant like the ones they used to catch. And her beant no zalmon neither."

He went sadly back to his mill, and we fished on down. Mother said, "Perhaps it was just as well you let the salmon go. I felt all the time we shouldn't do it, but it was so exciting when he got on I just had to go."

I hooked another small pike of six or seven pounds above the mill, and Mother took the rod and killed him. Below the mill we caught another big chub, and a fair-sized pike came at the bait and missed it. So we came again to the railroad bridge. I stopped to straighten the hooks of the wagtail, and Mother went a little ahead. She said quickly, almost in a whisper, "Look! He's there now."

I looked across and the pike was there, my pike, straight and still as a thick bronze rod, not a foot under the water. He was lying at the lower end of the eddy, nose almost touching the main stream, body slanting in toward the bank. Mother came quietly and slowly back to where I was standing—she knows about fish.

"Do you think you can catch him?"

"Not from this side," I said. "I'll go up on the railway and round. You wait here and tell me what he does."

It must have taken me ten minutes to cross the bridge and get to where I wanted to fish from.

"He hasn't moved at all," Mother said.

I made the first cast right across the stream from well above the eddy, so that the wagtail would swing round to my side opposite the upstream end of the eddy and well away from the waiting pike. I meant to fish right down the length of the eddy step by step that way, so that he would see the bait first at a distance, then gradually closer and closer to him. The second cast swung round. As the line straightened, I let it hang for a minute, then began to reel quite fast. I heard Mother say, "He's gone," and there was a splash and a great swirl in the water twenty or thirty feet below me, directly behind the wagtail. He hadn't touched it, and I let the bait hang there again, then brought it slowly up to me until I was sure he was not following. I lifted it out and felt despair. All too often when a big pike misses the first time, he does not come again. Then Mother said, "He's back in his old place."

"Exactly the same?"

"Exactly the same, except perhaps a little deeper now. I can only just see him."

I supposed I ought to wait and rest him, but I couldn't do it. We had two more days to fish, but he might not be in the mood to take again. I fished on down the eddy, bringing the bait to the edge of it at each cast from clear across the stream. I thought he would come, if he were coming at all, when it swung in three or four feet above him. But he didn't; and he didn't come at the next cast or the next. Mother said, "He doesn't seem to see it even," and I was sure then that we wouldn't get him. I took two steps down and cast again. The bait swung in ten or twelve feet below the eddy, and I began to recover it in quick jerks and stops. He took when it was right opposite him, within two feet of his nose. I don't think I struck. He just ran, pulling the rod down in my hands, tearing at the reel as the salmon had. Fifty or sixty yards down, right under the bridge, he jumped, not like a pike, half out and shaking his head, but like a trout or salmon, clear out so that the drag of the line flopped him over on his side with a splash that echoed splendidly from the bridge girders. There was much more to it than that: at least three good runs, several sulky, head-shaking jumps, a long straining and reaching with the gaff from the high bank above the eddy. But I had him at last and held him up on the hook of the spring balance for Mother to see.

"He's twice as big as the other one," she said. "He must be even bigger than you thought."

But he wasn't; the needle of the spring balance wouldn't quite come down to the eighteen-pound mark. And I still don't know whether he was the same fish I had made into a twenty-five-pounder on Waterloo Station or whether someone had caught that fish and let another take his place. Probably it was the same though; spring balances are notoriously unfriendly to legends.

The day that all this happened was February 22, 1926. I was eighteen years and one day old at the time and still six or eight months away from American soil, so I probably didn't realize it was Washington's Birthday.

"WHERE TO FISH"

THE North American is probably the luckiest fisherman in the world. He can range a whole continent of lakes and streams and up and down along the shores of two oceans; he can catch salmon and trout and char, bass and pike and muskie, sailfish and tarpon and tuna, and seldom enough run up against man or sign that seeks to bar his way. As a result he flourishes in his millions, learns his craft, finds his happiness and the growth of soul that his sport yields.

In Great Britain, too, anglers flourish, not merely in thousands or tens of thousands, but again in millions. This is hard to believe. Sitting here and knowing it, I still find it hard to believe. Yet there is ample evidence. Consider only the quantity and quality of British fishing tackle that has been used for years on this continent; an export trade such as that grows only from something that a home demand has created, and maintains its standard only under the exacting criticism of a lively home use.

Great Britain is tiny and crowded, it is heavily industrialized, cross-hatched with roads and plagued with private ownership of sporting rights, all circumstances that mark the ruin of fishing for the average man in North America. They have their effect in Great Britain, but it is a double-edged effect. Good angling waters have been ruined by pollution and overfishing. Against that, the people of the country are wise and strong in their efforts toward conservation, and there is powerful legislation directed against pollution. Private ownership prevents the access of the great body of anglers to the best salmon and trout fishing. But against that, it has done much to preserve and improve the resource, and with the increase of fishing clubs of all kinds, more and more anglers have access to fishing that might no longer exist had it always been in public hands. The island is small, tiny when measured against the hugeness of the North American continent; but this means that a man can reach a lot of fishing without the expense of traveling far from home. It may be pleasant for the New Yorker to be able to regard the fine streams of Montana or Oregon as part of his birthright, but he can hardly feel that he has free access to them when he is writing the check for his traveling expenses.

Perhaps the garden quality of England is the greatest single

February

factor in the country's yield of good fishing. Heavy rainfall and the lay of the land make for a multitude of river systems. Dense and long-established settlement has tended to conserve and increase this total acreage of water; everywhere there are man-made lakes and ponds, and almost every stream or river is controlled by weirs and hatches that hold and turn the water to irrigate fields and drive mills. Such water is stocked with fish and often cultivated as carefully as any garden, and every fish that swims is used by the angler. For the moment—but only for the moment—write off trout and salmon as preserved for the wealthy or the fortunate. There are still pike, perch, roach, dace, rudd, carp, tench, eels, grayling, chub and even the tiny six-inch gudgeon, all of which provide sport satisfying enough to draw men out from their firesides.

Perhaps the most popular fish in England, where the mass of British anglers live and do their fishing, is the roach. And most roach fishermen are craftsmen—mechanics, carpenters, plumbers, miners, blacksmiths, skilled workers of every kind who have learned their trade through slow and careful apprenticeship. Perhaps for this reason, roach fishing is an art whose mastery requires long apprenticeship and a high degree of natural skill. A real roach fisherman is an artist, and his art commands the respect and admiration of any angler—it most certainly has all of mine.

For one thing, roach fishermen use the lightest and finest of tackle. A friend of mine at Oxford, a plumber whose name was Tom, had six 2-pound roach in handsome glass cases. They were silvery fish, deep-bodied and scarlet-finned, and in the case beside each one was the hook and a length of the gut that had caught it. Tom was partial to a No. 18 hook and 6X gut, which makes the dry-fly fisherman with his No. 16 fly and 4X gut just plain crude, if not clumsy. The rod Tom used was what is called a "roach pole," fourteen feet long and weighing rather less than an ounce to the foot, but stiff and quick. At home over a pot of tea or elsewhere over a pint of ale, Tom was happy and easygoing to a fault; he loved a belly laugh and indulged himself frequently, to the disquiet of the heavy gilt watch chain that looped across his broad and up-borne waistcoat. By the river he was silent, still, intent and deadly. He would set up his fishing stool by a favorite swim, usually a twenty- or thirty-foot length of easy current about six feet deep, throw in his ground bait of bread paste and bran and aniseed oil, then bait his tiny hook with an even more suc-culent variation of the same mixture and begin to fish. Tom used a slender quill float with enough line below it to carry his hook to within an inch or two of the bottom of the river. Three or four small split shot sank the hook and cocked the float, and the lightest of light lines ran back from the quill through the rings of the rod to the reel that he always called a winch.

Silent on his stool, he would make each cast with a slow, easy swing that dropped the paste gently at the top of the swim; as the float cocked and started its journey, his concentration became thick as gloom. The strike is the roach fisherman's art, for roach have tiny suspicious mouths and love to nibble at a bait or take it in and eject it so quickly that the movement scarcely shows in a quiver on the float. Such playful creatures were never safe with Tom. His eyes were hard on his float, and his whole body was hunched toward it, keeping the rod top as nearly as possible above it right through the length of the swim. The tiniest check meant a swift, sure strike and generally a fish securely hooked. I watched him many times before going off with my fly rod to look for chub, and occasionally I tried my hand with his tackle. Whenever I did so, I learned humility; again and again I would strike too late or too hard or fail to strike at all. And Tom would take the rod and show me. "There. You see 'ow easy it is. Just keep your eye on the quill and 'it 'im as soon as it checks." As he spoke, he would have struck to a check that only his spirit could have seen—his eyes were no better than mine and I had not seen it—and be fast in a good fish. He played them as he fished for them, with a minimum of fuss and movement, generally on a tight line and following the runs and struggles of the fish by keeping his rod top as nearly as possible directly over it. With the fish on the bank, he would say, "You could do it, easy, if you'd keep at it. It ain't nothing but practice and a little patience. You'll come to it when you're older and not so flighty. Now you've got to be running up and down and flicking a fly abaht all the time or else you don't think you're doing any good." Tom would laugh then. "Young stuff," he'd say. "That's the ticket, boy. Keep running just so long as there's a jot or run left in you. Go on now and catch some of them there durn old chub. They're more your mark."

Roach fishing, as Tom went about it, takes skill and patience and a developed sixth sense; above all it takes concentration. There are thousands upon thousands of fishermen like Tom in the Midland and south of England angling clubs, and they match their skill in championship competitions that make the Puget Sound salmon derbies look like little family gatherings, though the prizes are nothing more than cups and medals. This, then, is the rock-solid base of British angling. For myself, I would choose to try for many other fish before roach—salmon, trout, pike, grayling, perch and chub, to name only a few—but I feel always that the roach fisherman is the highest and most orthodox symbol of all the great body of coarse fishermen, and that these men of the float and paternoster and ledger are more truly representative of British angling than all the trout and salmon fishermen about whom the books are written.

You can find coarse fishing in almost any part of England— in the Norfolk broads and the Cumberland lakes, in the Thames and in the fine rivers of the West Country, in the Ouse and Trent of the Midlands, in the Tyne and the Tees of the North, in hundreds upon hundreds of lakes and ponds all over the country. Sometimes this fishing is open to the public without question or payment of any kind. More often it is necessary to buy a daily or weekly or season ticket to the water, nearly always at a nominal cost, from some local angling club. Sometimes it is necessary to ask permission from a land-owner or his agent, and the permission is usually given for coarse fish. This means that in spite of private ownership and dense population a keen angler, even though he happens to be a poor man, can find a lot of fishing in England if he knows where to look for it and whom to ask.

There is a little book in gray cardboard covers, put out by The Field Press, which gives a tremendous amount of information of this sort. The book is called simply *Where to Fish*. My copy is the fifty-fourth edition, dated 1923-24, and I have had a lot of fishing out of it, both riverside and fireside fishing. Someday I shall get a later edition—preferably a postwar edi-tion, because there surely will be one—just to see how much has changed, but I shall never discard the old fifty-fourth, which was the first edition to be published after the First World War. The book starts out with a glance back to angling affairs of the previous year or so and slides quickly on to "A List of Notable Fish," about a dozen pages of them, and, what I mean, they *are* notable fish: salmon from 50 pounds to 69¾, trout from 7 pounds to 39½, pike from 30 pounds to 53, and so on through the whole list; then to England and Wales, county by county and town by town; then to Scotland, Ireland, Africa, Canada, the United States; back through France, Norway, Ice-land; thence to the Balkans, Australia, and even the Fiji Islands.

I like the parts about England and Scotland best because the authors, most of whom are local tackle dealers, really know their subject. There is page after page of "The hotel has six miles of water reserved for guests"; "Good pike and perch in Blank Lake—permission from the owner of Blank Manor"; "Good trouting; the proprietor of the King's Arms gives per-mission when properly applied to"; "Salmon and trout; fishing free for eight miles below the town; water above the town strictly preserved, but permission can sometimes be obtained";

February

"Chub, dace, pike, perch, good fishing; day tickets 1/-, season tickets 10/-, from Hon. Sec. Willow Bottom Angling Association." It is so easy to expand the pictures. You go to Willow Bottom, settle yourself in the warm and comfortable Black Swan or perhaps the Stuffed Pike, then search out the Hon. Sec. He is a large and cheerful individual, busy, but glad to take time out for a pint or several pints at the inn of your choice. Yes, the fishing is good. Be sure to give the Weir Pool a try—there's a big one there, always lies near the broken willow on the far bank; Joe Gain hooked him last month and broke in him. And the Long Wood Pool—be sure you don't miss that. . . .

Where would you fish and what would you fish for? Name it, because nothing is impossible. Perhaps the Dee in Scotland for salmon? Look under Braemar: "By staying at the Fife Arms Hotel, salmon fishing can be had in over seven miles of water, or Invercauld Arms has two miles." Or perhaps the Tay—the Tay, after all, has produced its sixty-pounders, while the Dee has only fifty-pounders to boast of. See under Aberfeldy: "By staying at the Breadalbane Arms, 4½ miles of the Tay can be fished free." Come down to the south of England. Really good trout fishing? How about the Kennet, where Sir Aubone Fife caught, in 1903, on the May fly, sixteen trout weighing fifty-six pounds? No river has such a May-fly hatch or such monster trout as the Kennet. "Hungerford," the gray book says, "Kennet and Dunn. The river is preserved and well stocked with trout and grayling; application for season ticket to be made to Mr. L. H. Beard and for day ticket to T. G. Freeman. May and June reserved for S. T. holders, fly only; no Sunday fishing. Commoners' days [I'm not sure what this means, but it sounds hopeful for you and me] Monday, Thursday and Saturday." Not the Kennet, something really hard? The Test at Stockbridge, the finest stretch of dry-fly water in the world, preserved, developed and used by the ancient and fabulous Houghton Club. The gray book admits it's not too easy: "Pre-

55

served by the Houghton Club above and below the town."
Then the ray of hope: "Below, most of the free holders of
Stockbridge have the right of fishing in the marsh on one side
of the river for half a mile; leave from one of these." So, even
this can be done.

Perhaps all this hasn't much to do with a day's fishing in February; I don't think Tom bothers his roach much in February,
and all the season tickets in the world will not let you catch a
February trout in the Kennet or the Test. But for some reason
I think I have turned to the gray book most often in February.
It was a February day in London when Gerry came up to my
Redesdale Street room. He circled the big, paper-littered table
contemptuously, then pointed to half a dozen pipes in an ash
tray.

"You're ruining your health," he said. "All you do is sit in
here and swot your head off and smoke your lungs black. You
look pale and sickly. You need to get out."

"Well," I said, "when did you get the call?"

"No, I really mean it. You'll kill yourself if you go on like
this. You've got to go out somewhere—go fishing or something
like that."

"Yeah?" I said. "Where for instance? Off Battersea Bridge?"

"No, really get away somewhere. Devonshire's pretty nice.
You could find fishing in Devonshire this time of year, couldn't
you?"

"Probably," I said suspiciously. "Whereabouts in Devonshire?"

"Oh, anywhere. Ever hear of a place called Totnes?"

"Yes, I have. Why Totnes?"

"I just like the sound of it."

"There must be a woman there," I said, but I reached behind
me for the gray book.

"No, there's not. Not a woman. I mean, of course, there's a
woman there, lots of women, but that's not it. I just want to

see you get out of this work rut you're in before you kill yourself."

"Well, there's the Dart at Totnes. Salmon start on the fifteenth. It's kind of good sometimes. I've been there before,
higher up than Totnes. But I'm not going now. I'm broke."

"Don't think about that, old man; it's my party—get your
health back and all that. Besides, I want to catch a Dart salmon.
Always have wanted to."

"Up till a couple of minutes ago you didn't know Totnes
was on the Dart, and you didn't know there were salmon in
the river."

The end of it was that I went with him, not for the sake of
my health, which was perfectly good, but because the Dart
was a strong temptation in February London and because
Gerry obviously had some plan that needed his presence and
mine at or near Totnes. We settled in at a place near Buckfastleigh, where the gray book had taken me once before. I
was up early on the first morning (we had arrived at dark the
night before) and tried to move Gerry to enthusiasm over the
possibilities of a Dart salmon.

"Can't go with you today, old man. Got to see a man about
some business. Take my rod and I'll join you this afternoon if
I can."

That was final. I took his rod gladly—it was a thirteen-foot
split cane and half the weight of my old greenheart—and went
out by myself. It was a sunny day, too sunny, but I couldn't
mind that because the whole air smelled of spring and sunshine belonged there. The river danced and sparkled and
begged for a fly to play with as our deep, quiet Dorsetshire
Frome never does. I went down to the first pool, a wide stretch
broken by big rocks, and found salmon showing there. I covered fish after fish without a touch until at last something took
near the tail of the pool; it was a twelve-pound kelt and I freed
him to find the sea. All day it was the same story, fish showing
everywhere, but only kelts were taking hold. The afternoon

went on, and Gerry did not come down. I felt sure now that it must be a woman. Seeing him in town, walking down Sloane Street, you might have doubts about Gerry; he is likely to be wearing a bowler perched on one side of his head, a light gray overcoat of quite spectacular beauty, pale-yellow chamois gloves and an umbrella of the slender, tightly rolled kind that we used to call dieted. But he can be a really grim and determined fisherman. Bad weather means nothing to him, and dangerous wading is only a challenge; a new river should have hurried him through any business with a man in no time at all. I tried to guess my part in the affair and decided comfortably that I was just a convincing piece of camouflage. Then, at dusk, I hooked a fresh-run ten-pounder and forgot about Gerry.

That fish rounded out the day perfectly. You do not, or at least I do not, really, deep in the heart, expect great things of places found in the gray book; they may be as good as they seem or they may not; the only way to be sure is to go and fish and find out; and if you have taken a blind chance on such things as the state of the water and the weather and the arrival or nonarrival of migratory fish, you really deserve a disappointment. So I went back to the farmhouse in a pleasant glow of satisfaction and ate a lazy and contented dinner before I began to worry about Gerry again. He came in almost as I started worrying, and I could see at once that his day had not been wholly wasted. Gerry, as he quite often is, was excited.

"Hello, old man," he said. "How was the fishing? Let's have a drink on it. Great place this, isn't it?"

I hadn't had a chance to tell him about the fish or anything else, so I took it that the roses of his day were bright enough to color mine for him. I began to mix the drinks.

"How did you make out?" I asked. "Fix things up O.K.?"

"Yes. It wasn't the way I thought at all. Gosh, she's fine. I want you to meet her."

"Gerry," I said reproachfully, "you said it wasn't a woman."

"She isn't either—not the way you say that. You don't know

how awful you make it sound—as if a girl has to be a mistress or something."

"I'm sorry. But you didn't tell me much about it."

"We'll tell you the whole thing tomorrow. You've simply got to meet her—she's wonderful."

"So's the fishing," I said. "You're not going to miss it all, are you? If it's cloudy tomorrow, we ought to be able to murder them."

"I'll get down there with you early tomorrow—really I will. Just as soon as I've got everything straight. Mix another drink now; I feel like celebrating a bit."

The next day was cloudy. Gerry took the car and went off about his affairs quite early, and I went to the top pool and started in. The top pool is wide and fairly fast, with a current badly broken up so that you have to do a real job of fishing to bring your fly properly through each little pocket that may hold a fish. There are high, steep banks on each side, but the right bank, from which I was fishing, is clear of trees, and for some reason I decided to fish from the top of it instead of going down to the water and using a roll cast. It is a contemptible practice and a lazy one, to stand up high like that when you don't have to, but that day it brought me a reward. I had fished through nearly three quarters of the pool, using a big Silver Wilkinson, thoroughly enjoying myself because I could watch the fly work through each cast and feel that I was really learning the pool. Over on the far side the river deepened under the roots of a big sycamore. I drew line off the reel, made a cast well short of the deep place, let it fish a little way round, then lifted and really reached out. The fly rolled over in a satisfying curve and laid itself in the water within inches of the sycamore's upstream root. I kept the rod point high to give it a chance to come slowly over the deep water. Then two things happened at once: the sun broke through the clouds, and I saw a big salmon rise slowly, slowly through the water, seeming to balance through his whole rise with head and tail absolutely level. He had judged the swim of the fly perfectly, and I saw his gills show scarlet as he opened his mouth to take it. The pull of the line struck him, and he went away upstream at once in a run that made Gerry's rod bend like a birch sapling in a gale of wind.

He was one of those bullheaded, unspectacular fish, but it wasn't altogether easy to fight him from the high bank. I could see every move of his fight, even see that he was hooked well back in the corner of the mouth as the sun caught the blue and magenta hackle of the fly. He seemed to know the rocks and worked his way sullenly from one to another, boring down under each and every one until the lift of the rod moved him on. He came in under my own bank at last and held there, still a strong fish, close under a willow stump. I worked my way cautiously down, keeping a tight line on him, worried because I had no tailer, and no gaff is allowed on the Dart in February. He moved up a little, clear of the stump; his head was hidden from me behind a clump of dead bracken, but I could see his back almost to the dorsal fin. His big tail was moving slowly and easily and his head was down against the lift of the rod; it was no time to try for him, but I managed to lie down along the bank without jerking the rod. Still keeping the strain on him I reached out my right hand, slid it into the water and got a firm grip on the wrist of his tail. He tried to go, but I have a big hand, and the tail of an Atlantic salmon has a slender wrist that a man can really hold on to. I held and lifted, dragged him on to the bank and rolled on top of him. He was a cock fish of twenty-one pounds.

It was a good start—so good that I felt I was hardly entitled to anything more. I knew even then that the vivid sunlit picture of that big fish coming up to the fly was one that I should hold and cherish forever. I can see it clearly now, more than ten years after. And I know now what I did not know then, that I had risen and struck my first salmon by the greased-line method; for that was what it was, in spite of the big fly and my ungreased line.

The next two pools gave me only a single kelt and a half-hearted rise from another fish. Then I came to the Abbey Pool, a fine pool in a rock basin under the high wall of the Abbey. Two brown-robed monks were leaning over the wall watching the pool as I came up. I said good morning to them and began to fish. One of the monks moved away, but the other stayed to watch me. He was a big man, with a broad, heavy face on which his beard showed blackly in spite of close shaving, but his blue eyes were interested and his fine big mouth seemed made for laughing. The monks of Buckfastleigh, as all the world knows, are craftsmen—masons, carpenters and architects who have hewn and raised and placed every stone of the magnificent Abbey.

I nodded toward the pool and asked him, "Fish?"

He smiled and held up three fingers. "They're lying together. Your fly crossed a few feet above them."

I let out line and cast again. "The outside one is following," the monk said. "No, he's turned away from it."

I cast again and looked up at him, but he shook his head and smiled. I cast a slack line to let the fly work down deeper, but still it was no good. I moved position to bring it across from a different angle, tried to hang it near them, took in line and swept the fly across short of them, worked it fast and slow, smoothly and in jerks.

"They don't seem interested," the monk said. "Let out a little more line and bring it across behind their tails."

I stripped line from the reel and made the cast. The monk said, "Now!" and I missed the rest in the thrill of the savage take. That fish was both lively and spectacular. He jumped almost as he took, then began a run that took him out of the short pool in a moment. "Quickly," I heard the monk say. "Follow him." I was already following, holding hard because I didn't know what was below or how far I could follow. The

strain checked the run in fifty or sixty yards and though the
fish ran again several times I brought him out at last, still under
the Abbey wall. I looked up to thank the monk and ask what
he thought of the fish, but he was gone, and I heard a bell
somewhere beyond the wall. Perhaps he was wondering, as he
knelt in the choir stalls, how it had all come out.

The fish was smaller than the first one, and my battered
spring balance made him just under seventeen pounds. I went
back to the pool and decided to give it a rest; the sun, which
had been in and out of clouds all day, seemed to be perma-
nently out now and it was warm. I went up a little from the
pool and lay where I could look across the river at a sloping
bank covered by dark firs and silver-barked birches. I thought
I could see faint, pale green on the birch branches, and daffo-
dils were blooming golden here and there under the trees. Up
the valley, on the line of the river, there was a distant sight of
Dartmoor. Beside me, bright and clean and beautiful, lay my
two fish.

Because of all this I was, perhaps, in a receptive mood when
I first saw the girl. But even so, she was really beautiful. I
thought of her at once as a blue-black girl; that may not have
been the color of her hair, but it certainly was its quality. Her
eyes were deep blue, almost violet, and showed strongly in
her dark face. I think there were freckles about her nose, rather
large ones and dark, but that was only an impression that I
never had time to confirm for looking at the rest of her. She
was wearing a blue, brushed-wool sweater, a pleated gray skirt
and square-heeled shoes that she set firmly and confidently
against the sloping ground.

I stood up, and she said, "You must be Gerry's friend. He'll
be along in a minute—he went down at the other pool to make
sure you weren't there. Oh, look what you've caught. Aren't
they beautiful?" And she knelt beside the fish to look at them.

Gerry came then and brought things back to ground level
by introducing us more or less formally.

"Joan and I are going to get married," he said. "Surprise you?"

"Well," I said, "you haven't given me much chance to be anything but surprised."

Joan laughed, and it was a good laugh to hear, happy, yet strong and full without a trace of giggle anywhere about it.

"Will you tell him, Gerry, or shall I? Perhaps I'd better. It's all my fault." She lay back on one elbow and crossed her ankles. "You see, Gerry asked me to marry him in London, the first night I met him. I didn't think it was very sensible to decide something like that all at once, but I didn't want to say no, so I told him a fine story about having a fierce family that wouldn't hear of suitors—you know, an angry papa and man-eating big brothers. It was fun telling him."

"Scared me to death," Gerry said. He picked up the rod and began playing with the fly. "Those are real fish. Any more where they came from?"

"It didn't scare him too much, though," Joan said. "He came down here to abduct me."

I looked at Gerry. "You were going to take a girl forcibly from the bosom of her family?" I said. "Abduct her? Ride away to the west with her, shaking off pursuit and all that sort of stuff?"

"You were going to help," Gerry said. "Lower ropes over walls, place ladders against casements, drive the panting vehicle of escape, attend to all the mundane details of making sure that the marriage was legal." He got up, dropped the fly into the water and began to pay out line.

"That's nice," I said. "That would have been good for my failing health." I looked at Joan. "Yes," I said, "I think it might have. How was it all this action didn't take place?"

Joan laughed again. "I haven't got a fierce family, I'm afraid. Just a very normal and gentle white-haired father and no brothers at all."

Gerry had let out a good length of line and he rolled it over in a graceful, easy cast. A good fish took hold at once. Joan scrambled to her feet and went over to him.

"Oh, Gerry," I heard her say. "You're wonderful. You do things so easily."

MARCH

Whatever else may be happening in Pacific coast streams, their task of raising and fostering the salmon runs goes on; it is their huge main theme, fading into the background at times, while other movements become more obvious, but always dominant and controlling. March is the alevin month, as January is the hatching month. You may never see them, but they are there, the millions of tiny salmon, each with the supporting yolk sac pendent on its belly, no longer egg but still not quite fish. At least fifty days must pass between the time they first break from the egg and the time they become free-swimming fry, the last of the yolk sac having been taken into them as food—fifty days at an average water temperature of fifty degrees Fahrenheit. For each degree of temperature below fifty, five days longer. The Campbell is a cold river in the winter months, often a shade below freezing, seldom above forty degrees Fahrenheit; so the whole period from the burying of the eggs in the gravel to the emergence of the alevins is a long one. But the clusters of fry in every eddy of the river in April tell the story of March, and occasionally there is the direct evidence of alevins in the stomachs of steelheads or cutthroats. If you have the heart for it, you may also dig in the gravel and find them. I have not—their troubles are enough without my curiosity.

It is interesting to wonder how generally March could be considered the alevin month in the Northern Hemisphere. There is so much variation on the Pacific coast alone. Salmon run to most of the streams, from the Yukon in Alaska to the Sacramento in California, but spawning times vary and times of hatching and full development must vary with the tremendous variation of winter temperature. And what of Japan and Siberia where Pacific salmon also run? The brown trout and Atlantic salmon of England and Scotland are late-fall spawners, so alevins should be working up through the gravel there, too, sometime in March. Generalizations about fish are shoddy and dangerous, doubly dangerous for one so little given to mathematical calculation and solid search of reference books as I am. But I like this picture of myriad tiny atoms, in rivers all around the world, struggling through silt and gravel to start their growth to trout or salmon at about the same time.

March, certainly for most Northern Hemisphere fishermen,

is the start of the trout season. Sometimes I think it should not be. Trout are hungry in March; there has been little for them in streams and lakes through the cold months, and now there is enough moving surfaceward to stir them into activity. In England, where the brown trout spawn in October and November, March fish are seldom in good condition, and many streams are closed until April first. On the Pacific coast, the noblest cutthroats spawn in January and February, and they are thin, sad, ravenous creatures in March. Even in May they are not fully recovered, and anyone who really loves beautiful fish slips them back to search the estuaries for sandhoppers and the aquatic cousins of the wood louse. And the nonmigratory rainbows have May for a spawning month, so that you must always catch some of them red and full of spawn in March or April.

Perhaps a too close consideration of spawning times is not sound. I have seen rainbow trout spawning magnificently in July, and in August every year I work my hardest to catch the big cutthroats that ascend the Campbell to hold in the Canyon Pool until they come to ripeness in January or February. The winter steelhead are full of spawn in the months they run to the river, and even the summer fish are developing fast toward the business of October or November. Catch a yearling trout of any species tomorrow, and you have made sure that he will not come to his mating in two or three years' time. I think a closed season should be measured rather in terms of the rest it gives to a fishery, so many months in which trout may not be and are not caught, so that the angler's total catch over a full year may be less; this for the sake of the fish. And for the sake of the angler it is best to pick a closed time when the trout are in poor condition and least inclined to respond to attractive angling methods. This means the winter months and leaves spring and summer and early fall as the trout fisher's season; but not too early in the spring nor too late in the fall, or the rest cannot be long enough for the fish. I have never felt that the Pacific coast cutthroats are given a fair chance. Their British Columbia open season runs from March first to November fifteenth in nontidal waters and all the year round in tidal waters. March fifteenth to October fifteenth in all waters should be enough, and more than enough, time for the anglers to do their work.

Yet I have fished for trout in March and greatly loved the fishing. There is a breathless expectancy about the start of a new season. Fishing the big steelhead flies through the pools in January and February, one may feel and see fine trout again and again. Sometimes a run of small steelhead is in, fish just under the five-pound mark, which makes them safe for the time being. I have seen the Main Island Pool so full of these in February that one dared not let the fly rest near the head or in the lesser runs at all, but had to fish only the flattening of the heavy water toward the tail—I went out eagerly on March first that year.

March is a good month for fishing beaver ponds. The water is high then for trout to climb into them from the lakes, and the shallow reservoirs, almost motionless, warm more quickly to release creatures still held by winter cold in other waters. If you are a fisherman at all or a woodsman at all, you have to like beaver ponds. Their variety of size and shape is almost infinite: they may be as large as full-sized lakes or nothing more than mudholes in tiny creeks; they may be sloughs cutting back from the head of a big lake; they may be whole segments of a lake or wandering backwaters from a river or a series of fine, flowing pools. Always there are deciduous trees around them, alder and willow, perhaps crab apple and barberry. Always the water seems rich, with deep pockets of mystery and a promise of big fish. Because the water looks fit for them, I often think of huge bass and pike laying in wait under the lily pads or among the waterlogged sticks on the bottom. In western waters they aren't there—only trout. But several times I have worked a good fly over a likely place and seen a fish surge at it with all the wicked swiftness of pike or bass. Once it was a cutthroat trout, monstrous-headed, black-backed, cruel-jawed, his body nowhere wider than between his gill covers, nowhere deeper than the depth of his head; he weighed three pounds for his hungry twenty-eight-inch length. Once it was another type of cutthroat, green-backed, white-bellied, strong and altogether perfect; his hog-backed eighteen inches weighed three pounds, and five others exactly like him came in the next dozen casts.

But at the start of the season I always remember a beaver pond that cut back from the Anutz River, above Nimpkish Lake. With Tommy Dickinson I started several seasons there, creeping on cold gray days into a slimy, fire-blackened dugout whose sole virtue was that it floated with the seats above water —that was a real virtue, because it was no craft to stand up in. The trout seemed to be schooled at that time. They were not big fish, and we caught nothing that would quite draw down to the two-pound mark; but they were clean and bright and sufficiently uncertain to be interesting. Sometimes the ponds were covered with a hatch of small blue May flies, and the schools cruised swiftly among them and responded eagerly to a small dry fly. At other times the ponds were still and seemed empty of fish; yet one could find them with a slow, deep wet fly or, strangely, with the same small dry fly. I remember two dry-fly patterns that I used there, a blue quill variant and that old chalk-stream stand-by, Tup's indispensable; it seemed strange to be setting that one out from a crazy dugout among the beaver houses under the white spires of drowned cedar trees.

There can be sunny days in March, mild and full of spring, but I do not think of such days when I think of March trout fishing. Instead, I remember a day of cold, heavy rain driven by an equinoctial gale that lifted spray from the crests of the current waves. I was standing thigh deep in the Sandy Pool, a few steps above the mouth of the little creek that comes in on the south side. Suddenly there were May flies on the water, out-of-place creatures on the black surface, torn at by the wind, seeming to cling with their feet to keep from being blown away upstream. A big trout rose untidily, then another smaller one, then another. I changed quickly from my wet fly and began to cover the rises. The wind picked my fly away from where I had tried to drop it above the big fish, hurled it upstream and in toward the bank, picked it up again and dropped it almost in the rings of a rising fish. I caught that fish and tried a hundred casts to cover the big fish; when I did cover him, he wouldn't come up to it. I tried again, and again he let it go by, rising contemptuously to a natural fly. I raised the rod top, and the wind caught the line and flicked the fly over above him again. This time he took, and I felt the small hook solidly into him. As he came to the net, the rain turned to sleet, and a great Douglas fir crashed down on the far bank of the river. But I fished on until dusk, when the hatch failed, and caught fish steadily. Then I came up out of the water and turned my face into the wind for home and a March fireside.

There is never the hardness and bitter cold of winter fishing in March, but the month has a wild competitive savagery of strength suddenly aroused from sleep. Under it, somewhere, the alevins shelter and grow.

HOUSE HUNTING

Wʜᴇɴ Ann and I first decided to get married, we did not worry greatly about where we should live or how. In Canada, we knew, and not in a city. The rest would take care of itself; after all, the first place need not be the last, and people always had found places to live. Since our freedom of choice was practically unlimited by any other factor, it seemed sensible enough to look for a place in good hunting and fishing country. Years of living with prospectors and trappers and stump ranchers had even persuaded me there was good economic reason for doing so, and I had known more than one household where regular visits to the butcher shop were considered outright self-indulgence, bordering on immorality when there was meat to be found in the woods and streams. I am not quite sure now whether I had actually adopted this belief myself or whether it was convenient to have an economic justification for hunting and fishing; but I know that for a long while I reckoned an empty larder the signal to go and look out a rod or a rifle.

We were not worrying, as I say. We were mainly concerned about getting married and we were more than satisfied that we could solve any and every problem that came up after that. But as time went on, I began to worry a little, all by myself. Ann was living and working in Seattle and would be until we were married; I was going my way about Vancouver Island, and Vancouver Island was where we would live, certainly at first. So the business of finding a house was rather squarely up to me. The prospect was a little frightening. I had never owned a house other than a cabin or rented a house or paid much attention to houses. I doubted whether I knew what to look for, and it seemed as though a house should be chosen to suit the fancies and foibles of a wife rather than those of a husband.

This problem was fairly well forward in my mind toward the end of March, 1933. I had spent the winter hunting cougars, trying to polish my knowledge of them to the point that would let me write a book, and now the snow was gone and the best of the hunting was over. Reg Pidcock came along then and reminded me of my promise to go up and fish for steelhead with him in the Campbell.

"Heck," I said, "I've got to start in and write a book."

"You've got all summer for that," he said. "Besides, I want

to see if you can catch steelhead. It takes a good fisherman to catch steelhead."

"I'll catch 'em, if they're there." The implied doubt of my competence was more than enough excuse to delay the painful start of a new book. "When do we start?"

"Right now," Reg said. And we got in the car and went.

Reg is a bachelor of sixty or so, a retired logger and a native son of Vancouver Island. He loves hunting and fishing with a deep and quiet intensity grown out of a lifetime of taking both sports for granted. He lived then and lives now on the bank of the Campbell River, five or ten minutes' walk below the Sandy Pool. The Sandy Pool, naturally enough, was the first place he took me to on the morning after we arrived, and he left me there to see what I could do while he went to arrange about getting a boat for later fishing.

I could see at once that it was a truly great pool, one of the rare ones that deserve something more than a merely local name. In a sense it is two pools. The river comes roaring out of the rapid at the head in a strong race under the far bank, leaving a wide eddy that drops sand to a sloping beach. The race spreads gradually through a hundred yards or more until it covers the full width of the river bed just above the big rocks. Twenty or thirty yards below the rocks is the tail of this first pool, a wide place, shallow enough for big sunken boulders to mark the surface. Almost at once the shallow drops away into ten or twelve feet of strong water, and this is really the lower part of the pool, more properly called Pidcock's Pool. It is deep through fifty or sixty yards, then widens into a broad fine sweep of current, almost even from bank to bank and a wonderful lying place for fish.

I had been able to see all this as I walked up the length of the pool under the tall bare alders on the south bank of the river. The far bank was beautiful; great dark Douglas firs growing away from the water through a steep slope, dead maple leaves showing brown under their banked green. A single tree, one

72

Leon Durling

of the largest, had recently fallen into the river and was held there, almost squarely across the current, by the grip of its big flat roots in the gravel; thirty or forty feet of the top had broken away and gone on down the river, but there were still green branches on the upper side. I was in a hurry to start fishing; but I didn't know the pool, and Reg had been discouraging about its possibilities unless one had a boat. "You can fish from the sandy beach at the top, but the best fishing is at the lower end and it's much too deep to wade there."

I started just below the rapids and began to fish carefully down, casting well across and spinning a devon minnow, moving down two or three steps between each cast. Rather quickly I caught a dark and ugly fish which I turned loose. That was a disappointment because I had suspected all along that it might be rather late in the season, though Reg was confident we should find bright fish. It began to rain as I got down to the big rocks, an unkind rain, cold and with snow in it, and I could see the stirrings of a southeaster in the tops of the tall trees across the river. I came to the lower part of the pool and was already wet and cold. Wading in thigh boots was impossible. Alders and small brush grew right out to the edge of the water and the bottom was steeply sloping sand that crept away from underfoot until water flooded over the waders and one clambered, gasping, up the slope again.

I found a fairly clear spot on the bank at last and managed a good cast well out into the deep water just below the fallen tree. I paid out a little line to let the minnow well down, felt it start nicely on its swing; then a good fish took. He jumped after a short run, and I saw that he was silver and I wanted him badly. There was much trouble he could get into; a good run downstream would have taken him among the boulders in the heavy current of the tail or perhaps beyond and into the rapid. Bringing him back would have been difficult in any case, almost impossible if he had chosen to swing over to my own bank, because a matted clump of spirea grew out into the water fifty yards below me. For some reason he chose to fight well out in midstream, almost opposite me most of the time. Once he seemed inclined to run up under the log, but I brought him back from that and in a little while I had him.

The first fish from a strange water is always a triumph. It is difficult not to be greatly hopeful of a new stream, but one learns to temper hope with skepticism and loses nothing by doing so. The thrill of expectancy is there as one starts to fish, the fine delight of picking this place or that as a good lie, of visualizing the swim of bait or fly through a swell of dark current or across the eddy behind a dimly seen rock. And then, when a fish comes up and is caught, there is a surprised sense of achievement, a feeling that something new has been found and is held proved for the future—one will never again fish through that spot without hope and confidence.

I should have gone home then, I suppose, but I didn't. I fished on and hooked another good fish and lost him as he rolled on the surface twenty or thirty feet out from the bank. Then I did go home. Reg was in the house when I got there.

"Did you get the boat?" I asked. "That pool needs it."

"Sure. We'll take it up tomorrow. How did you make out?"

"I got one."

"No," he said. "Did you?" He came out, and I showed him the fish. "You did all right; I didn't think you'd have much chance without the boat."

"Lost another," I said. "If I hadn't been so wet, I'd have tried it a while longer."

"You'd better come in and take a hot bath. I'll have supper on by the time you're ready."

The bath was really hot, and the bathroom was steamy and warm. As I lay in the water, I realized slowly that in six years on Vancouver Island this was the first house I had been in that had proper plumbing—running hot and cold water, bathtub, wash basin, inside toilet. The rest of the house was good too. It had a full basement, a small comfortable living room with an open fireplace, a neat kitchen with the sink just off it in a convenient pantry, two downstairs bedrooms and a large attic. But I did not immediately connect all this comfort with my search for a house. I don't think I had seriously considered Campbell River as a place to live; it had seemed to me a place where tourists came to fish for tyee salmon, and tourist places too seldom have a real life of their own.

As I fished and lived with Reg during the next few days, I began to think more sensibly. There was more to Reg's place than a comfortable house; there were ten or twelve acres of pasture land and alders, a good red barn, an orchard, a small vegetable garden with an asparagus bed and the fine river flowing by. There was more to Campbell River than the tourists; there were quiet, fine people there, fishing, farming, logging, running garages and stores, some of them attending to the tourists for two or three months in the year, but all very much concerned with other things through the rest of the time. And there was more to the fishing than just the Sandy Pool. There was the Canyon and the Islands, the tidal water below the bridge and a whole world of lakes and streams above the falls in the Campbell; good hunting country, too.

There are few men like Reg, in Campbell River or anywhere. I have fished and hunted and cut wood and lived alongside him for ten years now and I have never known him as anything but generous and gentle and overfair. This very afternoon I am going up to the Sandy Pool with him. He will fish the minnow, and I shall follow him down with the fly, and probably we shall both catch steelhead, because the river is in comfortable shape. Those fishing days in 1933 were wonderful. From the boat we caught many fish in the Sandy Pool and learned, in some surprise, that they were nearly all lying just above or just below the fallen tree—rather interesting evidence of the adaptability of migratory fish, because they had seldom held in that part of the pool before, and since 1935, when the tree went out, they have gone back to their old lying places at the tail of the pool. We went up and fished the Canyon Pool, and I caught two beautiful fish there, then hooked bottom about forty yards out and broke a brand new line at the rod top.

The next day after that was the last day, and we went to the Sandy Pool again. We wanted fish to take back to Comox with us and felt sure we could get them. It didn't occur to me to worry about my line. It was brand new, twelve pounds breaking strain, and I had had a hundred and thirty yards of it on the reel, so there was plenty left. We started in just above the fallen tree and hooked the first fish almost at once. He was a good one, about fifteen pounds and bright, and he ran strongly down to get under the tree. I tried to hold him, actually did hold him and felt him coming back to me, then the line broke.

"Damn it," I said. "Held him too hard."

"No," Reg said. "Your line's too light. That's a foolish little line to use for steelhead."

"It casts well and I've held plenty of them with it the last few days. It's just that I didn't feel this one right. Too clumsy."

So I cast again and hooked another, a little fish of six pounds which I handled lightly and Reg netted for me. Two or three casts later—the whole of this affair took only a very short time —I hooked yet another, a fish of about ten pounds, and he also went down for the tree. But I held him and humored him up, and at last Reg slipped the net under him. "This one's ours anyway," he said as he lifted. He swung the long handle to bring the fish into the boat, but there was a faulty place in the net and the fish slipped through, into the water, and the line broke again.

"Told you that line was no good," Reg said.

"Don't blame my line," I said. "It's your net that's bad."

"Well, you'd better get the next one if we're going to have anything to take down with us. How many fish do you think there are in this pool anyway?"

I hooked the next one without much difficulty, steered him

gently away from the log, brought him almost up to the boat, humored him through two or three short runs and decided he was about ready for the net. Then the line broke once again. This time there was nothing at all to confuse the issue; it was a bad line and I knew it was a bad line. Reg didn't say a word. I sat down in the boat and began to take the line apart, pulling gently on it between thumb and forefinger of each hand until I had broken away ten or twelve yards in small pieces. Then it became decently strong again.

"A fisherman like you ought to know better than fish with a line like that," Reg said.

"It's a new line," I told him. "Never been used till I came up here this time." But I knew that didn't let me out.

That, I suppose, was a fairly depressing afternoon of fishing; we didn't even hook another fish. But even so, it must have had something, because on the way home I asked Reg, "How's chances to rent your house this summer?"

I rented it that summer, and Ann and I lived there for three good years after, until we bought the house we now live in and moved a hundred yards farther up the river.

PICKING FAVORITES

Two or three days ago the editor of a sporting magazine wrote and asked me to name my favorite trout flies, wet, dry and streamer, and my favorite trout water. That sounds straightforward enough; a man ought to be able to answer questions like that almost without thinking. But I found myself mulling them over and over. I'd be thinking while I milked the cow, thinking while I was up the river, thinking in the bathtub or while the children were saying their prayers, or even in court while one of the boys from our local Tortilla Flat was explaining how he came to have a couple of extra beers Saturday night and set himself up against the uniformed force of the law. At the end of something like a week of odd-moment thinking, I sent in my answers; and I found that two of the flies I had named were old favorites that I hadn't used for years. They were good flies, the Gammarus fly and the brown and white bi-visible to be exact, but I know they'll catch fish under most conditions, so I don't bother with them much.

That made me wonder again: Just what is a favorite fly, one you use or one you don't use? The answer is that it's neither, but the one you'd fall back on if you were to have no other, something like the one book you'd take along to a desert island. I found myself answering that one too, back in 1939 when I thought I'd get myself into a fighting army within a matter of days. I didn't make the army, but if I had, I should have taken with me Taine's *History of English Literature*. It's a good long book, thirteen or fourteen hundred pages, packed with quotations and references that would call back to memory a thousand other books and give a taste of something for almost any need or mood. But you can't say all that for some particular fly or even for some particular trout water. Generally I choose or make a fly because it fits an idea. And my favorite fishing water would always be the one I know best. For some reason there is more pleasure in catching a fish where you have caught one before and know one ought to be lying than in catching one, more or less blind, from an unknown water. And obviously there must be greater pleasure and merit in learning a new thing about a well-known stream than in learning half a dozen new things in one day about a strange water.

There is something foolish about trying to name favorites and ideals—the whole business has the schoolgirl's giggle strongly in it. Yet there is a lot in it that appeals to human nature. There must be, because we go on year after year naming beauty queens and most useful ballplayers and men of the year and most worthy citizens, and there's never much let-up of interest. Much of the appeal is in the scope given the imagination: think of any girl you like, any one at all; look the whole world over for your man; name any fly you like of all the thousands or millions that anglers have made from silk and wool and hairs and feathers. For once your mind can really go to town, without any petty limits at all. And sometimes the choice is easy and clear—Joe DiMaggio in baseball a couple of years ago for instance. I have a fly like that, a natural—Preston Jennings's Lord Iris for winter steelhead. It must be about three seasons now since I tied one on to a ⅘ leader and I've hardly wetted another fly for winter steelhead since then. That fly catches fish, and that's all I need to know for winter steelhead, because I think there is so much more in the way the fly is worked for them than in the pattern itself that I don't feel a need for change.

The selection-of-favorites racket can become contentious at times. King Arthur's knights put on some ferocious shows to decide just who was the ideal girl, and presumably the zoot-suited knights of today feel as strongly about favorite hepcats. The sports writers have had their prickings of conscience some years about picking Joe Gordon over Ted Williams or vice versa. I don't think I could get fighting mad over a choice of flies, but talking up one's favorite fishing water—well, that's something else again. I'm likely to get in trouble right at the start, because I automatically rule out all lakes and the salt water; only a river can give what I really want.

When it comes to choosing between rivers of different types I feel less sure. I have never yet seen a river that I could not love. Moving water, even in a pipeline or a flume, has a fascinating vitality. It has power and grace and associations. It has a thousand colors and a thousand shapes, yet it follows laws so definite that the tiniest streamlet is an exact replica of a great river. This has always been important to me. I can lie for an hour at a time and watch the flow of a little stream, dropping

pieces of dry sticks into it to trace the current movements, following the midwater drift of clumps of diatoms or algae torn
from the bottom, marking the way sand builds behind a pebble
and the current eddies there. It is easy, in the mind, to magnify
such a stream to the proportions of a full river, and it is highly
profitable for an angler to do so, because the secret vagaries of
current are clearly revealed here. Later, drifting a sunk fly past
the edge of a big boulder, it may be valuable to remember how
the current sucked in and turned back on the downstream side
of the pebble in the streamlet.

Very often there is small-scale fish life in the little stream.
On the Pacific coast probably there will be orange-tailed coho
salmon fry, swift and active little fish that sample every passing fragment of drift. It is not so safe to magnify these into
full-scale trout, for the trout's movements will be slower and
more closely circumscribed; but there is much to be learned
from the choice of a lie or the approach to a morsel of plankton. In a small stream's pools it is possible also to watch the
free and natural movement of water insects, the crawling cad-
dis-fly and stone-fly nymphs, the flat May-fly nymphs that
cling by preference to the underside of stones, free-swimming
Callibeatis, quick and fussy beetles, menacing water striders.
This also is trout fisher's education and any man's entertainment.

A fold or break of current, a burst of bubbles or the ripple
of a stone in a little stream, sharply and vividly matched to
some known part of a big river, releases in me a flood of satisfaction that must, I think, be akin to that which a philosopher
feels as his mind is opened to a profound truth. I feel larger
and better and stronger for it in ways that have nothing to do
with any common gain in practical knowledge. I have tried
to rationalize this as growing from a sense of unity between the
great and the small or perhaps merely from the godlike position that finds a full, wide river between my feet, my own
body magnified as my mind has magnified the stream. Cer-

tainly there is a spell there that I break reluctantly and that hangs with me as I turn away to walk toward home across the fields or through the woods; and perhaps one day I may know truly what and why it is.

All these qualities of moving water help make up my preference for rivers over other fishing places. Next to fishing a river I think I should choose to wade the surf of a California beach and hurl a long line out into it to find what is there; but that too is moving water, and I have never tried surf fishing, so I don't really know. Of rivers I should always choose clear ones; not the glass clearness of the mountain streams nor the peat-brown clearness of Scottish burns, but something between the two, a clearness that gives the water its proper depth. That is the clearness of the English chalk streams and also the clearness of Pacific coast rivers below the lakes, a satisfying, natural clearness, revealing and yet not staring.

Chalk-stream fishing is beautiful. The gentle, chuckling current, the long, trailing wave of dark-green weeds, the fine trees and rich meadows, all these form a lovely setting. The trout themselves are fast and strong and wise, and they rise with noble freedom to the droves of natural flies that sail the river's surface. Ancient stone bridges, weirs and hatch holes and deep-ditched carriers all make for variety in the fishing. It is difficult to name any preference ahead of chalk-stream fishing, and to do so is to deny the water that most challenges every phase of an angler's skill. And yet, I like to wade. I like to reach out across a big river; I like to use the wet fly sometimes; I like the exciting possibilities of sea-run fishing and the sharp seasonal changes that test one's most intimate knowledge of rivers open to the sea. I like winter fishing and I like, perhaps perversely, to know that I am fishing water open to all men, not preserved for a favored few. No waters that I know fill all these conditions more exactly than do the rivers of Vancouver Island.

I have said that I like to wade. You can wade the English chalk streams (many anglers do so), but it is wise to wade

A River Never Sleeps

them as little as possible because the big brown trout are easily
disturbed, and clumsy wading may put a big fish down from
surface feeding for several days. Besides, there is no challenge
to chalk-stream wading; the bottom is easy and the current
smooth and even. The young rivers of Vancouver Island have
strong, white water piling over rapids, and there is dark, gliding depth in many of their pools. Generally these rivers have
floors of tumbled, round boulders, slippery and treacherous
under fast water, dismaying to the overcautious, positively
dangerous to the clumsy. Very often it is necessary to wade a
deep run of really fast water to reach good fishing. Sometimes
one has to work and shift position for an hour or more with
body braced into a little dam that builds the water a foot higher
on the upstream side. The sound and feel and look of all this
is satisfying. It is a test of strength and confidence, and the rewards are great. The water is free and open to all, but there
can still be fair and equal ways of opening a little more to
yourself than to the next man.

Not that I am a really bold wader. I wear breast-high waders
and use them to their limit when I need to. Occasionally I use
them a little beyond the limit, and I have more than once rid-
den with them through a length of water that was stronger
than I judged it. Down in Oregon I believe there are men who
don't find mere waders enough. They wear also waterproof
windbreakers, securely zipped up to the neck and drawn tight
over their high waders; then, when need arises, they plant their
feet firmly and actually shoulder their way neck-deep across
a fast run. I haven't got a waterproof windbreaker and, though
I sometimes think of getting one, I should prefer to watch the
exact technique of these artists once or twice before I try it
out. The possibilities are attractive—for summer fishing anyway.

Chalk-stream fishing gives some perfect moments of sport
that are given by no other type of fishing. There is the difficult stalk of a big fish rising surely in an awkward place; the

82

clear visibility of so many of the fish one covers or attempts to cover; the certainty that they are wise fish, educated to nice distinctions; above all the quiet loveliness of the meadows during the evening rise and their sweet, heavy richness in the early summer months. And a fly-fisherman must always love the brown trout for the free riser that he is.

There is evening peace, too, on the western rivers, though it is threatened sometimes by the prospect of a hard trip home. They have a richness directly and peculiarly their own—the glory of the salmon runs. Their beauty has a rugged strength and leaping vitality of youth rather than any calm serenity of mellowed age. Something of this is in western fish also. The golden cutthroat seems always such a workmanlike fish. He goes after his food with a slashing ferocity, hunting it through the tide flats, mounting the rapids to meet it where white water sweeps it from the rocks above the pools. The rainbow is an individualist, a pioneer searching always wider scope; mere rivers confine him, and he goes out with the salmon into the breadth of the sea, to grow himself to the silvered nobility of the steelhead.

Both types of river test a fisherman, the one more subtly than the other. But there are other kinds of trout waters, each with its own joys and fascinations. I have narrowed my choice, inevitably, I think, to the types I know best. In my earliest fishing years I fished between the chalk hills of Dorset until any change in the river Frome or the fish that swam in it or the duns that hatched from its weed beds marked itself instantly upon my mind. In the years since then I have fished one or two Vancouver Island rivers until I know them as well as I know the Frome; I feel at home on them, and everything I see in them or about them has its meaning for me, as the life of the Frome meadows had. These waters are favorites because they are the waters I know best; the choice is an artificial one really, having little to do with the merits of the streams themselves measured against the qualities and merits of other streams. In the same way and for the same reasons my final choice is an artificial one. Because I go out to find her fresh-run steelheads on a named day in December; because I know her big cutthroats will chase the humpback fry in April and climb the river again behind the first of the adult humpbacks in August; because the little summer steelhead lie thick in the Island Pools in May; because I live beside her and can learn something new about her each time I go out, my favorite trout stream is—the Campbell.

APRIL

WHATEVER one may say of March, April is the true opening month of the trout season. I have caught plenty of out-of-condition trout in April, brown trout not yet built back to shape by the release of underwater life in the warmer temperatures, cutthroats hardly finished with their spawning, rainbows full ripe and ready to begin theirs. April days can be as cold and wet and miserable with wind as December days. April rivers can be swollen and thick with flood. But April is still as beautiful as its name, the true spring month that breaks our world out of winter into something nearly summer. It could not be right to keep anglers away from their rivers at such a time, and I think they seldom are kept away, unless by the ice of a high altitude or a late year.

There is a tale that the willow and the alder are two anglers who offended the powers by fishing on Sunday and were transformed, to stand beside the river evermore. It would have been in April, I think, that this happened. The alder woods are a bright, fresh mist of pale green then; the willow whips are tall and supple, with the sap swelling under green and yellow bark and red and white buds thrusting forth. April, perhaps because it is the spring month, is a month of little pictures vividly remembered. I remember the high, wild, crying wedges of geese swinging splendidly northward, sometimes with the sunlight bright on their wings; and once, at dusk, three geese circling the house and looking for a place to light. I remember the bright mating plumage of the mallards and the drake mergansers all up and down the river and once, along the road, the first goldfinch of the year all black and sunlit yellow just ahead of me. I remember the approach to the Sandy Pool— under the white-barked alders a floor of freshet-swept sand pierced by bleeding heart and a thousand trilliums and the pink Easter lilies just breaking out of bud. Once, going up to the Canyon Pool along the far bank of the river, I crossed a little swamp where skunk cabbage flowers sprang strongly from black ooze in spaced and loveliest yellow. There is pink almond blossom in April and heavy white cherry blossom against blue and white skies. There are killdeer and yellowlegs on the tide flats, meadow larks on the fence posts, red-winged blackbirds in the swamps. Not to go out and meet all this would be a denial of the year's hope.

The humpback fry are out in the Campbell in April—other fry too, for that matter—but one notices the humpbacks because of their bright silver scales quite without parr marks. It seems to me I always see them first swimming about in the current within inches of my waders, half a dozen quick little fish, heads upstream, holding maybe, but going down very shortly. Then I look harder and see others, whole schools clustered in the eddies. The big cutthroats find them out and feed greedily —it pays to drop a fly in places where no fish lies through the rest of the year. Obviously a silver-bodied fly is the thing, fished fast; but that is a shade too obvious. It will take fish, yes, and sometimes take them better than anything else. But the cutthroats are seldom as single-minded as they seem. Many times I have opened up a catch of ten or twelve fish, taken in April when the river was full of salmon fry, and found that only one or two of my fish had been really feeding on fry, and sometimes not even one or two. Of the others, several perhaps would have fry in them, but well mixed with other feed, and at least half the catch would have been concerned with anything and everything except fry—May flies, caddis grubs, beetles, caterpillars, bees, even bullheads, but not fry. I suspect that free-swimming fry are overquick and difficult to catch. Not every fish can be bothered with them when the current brings other and better things straight to the open jaws.

So I seldom fish my silver fly very fast; I let it drift weakly, crossing the current but making no headway against it, tumbling down rather and, I like to think, rolling clear over sometimes. And I do not stay always with the silver fly or even with the wet fly. The trout are feeding, on the lookout, and I have risen April fish after April fish to the dry fly in pools where every little backwater was packed with fry.

I remember April fishing days, like other April happenings, in quick sunlit flashes. I remember an English garden, built narrowly along a trout stream, a thorn hedge, a narrow border, an edge of lawn, a red-graveled path, another strip of lawn, and then the river, and on the far bank, tall and graceful willows in wild growth. The river was shallow and straight through the garden, broken into three little falls by logs staked across it. Close under the far side of the center fall, in a deeper place where the bubbles showed white in green water, I could see the long dark shape of a big trout. He was a thin fish with a great wedge-shaped head, and he showed up very clearly against the pale sand of the river bottom. Grandfather, walking up the garden a few days earlier, had seen him and decided that he was a ne'er-do-well, a cannibal, who must be taken out by any method; and I was ordered to attend to the matter.

I had a medium olive quill tied on a No. 16 hook—double-o, we called it—and 4X gut. The chance of moving the fish to that, clear up from the bottom, didn't seem very great, but at least he deserved his chance. I dropped down on one knee and began to let out line in false casts. Then I saw the other fish, a pale, thick, hog-backed fish lying two or three feet over from the dark fish, well up in the water, his nose almost touching the little log that made the fall. As I watched, his body tilted slightly and his nose just broke water to suck in a fly.

I thought quickly over all the implications and complications; there were plenty of both. The pale fish was really big and really beautiful—I wanted him badly. He was a stranger, perhaps not yet settled into a permanent summer holt, and if I left him or disturbed him this time I might not find him again. He was difficult; the fall of water over the log made a close back eddy, perhaps five or six inches wide and running the full length of the little fall. He was taking flies held in this back eddy, and to catch him, I must drop my first cast so that the fly pitched almost exactly on his nose, with a slack line behind it to delay the pull of the stream which would eventually whip the fly out of the eddy in an unnatural drag that would scare the wits out of him. I considered a longer cast above the fall

that would let the fly drift down on him, but decided against that because the fly might be drowned or, worse still, the longer drift might use up the precious slack line and bring the drag on the fly just as it came into his vision.

Then there was Grandfather to be considered. Grandfather wanted his cannibal caught and would have a good deal to say about it if he was not caught—Grandfather hadn't a very high opinion of fishing as a sport, though he felt that one possibly had some excuse for indulging in it if one did a good job. Catching the pale fish would almost certainly disturb the cannibal and make him impossible to move. But I still wanted the pale fish and I promised myself that the affair of the cannibal would work itself out somehow.

I lengthened my line and dropped the fly on the water once, well behind both fish. The pale fish came up in one of his tiny, tidy, fastidious rises as I did so; his back looked six inches wide, which it was not and could not have been, but the impression made me want him still more. I let out more line, then took my long chance and aimed the fly for the narrow eddy. It came perfectly to the water, perhaps three inches to one side of his nose. He turned to it slowly, so slowly that I knew from the poise and set of his body rather than from actual movement that he was interested. The little olive danced there on the curling water in the April sunlight; I moved my rod point cautiously to delay the drag of the line until the last possible moment. Then he came, confidently and calmly, and the fly was gone. For a tiny fraction of time his back was broad again and quite still in the bright water. Then I touched the hook home. He did the right thing, by Grandfather and by me. Instead of turning across or down he went straight up, over the log like an explosion and on almost to the tail of a fine weed bed, where the rod turned him. I brought him back, and he ran again as he felt his tail come out over the log. Three times he did that; then I tumbled him down, and we fought it out in water well below the cannibal's lie. On the bank he was as perfect as I had hoped he would be, his red spots splendid against his pale coat, his body far too thick for my hand's grip.

And the black fish was still where he had been. I dried the fly and dropped it over him, but he made no move. I tried it again, half a dozen times, then a freak of the current smoothed the surface and I saw his head most clearly. Around the eye there was a circle of dead whiteness; I knew he was blind. I drowned the fly and dropped it to him again, several times. Once he moved, the slight restless movement that brown trout make when they are deciding it's about time to move out for some favorite hiding place. I crept back from the bank and made myself wait for ten or fifteen minutes, then changed the little dry fly to a much larger wet fly, for the small hook would not sink down to him. The big fly went down well, and I tried drifting it a foot or two away from him at first, hoping he would sense it and come across. I brought it closer and closer to him with each cast, and still he would not move. Then I dropped it squarely above him. It sank and slid down; it brushed his nose so that he turned away; it crept along his body, passed his tail—then he turned like a pike, his great white mouth opened and he had it. Grandfather looked over both fish as they lay in state on the hall table and was impressed.

Two other April days come sharply into my mind, and both are sunny days of fish seen clearly in bright April water. On the Nimpkish River we kept the gas boats tied to a rough landing two or three hundred yards below the house. One morning we went down to work on them, and as we worked, a good fish rose again and again with solemn, solid plops close under the bushes just above us. Buster said at last, "Go and catch him."

I started on him, using a small iron blue; and as he came to it, another fish rose twenty or thirty yards farther up. I netted the first fish, a green-backed, solid cutthroat of two and a half pounds. Little dark-blue May flies poured down the river in a narrow stream close under the bushes, and the second fish still rose. I went up to him, and as I cast for him, a third fish rose twenty yards beyond him. An hour later I came out of the water opposite the house, and I had with me ten white-bellied, green-backed cutthroats with not an inch in length nor a quarter of a pound in weight between them. I laid them out in the sunlight on the short grass of the bank. Buster was coming up to the house for lunch and saw me there. "You're a hell of a guy," he said. "I ought to have known better than let you go off the job." Then he came closer and saw the fish. "Oh, boy!" he said softly. "Oh, boy!"

Since Ann and I have filled the house with children, we go up the river together too seldom. But there was an April day a year or two ago when we arranged things and went. "We shan't find much," I said. "The fish seem to have moved up out of the Island Pools this year. I think the river's low for them. But it's a swell day and it will be fun up there."

So I went out into the main pool and hooked almost at once a thick golden cutthroat that looked to me like a four-pounder and fought me till I was trembling with the fear that I should never get him to the scales to find out. I have caught only one sea-run cutthroat of over four pounds in the Campbell, and he doesn't count because I was fishing for steelhead when he took hold. The fish came to the net at last, and I carried him proudly ashore. "He's a four-pounder," I told Ann.

She shook her head. "I don't think so. I've seen you catch them as big as that before."

The scales made him three and three-quarter pounds.

I fished lazily, bouncing a deer-hair dry fly down over the fast water of the pool, and caught other fish. We lay in the sun and ate lunch and talked. I went far out on the bar at last, because it seems wrong to go all the way up to the Islands and not try it out properly, however lazy the day. Just above the main run a great, bright steelhead took my fly. He seemed to love the fast, clear water and ran and played in it with little care for all I could do with my trout rod. Ann saw me in trouble and came out along the bar toward me. The fish came back, more or less of his own free will, and carelessly let himself into slack water behind a rock. I held hard, reached down and slipped a finger in his gills. I held him up, looking back toward Ann against the sun, then freed the hook and slipped him back. I heard Ann laugh and knew that the Island Pool was a good place to be on a spring day.

H. M. GREENHILL

As I look back on them now it seems to me that my male elders in Dorset fell into two astonishingly well-defined groups. There were the Victorians, men in their seventies and eighties: Grandfather and his two brothers; Thomas Hardy; Squire Sheridan, Grandfather's neighbor; Mr. Shepherd, the village carpenter; Knight, the river keeper on the club water. These make a cross section of examples. They were small, spare, wiry men, usually with short gray beards—though Hardy and my two great-uncles had only gray mustaches—very quick and keen, both physically and mentally. Dorset is kind to old men, or was before the world wars began. Squire Sheridan was well over eighty when I last saw him, but he was standing waist deep in the river, cutting weeds with great sweeping strokes of his scythe. Grandfather had to break his ankle twice in the hills to be convinced that eighty is too old for hard shooting days. Knight was walking his twelve or fourteen miles a day through the water meadows, summer and winter, when he was well into the eighties. Hardy, though the scope of his labors bore little relation to that of these mere mortals, was in no greater haste to lay down his burden than they were; his greatness did not fail him in his lifetime and his stature grows steadily now that he is dead.

Among these men there was something of the closeness that there is among the elder citizens of an American small town. Grandfather and my great-uncles had been at Dorchester Grammar School with Hardy, and though the way of the three brothers branched widely from Hardy's way after their school days, there was much that held them together. Grandfather loved Dorset county as Hardy loved Dorset people and he respected Hardy with a sincerity that was wholly admirable in such a practical and autocratic old gentleman. I think he rarely missed a quarterly teatime visit to Max Gate, and I know that when he took me with him, we entered the house and met the great and gentle little man with a humility that seemed to reduce Grandfather to my own schoolboy age. Between Grandfather and Squire Brinsley Sheridan there was a different respect, grudging and born out of a lifetime of disagreements, but real. Mr. Shepherd and Grandfather met squarely as equals, craftsman to trader, though one was employer and the other employed, and I think the fraternity of old age was stronger between these two than between any of the others. Knight was Knight, the friend of every keen fisherman, wise in the life of his water meadows and a truer countryman than any of the others. Knight could not read or write properly, and he regretted it. Once he told me, "I ain't never learned 'ee. My zister, her can do 'un, but her beant so oold as I be. You zee, when they passed this 'ere law 'bout 'avin' to 'ave schoolin' it du zeem I were just too old for 'un." I often wondered how great was the loss through that, not Knight's loss, for he was great in his work as were the other Victorians I have listed, but the country's. Sixty years of walking the meadows is a long time, sixty years of knowing birds and beasts and fish and seeing them with sharp gray eyes that never needed spectacles is time to have yielded much knowledge. An educated Knight might have been another such as William Lunn, the inspired keeper and manager of the Houghton Club water. He might even have been a Gilbert White or a Jefferies.

The other group of my elders was Edwardian, as clearly as Grandfather's group was Victorian. They were big, heavy, broad-shouldered men, often soldiers, black-mustached and deep-voiced, lovers of all forms of sport. Nearly all of them were magnificent with the shotgun, most of them were cricketers, and some were good fishermen. I can think easily over a long list of names—Colonel Saunders, Major Radclyffe, the Hambro brothers of banking fame, my uncle Alec who died of wounds in 1919 and John Kelly, the wonderful Irish gardener who was as truly a Dorset man as William Barnes himself. Of them all, none was truer to type than Major Greenhill, and from Greenhill I learned most of those things about fishing and wing shooting that a boy generally learns from his father.

The First World War took hold of my father when I was six years old and held him until he was killed at Bapaume in March, 1918. Nearly all my Mother's eleven brothers were kept busy during the war and for some years after. As a result, I grew up beside a fine trout stream and in the midst of good shooting country with only the crudest ideas of how to go about either business. I caught a few fish by most reprehensible methods and stalked rabbits and pigeons, even partridges and mallards, with a variety of weapons at once less effective and less artistic then the shotgun. In the summer of 1922, when I was fourteen, one of my uncles—the best and keenest fisherman of them all—was at home long enough to teach me the elements of dry-fly fishing. And during the Christmas holidays of the same year Greenhill came, it seemed to me from nowhere, and took over.

At that time Greenhill was already a heroic figure to me. He had always been held up to me as one of the best wing shots in England, and I knew he was a fine salmon fisherman. He was a huge man, an inch or two over six feet and weighing about 220 pounds, which he seemed to carry mainly on his chest and shoulders. I had seen him play a brave part on the cricket field, lifting the ball in full-shouldered drives to bounce its way among the mounds of the cemetery. Seated in glory at the edge of the ring, I had watched him referee the army boxing tournaments. And now his talented bulk rested itself deep in one of the dining-room chairs, and his strong, heavy voice told Mother that he would look after my sporting education. Someone, he said, had to make up for the war.

He taught as good teachers do, by example, by opportune and unhurried explanation, by occasional strong direction. The strongest lesson he taught, though he never named it, was complete concentration on, and devotion to, the matter in hand. I learned quickly that if there was a chance of going shooting on a certain day, I must not tie myself to anything else; that while we were out I must see everything and know everything —the identity of birds by their flight, the line that rabbits would take in bolting from a certain place, any shift of wind, the change of a field from stubble to plow, any lowering or raising of the river by a farmer's manipulation of irrigation hatches. I must never tire, because I was younger and stronger in proportion to my weight than he was—a point that it was not difficult for me to recognize. No walk must be too long, no hour of creeping in wet meadows too painful, if there was a chance of a shot at the end of it. Above all, I must be ready when game flushed; I could miss and be forgiven, provided I offered no excuse for missing. But if I failed to get my gun off at a fair chance, I must walk with it unloaded through the rest of the day. Safety was provided for by an even stiffer penalty; if I fired a dangerous shot, if I failed to break my gun before climbing a fence or crossing a hedge, I must go home at once in disgrace. But this penalty was never invoked, because I had been already well trained in safety.

Such an account of penalties and forfeits makes our shooting days sound gloomy, but they were not. I made him angry perhaps half a dozen times in all the years we fished and shot together—two or three times because I was lazy or fainthearted, two or three times because I missed, through sheer carelessness, golden chances we had worked hard for, once because I lied to him. It was a simple thing, this last, yet it taught me clearly, as nothing else has, the urgency of being honest with yourself if you want to learn. I had planned to take the ferrets and terriers out one day to kill off the rats that infested a corn rick. The day turned out badly, with a southwesterly gale and driving rain, but I wanted to go anyway and I asked Greenhill to go with me. "No use," he said. "Rats won't bolt a day like this. You'll get your ferrets all bitten up and you'll just be wasting your time." I went anyway, with a couple of friends; and my favorite ferret got badly bitten, the rats wouldn't bolt and we finished the day with six or eight dead rats instead of a hundred or more. A few days later he asked me how it had been.

"All right," I said. "We didn't do badly."

Greenhill snorted. "Bet you didn't get half a dozen rats."

"Yes, we did," I said. "More than that."

"How many? Twenty? Thirty?"

I nodded. "About that," I said, and he said nothing more until the next day. Then he said, "You lied to me about those rats, young fellow. You only got six or seven the whole day."

I tried to get out of it, but there was no way. He was really angry then and so was I, angry and afraid. But what he meant was clear enough: rats and rabbits won't bolt well to ferrets on a bad day—that is a piece of knowledge by which one must be guided again and again in planning a day. Any exception to it is important, for it may disclose some other factor that has entered into the business. A lie such as I had told is aimed at the roots of useful knowledge.

One other incident taught me early just what sort of training I was under. Greenhill had a Labrador bitch named Dinah, and Dinah was a model retriever. By some standards she was too sedate and dignified and slow, but her calm eyes and mind missed nothing. Greenhill could stand and drop a dozen birds, with Dinah moving only her head behind him to watch the flight and fall of each one. Then, when the drive was finished, he would move her out, and she would pick up every one of them on her own, without help unless there happened to be an exceptionally bad runner. She was the same in the meadows, phlegmatic about the rise of a bird, unmoved by the shot, unconcerned about the retrieve until he ordered her out. Early one January we had a quick spell of hard weather, a light fall of snow and more frosts. Working the meadows for snipe, we found a flock of mallards on the river, stalked them and killed four. Two fell in the water on the far side of the river and were caught up by low-hanging willow branches. We picked up the other two, and I waited for him to send Dinah across. He didn't. Instead he said, "All right, young fellow, get on with it."

"Get on with what?"

"Go across and pick 'em up. It's too cold for Dinah; she's getting old."

The nearest bridge was a mile upstream, and the water was high and dirty in spite of the frosts.

"You mean swim?" I asked. "It's too cold."

"If you want to come out with me you do what I say and don't argue."

"I haven't got anything to dry myself with."

"You've got a handkerchief, haven't you?"

I took my clothes off and fetched the ducks, and the handkerchief did its job well enough. That wasn't the last time I worked for Dinah.

"She works hard enough for you," Greenhill said. "You can do something for her once in a while."

Because he infinitely preferred shooting and salmon fishing and because I knew my way about the river well enough,

Greenhill did not come trout fishing with me very often at
first. As a matter of fact I began, in my dry-fly man's ar-
rogance, to discount him as a trout fisherman. My uncles and
my father had, so far as I knew, used nothing but the dry fly
on Grandfather's lengths of the Frome and the Wrackle and
on the Club water as well. The uncle who taught me to fish
had taught me only dry-fly fishing, and I was, at fourteen, a
hidebound purist. To make matters worse, I got pretty good
at the business and kept on improving steadily, which was natural enough because I had every opportunity to know the
water well and had a fanatical keenness as well as a complete
disregard for weather conditions or discomfort of any kind.
Such things simply didn't register.

I am not sure just when or how I discovered that Greenhill
was not a very experienced dry-fly fisherman. Certainly he
never told me or admitted it by remotest inference, nor did he
ever attempt to suggest that the wet fly was a better method.
But I knew somehow; and after the original shock of surprise,
the knowledge gave me a very pleasant sense of superiority—
there was at least one thing in which I could match him.
Greenhill took whatever offensiveness I had to offer—I can't
remember any of it exactly, but I am sure it was plenty—and
began to fish with me more often. He used the dry fly for the
most part, out of respect for the unwritten rule of the water,
but occasionally turned to the wet fly. Very offhandedly he
began to explain to me and show me some of the difficulties
and complications of wet-fly fishing. We treated it as something of a joke, a method to play with occasionally, just for a
change. I was glad to keep it that way because I was in no
hurry to lose my sense of superiority. Wet-fly fishing was
chuck-and-chance-it, a fair-enough method for the little trout
of the Scottish burns or the Devonshire streams, but mild sacrilege on a chalk stream, even on a minor edition of a chalk
stream such as the Frome was. But unfortunately for my sense
of superiority, I liked fishing and I liked to know about fish;

watching Greenhill and trying the method occasionally myself I began to see that there were satisfactions and difficulties in it as great as those of dry-fly fishing; more important, trout responded differently to a fly moved across or against the current than they did to one floating on the surface. Fishing the wet fly, one found trout in unexpected places; they came to it sometimes over the top of weed beds in great smooth arrows of disturbed water that checked sharply into a boiling rise. The sudden direct pull of a fish on the line and back into the hand was fully as exciting as the gentle dimple in which a dry fly disappeared.

The Frome fish were every bit as shy as chalk-stream fish are likely to be—any clumsy approach would put a feeding fish down for the rest of that day and perhaps for longer. Fishing a dry fly, one learned to kneel and crawl upstream, spotting rises carefully, studying the approach, working carefully into position for the cast. Upstream nymph fishing was fascinating and profitable, as I already knew, and the upstream wet fly offered most of the same advantages, except that the fish usually turned to follow it downstream before taking and so would sometimes see the rod or simply turn in disgust from the too swift swimming of the fly. But Greenhill wanted me to fish the downstream wet fly, and that was really difficult with shy fish. It meant an altogether more intense form of crawling and creeping, a closer study of lies and approaches and current, longer and in some ways more accurate casting. Greenhill was good, and I wanted to be as good myself; so I began to work at it.

As soon as I had thoroughly committed myself to learning the method, Greenhill began to rule and guide my learning as he ruled what I did when we were shooting. I started out with one bad fault, an almost unbreakable habit of recovering line in my hand, developed by years of upstream fishing. This brought the fly across too fast and too shallow, and Greenhill, after a period of patient explanation, began to take the rod away from me whenever I fell in to it. In a little while we were fishing with only one rod between us, changing over whenever one or other of us hooked a fish and whenever I made a clumsy or careless cast or fished the fly badly. I became a respectable wet-fly fisherman rather quickly, and from then on Greenhill was little concerned about whether I fished wet or dry or with the nymph.

All this, I realize now, was his way of preparing me for salmon fishing. Greenhill was not by any means a rich man; he lived frugally in the barracks at Dorchester and spent what little money he had where it would give him the most of the sports he loved. He had a pair of beautiful guns and loaded his own cartridges. His salmon rods were greenheart that he had made up himself; he made all his own traces and flights and minnows and prawn tackles, though not, I think, his flies. The one extravagance he allowed himself was the renting of a stretch of salmon water on the lower reaches of the Frome, between Wool and Wareham. During the season he fished there almost every day, alone or with his friend Charlie Baunton, with whom he shared the water.

At that time the Frome, like several other fine salmon rivers in the south of England, was slowly and painfully recovering after bad days. Early in the nineteenth century it had been a great river with a magnificent run of fish. Uncontrolled netting and some pollution had made it almost worthless, but evidently the run of fish was not quite killed out. I don't know the exact history of its recovery, whether the riparian owners bought off some of the nets, as they did on the Wye, or whether the scarcity of salmon simply discouraged the net fisherman, but the recovery was a fine thing. In the early 1920's there was a good run of fish in the spring months, and they were really large fish—over twenty pounds as often as not and thirty-pounders were common. One April, during the Easter holidays, Greenhill suddenly told me that I was to come salmon fishing with him, not just once or twice, but every day I wanted to. This was like a sudden opening of heaven's gate. For years I had listened to my uncle's talk of salmon fishing and read books about salmon fishing and dreamed dreams of it. Now I was to start fishing with the almost certain chance of really big fish, and I knew I should be learning the business properly.

The Frome is a slow, deep river in its lower reaches, and the meadows through which it runs are wilder and rougher than those farther up. Strong weeds and sedges grow up in the pasture land, and the irrigation ditches are deep and wide; the river was not tidal where we fished it, but as I remember it now the country had some measure of the bigness and wildness of the tide flats at the mouths of British Columbia rivers that I have known since. There were ravens there and big hawks and ducks and wading birds of many kinds. Small birds were there also, sedge warblers and reed buntings and black-headed buntings, pippits and pert wagtails; they sang and mated and nested in the reeds and the rough grass, the wagtails fussing and fluttering and strutting at the edge of the river. And always things were happening in the wide meadows and the willow beds: a nesting plover would be chasing a raven, or two ravens chasing a hawk; a polecat would be glimpsed hunting a hedge; or a sudden rush of wings would reveal a sparrow hawk's stoop at a bunting.

But the river itself was the greatest fascination. Its slow current hid things that I could only vaguely imagine: the lies of great pike and salmon, deep silent places from which they might fiercely turn at any moment to seize the fly or minnow or prawn that I dared to hang there. I was almost genuinely afraid at times, afraid of dragging the fly away from some crashing rise or of jamming the reel as a great fish jumped or of doing any of the hundred other things I could do to throw away a golden chance that might better have been in Greenhill's capable hands.

Wisely, Greenhill started me with the fly. The Frome is not

a really good river for the fly; for the most part it is too slow
and too deep for attractive fishing, though many fine fish have
come to the torrish or Jock Scott or green highlander. But I
was given the fly rod because it was easy—minnow and prawn
were for those experienced and fortunate individuals who
knew the bottom of the river as well as its surface and could
handle them properly.

We started fishing at an off time. Fish were being caught in
the pool below Bindon Mill. We heard about them and even
saw them caught as we passed the mill each day. But in the
rest of the river there was little moving; in a full week's fishing I had moved two fish to the fly, and Greenhill had felt perhaps five or six touch his prawn, only one of them hard enough
to take out line. We had not even killed a good-sized pike,
something I had hoped for, though Greenhill had warned me
carefully that we were not fishing for pike and should not
catch them unless we fished too fast for salmon. Before the
end of the week I had tried prawn and minnow several times,
gladly and hopefully, but they had done little more for me
than the fly—one good hard pull to the minnow in the Railway
Pool.

On the morning of the ninth day we got to the river late and
found that Charlie Baunton had killed two beautiful fish on
the fly before we got there. We caught nothing. On the tenth
day we took out only the spinning rod and fished alternately.
The Railway Pool was blank and so was the next pool below
it. That brought us to the Ivy Pool, a deep pool where the fish
sometimes lie well in under the bank in a sort of cave that the
river has cut away. Greenhill worked his prawn into this place
and hooked a fish. For once all went well, and I gaffed it for
him ten minutes later—a fourteen-pounder.

I worked down the rest of the pool, fishing my most careful
best, dropping the prawn within six inches of the other bank,
swinging it across deep and slow, holding it as long as I could
wherever the fish should be lying. Greenhill watched closely

and once or twice nodded his head in approval. I wanted that because I knew that a bad cast plopping down in midstream or a few turns of the reel too fast in bringing the prawn through a good lie would be his signal to take the rod away for half an hour. But fish how I would, the rest of the pool was blank.

The next pool was the Hut Pool, a pool on a curve and shallow at the head, so shallow that I could see the prawn as I brought the first cast around. I moved two steps and cast again. Again I saw the prawn coming up to me under my own bank; then there was a fish behind it, a silver-gray fish, big and beautiful. He came in a wave and turned in a boil, and then Greenhill was shouting anxious directions to me.

He was only a ten-pounder, and Greenhill lifted him on the gaff five or six minutes after I had hooked him. He half-apologized, half-scolded me, "I wanted you to get the first one, young fellow. Next time you can play him out and bring him to the gaff properly."

I don't think I cared whether I fished at all in the rest of that day. My salmon was on the bank, clean silver and beautiful, with the violet sheen of the sea faint on his scales. Greenhill fished on, and we came to the long pool called the Salmon Water. He was fishing as only he could, swinging the prawn out easily, letting it almost brush the reeds of the far bank in its fall, working it deep down to the floor of the river before he began the slow recovery. His big shoulders hunched over the rod, his hands on rod and reel were ready and sensitive, his whole being seemed projected out into the swim of his prawn, concentrated on what it was doing down there on the bottom of the river. Beside him Dinah sat in trembling concentration as tense as his own. Suddenly, almost in the exact moment that he began the recovery of a cast, he lifted the rod in a heavy strike. Dinah stood up, ears pricked forward. Right under the far bank a big fish crashed to the surface in a heavy, shattering jump. The fish ran as the others had not, deep down and strongly, taking out a lot of line. For fully twenty minutes he bored and struggled and twisted, while we followed him as closely as we could along the bank. Then Greenhill brought him to the gaff, and I saw he was big, so big I didn't want the gaffing of him for fear I would muff it. I reached over, slowly and carefully, then struck and felt the gaff slide solidly home; I lifted and the fish was on the bank.

"Well done," Greenhill said.

"Gosh," I said. "What does he weigh? Forty pounds?"

Greenhill shook his head and smiled. "Not quite thirty. We'll see when we get back to the mill." He began to mount a new prawn. "You get on and fish before it's too late. You won't get many days like this one."

So I fished out the rest of the Salmon Water, and near the tail of it an eighteen-pounder took me, and I killed him, properly and alone as a salmon fisherman should, even gaffing him myself. As we walked back up toward the mill along the railroad, I felt my face hot and my knees weak from sheer joy; the thirty-pound weight of salmon slung clumsily on my back was something I remembered only because it was salmon—salmon Greenhill and I had caught.

I fished many more days with Greenhill. Once I gaffed a forty-pounder for him, and within an hour of that he gaffed a twenty-eight-pounder for me. But right up until the last day I fished with him, I fished on probation. Sometimes, despairing of salmon, I would fish the minnow a little faster in the hope of attracting a big pike. "When you come out with me for salmon, don't waste time fishing for pike," he would say. "Give me that rod." Or, when I made a clumsy cast, "What are you trying to do? Knock their brains out? They don't want it on top of their heads." I think I learned the lessons. I know I still think of him almost every time I fish a pool and try to cover it as carefully and cunningly as he would have.

The very last day I fished with him we fished for pike in the river Stour near Wimborne. We often went out in high hopes of big pike during the winter months, and I was not surprised when he suggested the Stour because I knew a forty-pounder had been killed there years earlier. We crossed the river on a bridge some way above where we were to fish and saw it was high but in good shape. "You ought to get a twenty-pounder today, young fellow," he said. At the farm where we left the car, they told us the river might be flooded over its banks in places, but it should be fishable. This was accurate enough, and I killed a ten-pounder in the first few minutes by wading over the tops of my boots. I offered Greenhill the rod, but he shook his head. "I want to see you catch fish today," he said.

I caught them. An eight-pounder, a fourteen-pounder, two or three small ones, then a sixteen-pounder. Each time I offered him the rod, and each time he refused it. He stood behind me all the time, leaning on the long handle of his gaff, watching closely and yet not wholeheartedly interested in the fate of every cast as he usually was. It was still early in the day when the sixteen-pounder was on the bank. Greenhill said, "You know, I was born a few miles from here."

I was surprised; I hadn't known that. I think I realized then how little I did know about him. He said, "You've got all the fish you want. I'd like to drive round and look at two or three places."

So we took the rod down and went back to the car. He directed as I drove along narrow lanes until we came to the gates of a big stone house in a fine park. I stopped the car, and he looked at it for a long time. I knew it was the house where he was born and I asked, "Who lives there now?" But he didn't answer. Later we drove on farther, to a cemetery, and he showed me the graves where his mother and father were buried. After that we drove home. I felt I had been taken close to him, but I couldn't understand why and I held back into myself a little, afraid. After a while, he said, "Sorry I took you away from your fishing, young fellow. But it's not like salmon fishing; it was only pike." I hadn't minded about the fishing, but I knew it was strange that he had wanted to leave it and strange that he hadn't taken the rod all day. At seventeen I was perfectly willing to call a thing strange without wondering much just why it was strange.

Three weeks later Greenhill went up to shoot pigeons in a wood on a windy hill. He died there, and Dinah howled beside him through the night and part of the next morning.

LITTLE LAKES

THE little lakes of Vancouver Island and the British Columbia coast are uncountable. If they were to be counted, someone would have to lay down a law that distinguished between a lake and a pothole and a pond and a swamp. Then all the ground would have to be resurveyed and all the maps drawn again to make quite sure that no little lake, anywhere, was left out. And that would be an awful job because they nestle in a thousand unexpected places—on the breasts of mountains, in wide river flats, up draws and gullies, on forgotten plateaus and on the round tops of big hills.

To be little, I think a lake should be not more than a mile or two long. To be a lake at all, it should have a respectable flow of water into it and out of it, some lakes, I know, are fed by springs and drained by underground streams; but a little lake that has nothing more than an overflow channel leading from it is in grave danger of being reckoned a pond. Swamps, very often, are lakes filled in by the slow deposit of each year's algal bloom and weed growth until reeds and hardhack can spread their roots out into it and still keep their heads above water. It is not always too easy to decide when a lake has ceased to be a lake and become a swamp. Potholes, for my purpose, are flood pools in the swamps and wide places in the creeks where there is just room for a few ducks to light and feed. Beaver ponds usually are something all their own, good places to fish, but still more nearly potholes than lakes.

Most of the little lakes on the British Columbia coast have trout in them, and the time to go to them first is in April. May can be a good month too, but in July and August, even in June, the water is likely to be too warm for good fish or good fishing. In late September and early October, when cool nights have lowered the water temperature, they are good again. Generally the trout in the lakes are cutthroats, generally they will come well enough to the fly and generally there will be plenty of them; but that's about all the generalizing it is safe to do because little lakes can vary in fascinating ways, even when they are on the same watershed.

I like them best when they are back in the standing timber. They are secret and silent then, closed in, and few people go to them. It is a great moment when you come down through the woods to such a lake. You stand there and look at it, judging its shore line, measuring its islands, noticing a deep bay here, a sloping beach there, a rock bluff across on the other side; it is untried water then and it looks full of promise. Every windfall, thrusting out into the water, may be the haunt of a big fish; the shallow water behind the island, where the lily pads show, will surely be a good place for the fly; the mouth of the stream at the head will be worth trying; the deep, still water may hide anything, even a short, thick ten-pounder, perhaps a whole round dozen of them. True, that miracle never happens, but a man would be a queer sort of fisherman if he did not let his mind play with the idea of it at every first sight of new water.

There is a whole chain of little lakes above the fourteen-mile length of Nimpkish Lake—Anutz, Hustan, Atluck, Wolf, Crescent, Loon, to name only the larger ones. Each lake, and its fishing, is sharply different from the others, and each has its surprises. I fished Anutz for a whole year before I caught anything much bigger than a pound. Then one day I ran a canoe clear to the head and pulled it up on a gravel bar where the stream came in. I had meant to take the trail and go on through to Hustan Lake, but as I watched there was a quiet little rise at the edge of the fast run of water that poured into the lake. I got ready lazily to fish over it, but because the day was bright I put up a 4X leader and a No. 17 greenwell nymph. The fish rose again while I was tying on the fly, but I still didn't suppose he was particularly big. I cast upstream of the rise, saw a faint movement underwater and struck into something solid. The fish rolled out as he felt the hook, then turned and ran down into the lake until he had half the backing off the reel. He weighed over four pounds when I netted him, and I caught two others of about the same size without moving from the gravel bar. The next week I caught three more in the same place and with the same fly, one of them only a few ounces under five pounds. I can't recall that I saw any others or lost any, and each rise meant a fish fairly and solidly hooked. The little greenwell does its work well.

Hustan lies farther in toward the high mountains and is more beautiful than Anutz. It is almost two lakes, divided by a thirty-foot neck of moderate current. The best fishing is in this neck, good, free-rising little cutthroats running from three quarters of a pound up to a pound and a quarter at most. The lower half of the lake is a great jam of floating logs and smaller drift, sucked in against an underground outlet. There are two layers of splendidly arched limestone caves, the upper layer bone dry and with funnels that lead down to the river on the lower level. There were fish here in the semidarkness, little, thin half-pounders that took the fly greedily and fought gamely for their size. They were not blind, even far down the caves where only a shadow of light penetrated, and it was strange to hook them and play them and net them entirely by feel.

Little lakes have a way of hiding themselves in the woods, and it is easy to pass within a few hundred feet of one and not see it, particularly if it has an underground outlet, as is very often the case in limestone country. Unknown Lake is within a hundred yards of the main trail to Buttle Lake, or what was the main trail until logging destroyed it a year or two ago. Even though a stranger passing may see light on the water through the trees, he will not suspect there is a lake there because he has just passed a great wide backwater of the Buttle River and it is easy to imagine that the trail has curved to pass the head of this. I heard reports of Unknown Lake long before I found it, and wonderful reports they were too: the trout took with fierce carelessness; they were hog fat from feeding on nothing but leeches; they averaged three pounds or more in weight. The truth, when I found it, differed somewhat from the reports, but was almost as spectacular. The truth was not revealed the first time I found the lake—only suggested. It was a hot day in July, and Edward and I ran down from the trail on our way out from Buttle Lake. The lake lay in the sun without a ripple, and all over its surface there played great mottled-wing dragonflies, mating and hunting and feeding. They swooped and dove and pounced and hovered, and the warm, still air seemed to nestle under their wings and click with their sharp maneuvering. There were other, smaller dragonflies among them and gray and blue damsel flies also, but not a trout moved anywhere that we could see. We found an old dugout at the lower end of the lake; but it was leaky and waterlogged, and we had only an hour or so to fish, so we worked along the shore, wading in where the bottom was right. We caught and killed three fish that weighed about a pound each and returned two others that were smaller. All of them came up from deep water, in fine slashing rises, but after that fought poorly. Fortunately I had a thermometer with me, and when I read the water temperature at sixty-eight degrees Fahrenheit, I knew we had not given the lake a fair chance. When I examined the stomachs of the fish we had caught and found them packed with beetles and caddis larvae and chironomid nymphs, in hundreds, and fresh-water clams and dragonfly larvae, I knew the lake had possibilities.

So we tried it again the next year, in April, before the water had time to get warm. One or two fish showed far out, near the islands, while we were putting our rods up. I tied on a fly and flipped it out along the log I was standing on. It was taken fiercely and at once by a fish about fifteen inches long. All around the lake it was the same: the second a fly touched the water, a fish had it. They came to wet fly or dry, to fly worked or simply sinking down through the water, to fly cast well out or flicked in close to shore. Often three or four fish came at once, and the disappointed waited their chance until the barbless and pointless hook—for we cut away barbs and points almost at once—dropped away from the first fish. We caught no three-pounders—a pound and a half was the largest; but we caught no really small fish, nothing much smaller than ten inches long. Later I went into the lake again and built a raft so that we could fish the deep water in the center and the shoals near the islands. We tried in May and in September, but still we could find no three-pounders even though we tried a little halfhearted trolling for them.

Burnt Lake is another lake with no outlet and only a small stream running into it in times of heavy rain. It is a tiny lake, not more than twenty acres, and I first heard of it from hunters ten or twelve years ago. A wonderful place for big bucks, they said, if you can find it. It's somewhere in the flat above the Quinsam, not more than a mile or so from the road and nearer the bluffs than the river, probably draining into Coal Creek.

Then the timber was cut away, and the hunters seemed even more vague than they had been about it. So I took time out one day when I was hunting willow grouse and found it myself. It wasn't really so very hard to find, because there were a few tall, slim trees standing around it amidst all the devastation of high-lead logging; and when one marked their line from Coal Creek, it was fairly obvious that the lake was near them. It was a calm day, and the surface of the lake was not stirred by the least ripple. I watched it for nearly an hour and saw no sign of fish.

A week or two later I took the rubber boat in there and learned a little more about it. I fished with everything—flies and spinners and even worms—and could not move a fish of any kind. I took soundings and found over seventy feet of water in the center, with depths sloping almost evenly down to that from every side. The lake was quite cool enough for fish— fifty-two degrees Fahrenheit at six feet, forty-two degrees Fahrenheit at twenty-four feet—and I found many kinds of good trout feed in it. It seemed a perfect chance for an experiment in stocking. I made a few calculations and decided that an annual planting of about 500 fry should keep the lake producing a steady harvest of two- and three-pound fish. Kamloops trout would be the best prospect, because they will seldom spawn without running water, and I felt confident that the intermittent flow of the creek at the head would not be sufficient encouragement for them. So long as there was no natural spawning to confuse things, it should not be difficult to keep the lake exactly controlled.

I reckoned without the freehandedness of the powers that be. I wrote and asked them for the first stocking, 500 fry. When the cans came up, they had in them a thousand little fish instead of five hundred, three-inch fingerlings instead of one-inch fry, and all were solemnly dumped into poor little Burnt Lake. This meant a survival far in excess of anything I had counted on, and I saw that my hope of two- and three-pounders was gone. The next year, which was 1928, the powers sent along 500 more fingerlings in the spring, and then, during the summer, a great forest fire swept down Vancouver Island. For two or three days Burnt Lake was in the hottest heart of the fire. The last few standing trees burned away, the salal brush burned and the hardhack around the edges of the lake, and the soil burned away from the gravel of the ridges. Even great

Douglas fir stumps were burned to nothing, leaving three or four deep holes in the ground where their largest roots had gone down.

I saw Burnt Lake soon after the fire passed through. Its whole surface was covered with a gray scum of ashes, and I tried to imagine it as it had been in the fire, with the red glare all around it and reflected from it and smoldering pieces of bark and debris, wind-borne, falling into it and hissing their heat away into the water. I wondered if any fish still lived. Such a little lake in the midst of such a huge fire seemed no more than a kettle on a hot stove, but I remembered that heat goes up, not down, even in water, and that the lake was seventy feet deep. There would have been plenty of cool water down there. Then I wondered about the ash, whether it would choke the oxygen out of the water or perhaps sink down and clog the gills of the fish. I felt less certain about this; it might not kill them all but surely would affect a fair number, and that would be no bad thing for my hope of three-pounders.

I fished the lake the following April. It was full of fish, lively little nine- and ten-inch Kamloops that came hungrily to any fly. I waited a year and tried again; there were eleven- and twelve-inch fish now, rather thin and dark, but red-fleshed, pretty and lively. Many of them were fully ripened to spawn and some of the females had begun to reabsorb their eggs, I thought.

I still go occasionally to Burnt Lake. It isn't so pretty since the fire, but there is something attractive about its small, almost perfect roundness and the way the ridges circle it close and hide it. The salal and Oregon grape are starting to grow again, with yellow violets among them; willows are creeping down again from the swamp that feeds the creek; and not all the hardhack along the edge of the lake was killed. The fish are still there, and I keep very quiet about them and the lake. I don't think anyone has remembered to stock it since the war started, and in time the surplus stock of fish should die out.

Then, if there has been even a little successful natural spawning, there may be a chance of two- and three-pounders. I like to think of that and I like to think, too, that the ridges all around the lake will be green again with salal, perhaps even with the start of fir and hemlock and cedar. Some day, hunters may talk again of the little lake lost in the woods on the wide flat above the Quinsam. "A fine place for a big buck," they'll say. "And there's big fish in the lake too; you can see 'em jump sometimes, if you watch."

Ax and fire and logging machinery come to nearly all the little lakes of Vancouver Island sooner or later. Some are still lost in the deep woods, a few are protected in parks, rugged mountain country guards others; but the near ones, those one lives with, are passing through the change or must pass through it soon. And the change is not all loss. I wonder often about logged-off land, whether or not love of it is an acquired taste. The first days and months of the change are shocking—scarred earth, splintered stumps, dead, brown treetops, broken saplings, everything torn and shattered and flattened into a chaos of waste. The summer sun bleaches the raw red scars, dries the glistening sap where the bark is torn away, shrivels the needles from the broken tops; in the fall there is fire, and the waste becomes black logs and stumps against red gravel. Sooner or later after that the healing starts. Little shoots of salal and Oregon grape show the earliest green, and then the brambles and bracken and fireweed make light ground cover out of the exhausted soil; after these, willows and poplars in the creek bottoms and along the lines of swamps, spreading out even to dry ground where the country is fairly flat. Dogwoods spring from old stumps on the slopes, and in a few favored places the broad-leaved maples seed thickly and grow to tree height in a few short years. Wherever there are seed trees left alive after the burning, Douglas fir and hemlock and cedar show again; often the white pine comes, far more thickly than before the logging. But no fire kills blister rust. Its spores settle from the high air, and one by one the little pine trees wither and bleed and die. Slowly the old botanical wars fight themselves out again, and the forest builds back to itself through a changing loveliness surely as satisfying as the heavy magnificence of virgin timber.

The first little lake I ever saw on Vancouver Island was Theimar Lake, and my first duty was to stake out the line of the logging railroad that harvested its timber. Our line ran eight hundred or a thousand feet from the lake, but I went down there the first day. Mac, a little Irishman who was working on the same crew, came down with me, and I asked him about the fish. "Lots of them," he said. "The boys go out from camp every Sunday. We can come back and try it after supper if you like."

We did that, and the fishing was pretty good. It was an exciting lake too, deep and fairly wide at the upper end, suddenly narrow where an island came up out of the deep water and little more than river width from there down through a mile or more of swamp. I wanted to explore, and Mac was willing enough, so we poled the clumsy old raft all over it until the sun was down and the moon was up. Then we hit back for camp, and the moon went in and we lost ourselves somehow between the lake and our survey line. We walked around a little until I fell over a twenty-foot bluff and told Mac I meant to stay put until there was some light. Soon after that the moon came out again, and we found the line and saw lanterns along it— our boss had come out with the skidder rigger to look for us. Mac didn't like being kidded and he was pretty gloomy on the way home. "We'll never hear the last of this," he said. "The only way is to pull right out of camp tomorrow." But we survived it somehow and both of us were still working on the same crew a full year later.

I fished Theimar Lake a good many times during the next several years and learned the full length of the little stream that runs from it down to the salt water. There were beaver dams in the stream where big sea-run cutthroats sometimes lay, and in October a fine run of coho salmon came through to the lake to spawn. In the winter months I shot ducks and geese in the marshy lower end of the lake, and once, at dusk, half a dozen swans circled the island where I was hidden. I remember the work of the graders and steel gangs as they put in the railroad along the line we had laid out; I remember the fallers coming behind them and how I worked myself to load the logs on the cars as the yarding donkey brought them up to the track from the edge of the lake. I felt then that the lake was almost dead and finished. There was scrub timber still around the heronry and the swampy lower end of the lake, scrub timber around the swamps at the head; but the main part of the lake was stripped bare, and dead tops lay dismally out in the water in all the little bays we had fished. I fished it no more, though I passed it often on the way to other fishing places, and in fall and winter I hunted in it and near it for ducks and geese and grouse and deer.

Then I was away from that country for two or three years. The April after I got back I thought of lake fishing. Theimar Lake was only four or five miles away across the logging slash, so I took blankets and a light pack and went there. On the way to the lake I passed through two heavy hailstorms, cold lashing storms from black clouds, but the clouds blew over and the sun came out again in a blue and white sky. I began to notice how the logging slash had healed: alders were thick along the grades, willows and young conifers grew in the old settings, the raw red earth of the skid roads was weathered and overgrown by brambles, and salal brush was thick and glossy green among the burned stumps.

Even so, I did not expect that the lake would please me; the trees had been cut away from it, and the slope of Mount Holdsworth was bare for two thousand feet above it. I could see how the benches and gullies had logged out to the railroads we had laid along them and across them. I came upon the lake almost suddenly. It was blue and white, broken by the wind, very clean and clear in the sunlight. On the islands and at the far end the scrub timber was still standing; the swamp grass was thick, still brown from winter frosts, and Hudson's Bay tea grew in the drier places. At the head was the long, level swamp, and at the upper end of that stood the tall white pines that had not been reached by the high-lead machine. The lake seemed as fine as it had ever seemed, and now it was lonely and lost in the logging slash as little lakes are lonely and lost in the Scottish moors. The loggers who had taken the timber had moved far away; the steel and the ties were stripped from the railroads, and there was no threat of ax or donkey whistle or saw. No one wanted the country or the lake or anything in it, so it was mine as it never had been before. I was suddenly conscious of the other little lakes that lay near by, Soo Lake and Roselle Lake, and of the length of Theimar Creek toward the salt water and the sweep of land over toward the mountains along Nimpkish Lake. It was a big empty country, left to its own devices, to its own fascinating growth back into something that some day men would want again.

It was late afternoon when I came to the lake, and I had decided to build a raft because I knew the old ones would be waterlogged and falling apart. I made camp quickly near the larger of the two creeks that came in at the head of the lake, then walked two or three hundred yards up to the old logging trestle. The lean-to shelter where Sam Ford's bridge crew had cooked their lunches was still there, and I found a handful of spikes, as I was pretty sure I would. Then I picked out two of the sawed bridge ties left on the deck and dragged them down to the lake. There was enough shiplap lumber lying around the trestle to floor my raft, so I packed that down too. Then I put up my rod and caught two or three fish for supper.

The wind died down at dusk and a full moon was in the sky almost at once; it was a still night, crystal bright in the stars and the moon and the water. All day long the big blue grouse had been hooting in the logging slash and the ruffed grouse drumming in the swamps; now the hooters were silent, but the ruffed grouse drummed and courted all around me in the moonlight. I lay and listened to them and thought of Sam's good bridge crew—Roy Davis, Curly Brown, George Boxall, Ozzie, the engineer, Sam himself. I knew where some of them were and could guess at what they were doing. I wondered if they ever thought of this one of the many, many logging trestles they had built together, this one near the head of little, lost Theimar Lake.

I made my raft the next morning, dapping the bridge ties across three slender, sharply pointed cedar poles, nailing the shiplap deck to the ties. By the time I had finished the wind was strong again, blowing up from the foot of the lake. I poled my raft up to the island, drifted back and caught a few fish, poled up again, drifted once more and caught a few more fish. But it was hard work and uncomfortable, so I decided to wait for the calm of the next morning and spent the rest of that afternoon in walking to Soo Lake and Roselle Lake to see how they looked with the timber away from them.

In the calm of the next morning the fish were really feeding, coming freely to the surface in deep water all down the center of the lake. I used a small, dry iron blue on 3X gut and kept everything larger than fourteen inches. It was fine fishing, exactly what I had come for, and by the time the first ripple of wind came up the lake I had twelve or fourteen good, clean fish on the raft. None of them was larger than a pound and a half, but I was not looking for large fish because I had learned long before that Theimar Lake's big ones were dark and thin in April. I was near the island, almost a mile from my camp, when the wind began to freshen. I hooked another fish, and by the time he was in the net there were whitecaps all over the lake. I thought I saw a quiet rise on the slope of one and cast to it. A fish took the little fly at once and ran with a solid determination that told me he was big. Had he broken me or shaken loose in that first run, I should hardly have cared, because I was certain I knew his type—twenty-four inches long, a bare two pounds in weight, dark, with a big head and red on his gill covers. But he came back from the run and ran again, near the surface this time, so that I saw his broad, clean side under the crest of a whitecap. Then everything was difficult. The fish went down, and the raft wanted to drift over the line. I paddled awkwardly with one hand, holding the rod in the other. The waves swept over the shiplap floor of my raft, and the raft itself creaked and groaned. I couldn't raise the fish in the water; then I could raise him and he came back to me, but I couldn't net him. And the raft drifted over him again and I straightened that out, but he ran again, strongly, upwind, and I dared not hold him on the light rod and the light gut. Then the raft jarred suddenly, hard on the shore at the head of the lake. I jumped out into the shallow water and knew that the fish was tiring. Two or three minutes later he was on his side, with the swells lifting him as I slipped the net under. I looked at him a long time when I had him, because he was the only really fine fish I ever caught in Theimar Lake—nearly four pounds and fat as a fish from the Test in June. I forced the hook from his jaw and loosed the gut from my line. It was no time to make another cast.

MAY

I<small>N</small> May the Kamloops trout
spawn. Most of the spawners are four-year-old fish, and they
migrate from their lakes into the feeder streams exactly as their
steelhead cousins on the coast move from salt water into the
rivers. The Kamloops trout has made a great name for himself

as a game fish, and he deserves it: I know of no other fresh-water fish that runs more strongly than he does or jumps with a finer freedom and recklessness. A two- or three-pounder hooked on a fly cast over the shoals of some interior lake is the spectacular model of all that a fighting fish should be. And three-pound Kamloops are common enough in the interior of British Columbia, ten- and twelve-pounders are not absolutely rare and forty-pounders have been caught, though not, so far as I know, on the fly.

Yet the Kamloops is a simple product of environment. He differs from the steelhead and the Pacific coast rainbow (which differ from each other not at all) only in that he has rather smaller scales, 145 or so along the lateral line instead of about 135. Even this superficial difference can be wiped out in a single generation by hatching the eggs of Kamloops trout at slightly higher temperatures than those normally prevailing in interior streams.

The Kamloops at his best should be compared to the early summer-run steelhead, which is the coast rainbow at his best, a fish built to full strength and vigor by two or three years of sea feeding and not yet slowed by the drain and weight of developed ovaries or milt sacs. One catches the summer steel-head in rivers, usually in fine, sparkling, swift rivers whose current and obstacles give him great advantage. The Kamloops at his best is usually a lake fish; but there is no other lake fish like him, and if the tackle is anywhere weak or the hand on the rod too clumsy, he will find it out.

Though the Kamloops spawns in May, running then, gravid and red, to the streams, May is also one of the best months in which to catch him. One is not concerned with the spawning four-year-olds—they are in the streams, out of the way. The three-year-olds, still a year away from spawning, are coming into their noble prime. Dark-gray backed and silver-bellied from a full winter of deepwater feeding, they come to the sur-face as the ice breaks up and by May, unless the lake is a very

high and cold one, they are feeding well on the shoals and over
the chara-weed beds. There is plenty for them in the lime-
rich water that few other fresh-water fish can hope to find:
Gammarus, the fresh-water shrimp, Daphnia, the water flea,
many sedges, dragonfly nymphs and damsel-fly nymphs, crane-
flies and midges, stone flies and snails and leeches, all in the
abundance that grows Kamloops trout to three, six, twelve,
even eighteen pounds in three or four years.

Many of the wonderful interior lakes were troutless only a
few years ago, their masses of feed multiplying in chara-weed
beds, feeding upon one another in a never-ending cycle of
productivity too small for human interest. A few trout from
a lake with a natural stock, painfully transplanted by some
local enthusiast, often built a cycle of fish upon the teeming
cycles of insect life, and anglers from all over the world began
to find that the Kamloops trout lakes held great things for
them. Knouff Lake and Paul Lake came into their famous days;
and by that time things were on a more organized basis, and the
government took a hand, with hatcheries and large-scale plantings. More and more lakes came into production, and fishermen learned to watch and wait for them. "Peter Hope ought
to be pretty hot next year," they'd say. "They've made some
big plantings there." Or, "Tawheel's going to be open this
season. Boy! I'm sure going to try that one out."

It isn't all just perfect, by any means. Nearly always the
plantings of fish are made "blind," that is, without proper survey of the lakes to be stocked and without consideration for
the type of fishing most needed. Once stocked, a lake is usually
left to control itself. Further plantings of fish will probably be
made, but there will be no effort to limit natural spawning. As
a result, many of the lakes quickly spoil themselves. For a few
years they give great fishing; then natural spawning produces
an overstock, and the average size drops far down, or the lake
becomes unbalanced, with an overstock of fish one year and
a small stock the next. This uses up lakes pretty fast, and one

soon hears that "X lake isn't what it was," or, "You can't get big fish in B lake any more." But there are plenty of lakes in British Columbia, and more and more of them become accessible all the time, so that the feast of plenty goes through its extravagant courses and only a few of us worry. There's good fishing, the Lord knows; there's always good fishing.

That is why I always feel happy at Paul Lake. Paul Lake is one lake that is controlled, because there is a hatchery at Paul Creek where all the spawners are caught up. Their eggs are hatched artificially, and the fry are shipped out to other less fortunate lakes. Only a set and limited number is turned back into Paul Lake, and that number is just enough to yield plenty of fish between one and three pounds. Paul is a beautiful lake, set narrowly in the mountains, with fine shallows where the trout come splendidly to the fly and deep beds of chara where feed of all kinds multiplies. Two men are closely identified with it for me, and they always will be. One was a great fisherman—Bill Nation. The other is a great fishman—Charlie Mottley.

Charlie is a biologist with soaring vision; he has all a biologist's patience for detail, for controlled experiment, exact proof. But his mind does not stop there; it leaps ahead to put to use what has been learned. Working at Paul Lake, Charlie learned a lot, and from what he learned he developed the stocking formula that keeps the lake producing some ten thousand fish a year with a total weight of about five tons. The formula is simple enough and would apply to all the artificially stocked lakes of the interior. But Charlie, like many another good man, has left British Columbia for the United States, and no one bothers to apply his formula elsewhere than at Paul Lake.

Bill Nation was a wise, gentle, wholehearted angler. He was Paul Lake's best guide and the best guide to a hundred other interior lakes. Bill was no scientist, though he sometimes liked to set himself up as one. But he knew how to fish for Kamloops trout; he knew where to look for them, knew what they would be feeding on, knew how to give them a close enough imitation of whatever that feed might be. Bill's mind, like Charlie's, loved to take long flights ahead of sure knowledge, using a base of knowledge for imaginative and often very effective experiment. Bill's vivid theories lacked the close, hard logic that Charlie's ideas always had. Bill loved a poetic flight for its own sake—a wet fly, for instance, tied to represent mating damsel flies and fished several inches under water, on the supposition that the fish, by some process of their own, would reverse the relationship of the fly's position to the surface of the water and consider that it was flying some inches out in the free air, yet strike at the submerged improbability. Of course, the fly caught fish and caught them well, so Bill's idea must have had something.

Charlie learned a great deal from Bill, poetic flights and all, and Bill learned a great deal from Charlie; I was lucky enough to come between and learn from both of them. But I don't remember them for their work or their theories, but for their companionship and for what they gave to the lake. A day at Paul might start with a big batch of trout to be checked over, a sample of the previous day's catch. We would be curious about what their feed had been, and for an hour or more we would open stomachs, identify and count insects. Always there were surprises in this—perhaps a selective feeder with a stomach full of nothing but copepods or Daphnia; what had persuaded him to take bright fly on a No. 6 hook? Or a fish of more catholic tastes, crammed to the gullet and beyond with every variety of feed the lake offered; how had he supposed he could take and hold one more thing? Perhaps one or two of the fish would be spawners of the previous year, carrying Charlie's numbered tags in their tails. Bright fish, but thin and not brave when you hooked them as the maiden fish were. The spring balance told the tale of these, for almost without exception they weighed less than they had when running to spawn the previous year. And their scales under the microscope repeated the story—a ragged edge eating back into four good years of growth, with nothing at all formed beyond it. "They're nothing but a drain on the lake," Charlie would say. "A spawner recovering won't put back two ounces while a maiden fish is putting on five. Kill them, cut their swim bladders, turn them back for the sedge larvae to feed on."

Later in the morning we might go up to the traps in the creek to weigh and mark fish, and all the time we'd talk of fish, not only of Kamloops trout, but of brown trout and cutthroats, of Pacific salmon, of herrings or grayling or kokanees or anything else that balances itself on fins.

On the way back down the lake from the creek we would almost certainly fish, but lazily, because the afternoon would be hot and the lake calm and we would be thinking of cool beer back at the camp and some intricate argument we wanted to settle with reference book or microscope.

Toward evening we would go on down the lake to the lodge for a quiet drink with Bill and some of the guests and hear talk of the day's fishing. Bill would develop some new theory of imitating dragonflies, a new tying of an old fly perhaps, or simply a new and more realistic method of working the fly through the water. About then someone would start kidding, and Bill would answer in his soft voice and stories would begin to grow tall. And then it would be time to go down to dinner.

After dinner we would go to the boats, a little excited by the thought of the best fishing hour of the day ahead of us, the time when two- and three-pounders, perhaps bigger fish, came boldly onto the shallows near the outlet. "There's no hurry," Bill would say gently. "No hurry. They won't start to move much for half an hour yet."

But we would climb into the boats and start off anyway, cruising gently over the still water. In our boat Bill himself would have a rod, trailing one of his big dragon-nymph imitations on a long line while Charlie stood in the stern and I used some fly of which Bill did not approve from the bow.

Sunset took the color from the water, leaving it gray and black, rippled by the movement of oars and boats but otherwise still: some fish rising, but nothing really big within reach; a good rise well down toward the outlet, just in the gentle draw of the current. Bill swung the boat to it, and we covered it, Charlie and I. Then Bill's rod jumped—the big dragon nymph, fishing deep, had moved him. By the time he was netted, it was real dusk. Bill picked up the oars again and moved the boat gently and silently back to its hunting. I covered a good rise and hooked a fish of nearly two pounds. Charlie dropped a fly beside my hooked fish and struck at once to a solid pull. By the time both fish were in the boat, we were across the outlet, within casting distance of the far shore. It was harder to see now and difficult to judge distance.

I covered the little dimple of a rise under a bush that leaned out from the shore, but the fish would not take. I brought the fly in. "Going to put on a dry sedge," I said.

Bill shook his head. "No. Waste time. Too late to change. Keep fishing."

But I changed anyway and was lucky enough to get it done quickly in the dim light. The rise had come again near the bushes, twice, but Charlie's wet fly had not moved him. I shot the sedge into the rings of a third dimple, saw it disappear and tightened. A silver Kamloops caught the last light as he walked the water in five great jumps. "You were right," Bill said. "I was wrong." The reel talked as it had not through all that day, and the fish twisted his body against the pull of the line, deep down now. Suddenly he was at the surface again, jumping and jumping back toward the boat. I hand-lined fast and came up with him—lucky. A little while longer and he was on his side and Bill slipped the net under.

"Might be three pounds. We'll have to weigh him."

Charlie laughed. "When you check a batch for me, you say you can guess the weight close enough."

"Little fish," Bill said. "All about the same. Weigh two or

three and you've weighed them all. Go on fishing. There's time to catch another on the way back to the float."

So the boat stole on, and we cast to the rises we could reach until Charlie hooked the last good fish of the evening, and we netted it with the lights shining brightly out from the lodge.

Bill has had the chance now that he sometimes used to talk about—a chance to size up the fish and fishing qualities of the Styx. Charlie's excursion into mythology has taken him only as far as Ithaca, where he watches Cayuga's waters and plans for the Finger Lakes, but even that is overfar for the good of the Kamloops lakes. Paul Lake is a monument to both men— to Charlie's fish sense and Bill's fishing sense, but whatever the fish may do, should they become twice as numerous and grow twice as large, a day there can never be quite so full and good again.

SEA-RUN CUTTHROATS

M AY is a great and generous month for the trout fisherman. In the English chalk streams the fish are coming to their best and the hatching May flies drift in squadrons and flotillas and armadas, their proudly upright wings a mark that stirs both fish and fisherman. In the Adirondacks and the Catskills trout fishermen are out with the Hendrickson. Here in British Columbia the interior lakes are warm enough, but not too warm, for good fly-fishing, and the great native-stock Kamloops trout come up out of Shuswap Lake to their fierce feeding on sockeye and spring salmon yearlings at Little River and off the mouth of Adams. On the coast the summer steelhead are running. In May each year I used to return to General Money his big thirteen-foot salmon rod; through the winter months it was mine because, the General said, he was too old to give it proper work to do, but by mid-May he would be thinking of early summer fish in the Stamp and would take the big rod over there to fish its easy, graceful way down the Junction Pool or the General's Pool. In May I turn to a smaller rod and go to the Island Pools to find our own run of summer fish, little fish seldom over five pounds, seldom under two, but sea-run steelhead just the same and brave fish that hit the fly hard and jump freely in the broken water. The twenty-fourth of May, a good Canadian holiday, is a day I have often celebrated with the little steelheads of the Island Pools.

The Pacific coast is great trout country. If we consider the chars as separate from trout—and I am quite certain that we should—there are in the world only three species of trout, the brown, the rainbow and the cutthroat. Of these, two are native to the Pacific coast and the slope of water west of the Rocky Mountains. This, by itself, seems to argue that the Pacific watershed has in full measure whatever it is that trout need and like; all the testing and sorting processes of evolution have left it with two trouts and given only one to all the rest of the world. The variations of environment in the watershed have developed at least two subspecies of each of these native species: the rainbow or steelhead of the coast proper becomes the Kamloops trout at medium elevations and the mountain Kamloops at high elevations; the Yellowstone cutthroat and the mountain cutthroat, as their names suggest, bear similar relationship to the coast cutthroat, the type of the species.

I suppose it is most improper to talk of degrees of nativeness. A fish or a bird or a mammal is native to a country or not native, and that is all there is to it. But for many reasons, most of them emotional and quite illogical, I feel that the cutthroat is the most native of Pacific coast game fish, just as I feel that the ruffed grouse is the most native of the continent's game birds and the cougar and the raccoon are the most native of the mammals. The cutthroat, the coast cutthroat of tidal waters particularly, is such a down-to-earth, workaday, unspectacular fish; he fits his environment so perfectly and makes such good, full use of it, following the tides and the salmon runs and the insect hatches to the limit of their yield; and he has not been, as the rainbow has, more or less successfully transplanted to all parts of the world. He lives in his own place in his own way and has his own special virtues. He is a little like the burned stumps and slash and new growth of the old logging works in that one must know and deeply love the country to appreciate him properly.

In writing of the "Game Fish of British Columbia," Professor J. R. Dymond gives an opinion of cutthroat trout that is undoubtedly shared by many anglers:

Were it not that it (the cutthroat) occurs in the same area as two of the hardest fighting game fish known, its qualities would be more highly regarded. At times it does leap from the water when hooked, and often puts up quite a prolonged struggle before being landed. It generally rises quite readily to the fly, although as a rule it takes the fly sunk and drawn as a minnow, more readily than the dry fly.

The implication of this is that the cutthroat is not to be compared with either the Kamloops or the steelhead as a game fish. My own opinion is that, at his best, he is in every way comparable; and under some circumstances a discerning angler may even find him superior.

The qualifying phrase "at his best" is important, because the cutthroat is too often caught when he is not at his best. When the humpback fry are running in March and April, anglers catch two- and three-pound cutthroats that are thin and feeble after spawning. Many cutthroats are caught in low-producing lakes where the average fish are too small to give a good account of themselves and the larger fish are always in poor condition; and many are caught, quite unnecessarily, with spinner and worm or other such clumsy gear and have no chance to show what they can do. The cutthroat is at his best in a river that is open to the sea; he should then be a short, thick fish of two pounds or more, not too long in fresh water, with a clean white belly and a heavily spotted, green- or olive-brown back. Such a fish will come nobly to wet fly or dry—better to the dry fly than will Kamloops trout and far better, certainly, than steelhead—and when you set the hook he will run as boldly as any fish of his size, and probably he will jump too. Beyond this he has a way of his own that is fully as dangerous to tackle as the more spectacular antics of the Kamloops, a way of boring down and out into the heaviest stream against the lift of a fly rod and sometimes twisting his body and shaking his head in solid, sulky strength. I have had more moments of straining anxiety with big cutthroat trout half played out than I have with any fish, except, perhaps, big brown trout among the weed beds and other obstructions of the chalk streams.

The cutthroat's habit of going to sea is what makes him a really fine game fish. There are good cutthroats and good cutthroat fishing in the cold mountain streams that drain into the big lakes and even in ordinary landlocked rivers that owe nothing to lake or stream; but the true sea-run cutthroat is a very special fish and makes very special fishing. He is not truly migratory, like the steelhead and the salmon: that is, he does not run out to sea from his river in early youth and range freely through deep water until grown to full maturity. He is at once less businesslike about his migration and more practical. Somewhere toward the end of his first or second year he finds that the food available to him in fresh water is not enough, and he simply moves downstream to find more. In tidal water or in the sea just beyond the mouth of his river he finds what he is seeking, so he stays there awhile and feeds; sometimes he moves on out as far as five or ten miles from the mouth of his river, feeding as he goes; he may even (though I am not sure of this) school with other cutthroats to feed for a while off the mouth of some stream quite distant from his

own—certainly schools of big cutthroats lie at certain times off
the mouths of little creeks that seem far too small to support
them even as a spawning run.

But in spite of all this wandering there seems to be no sharp
break between the salt-water and fresh-water life of the migratory cutthroat. He may return to the fresh-water pools of his
river at any time: in spring when the salmon fry hatch, in fall
when the ripe salmon run, in summer when the sedge nymphs
crawl thickly over the round rocks of the stream bed. And he
is seldom beyond reach of the fly-fisherman's search; by studying the tides and his movement in them you may catch him at
his feeding in the estuary; by knowing a favorite bay or sandbar and his chosen time there you may even find him right out
in salt water. In Puget Sound keen cutthroat fishermen search
water as far as six or seven miles from any stream, trolling a
small spinner until they hook the first fish, then changing over
to the fly.

My own first meeting with sea-run cutthroats was in the
Nimpkish River. I was working in a logging camp seven or
eight miles away and started out for the river immediately after
work on my second Saturday in camp. I took a blanket and
enough food for a meal or two and promised myself a well-
spent Sunday. On Saturday evening I fished one pool in the
short hour or so before dark and caught three fish of about a
pound. The Sunday was a bright, warm day and I started early.
The Nimpkish is a broad, fine river, fast and fierce in most
places, but with a few long, slow pools. On the first of these
pools I wasted far too much time, but there was a strong deep
run below it that spread into something less than a pool, no
more, really, than a slackening in the rapid. Right in the
deepest and fastest water a fine fish took, and I landed a three-
pound cutthroat. At the head of the next pool was another
deep, broken run, and there the second fish, a little larger than
the first, came boldly to my fly. From then on I fished the fast,
heavy water whenever I could find it, and by the end of the

day I had four cutthroats and two rainbows, all over three pounds and one of them over four.

Since then I have caught sea-run cutthroats in the salt water, off the mouths of tiny creeks, over the tide flats of big rivers, in fresh-water pools and in the brackish water of shrunken river channels on the ebb tide. About ten years ago I used to fish the mouth of the Campbell regularly with Cliff Whitaker, who was my next-door neighbor at that time. Cliff had learned to fish and hunt in Alaska and was a good man at both sports, aggressive and determined, a fine woodsman and a tireless walker. He also loved human competition in hunting and fishing, which I do not, but we found a way around that which left both of us happy and comfortable.

There are half a dozen or more good places to catch cutthroats in the tidal part of the Campbell; two of them are sloughs, which make dull fishing; three of the good places are best fished from a boat; and only one offers the real variations and complications of current that one hopes for in river fishing and can, at the same time, be fully covered by wading. On a fair run-out of tide the river breaks into a sharp rapid just below the upper slough, and this runs for two hundred yards or more—water where there is always a chance of picking up one or two fish on the wet fly. At the tail of the rapid a small creek comes in, and since the creek has a run of cohos, the cutthroats wait near its mouth when the fry are moving down. But the best of the fishing was in a fairly big pool below the rapid. The main current of the pool swung away from the bank from which we fished and left a wide eddy where feed collected; this was a good place. The run of current itself was fairly good and became very good where it spread out among the short butts of rotten piles at the tail of the pool. All this water was uncertain; on a good tide during April or May the fish were sure to come into it, but just where they would be and how they would be feeding depended on the stage of the tide, the strength of the river and the type of feed that was most available. The mood of the fish also seemed to depend on just what kind of hunting they had had during the full tide before the ebb—a fish with a really fine bellyful of sand launce or sow bugs or sand hoppers could be a very fussy feeder when he came into the pool.

Cliff and I made a habit of going down to the pool whenever there was a good tide, and it wasn't long before we were getting very fine results on the last two hours of the ebb. We caught most of our fish on flies of the streamer type, tied, not in the American way on a long single hook, but on two or three small hooks in tandem, what the English and Scottish sea-trout fishers call "demons" or "terrors." Several Hardy patterns were very deadly: one with long dark badger hackles laid back to back, two tinsel-covered hooks and a red tag on the second hook; another with long blue hackles, strips of light mallard and three hooks each tinsel-covered and with a red tag; a third, called the "dandy" and made up of two hooks, mallard strips and a red hackle at the throat, was deadliest of all. But in the course of this fishing two things became evident: first, that streamer-type flies were altogether too effective under certain conditions, particularly when fish were taking freely on the last of the ebb; and second, that we were not catching fish at all well on the start of the flood, though big ones commonly moved up into the pool and began a lazy sort of feeding at that time.

Cliff and I discussed the deadliness of the streamers and agreed that we had better limit ourselves by giving up their use. At about the same time we discovered we could pick off some of the lazy feeders of the flood tide very nicely with a dry fly. From then on, all Cliff's competitive instinct was directed toward catching the fish by more and more delicate methods. We almost gave up fishing the ebb and always gave our main attention to the glassy slide of water near the piles at the tail of the pool; as soon as the tide began to slow the current there, we went down and waited for some sign of fish moving in.

They came early one day, and Cliff saw a quiet rise just behind the lowest pile. He dropped a brown and white bi-visible into the rings and hooked his fish almost as the fly touched the water; it was a three-pounder. His fly was hardly out free and dried off again when another fish rose within reach; Cliff covered him, played him and netted another three-pounder. Ten minutes later he dipped his net under a third of the same size. "That bi-visible's too deadly," he said. "Guess we'll have to quit using it."

And we did. The bi-visible we had been using was brown and white, tied on a size 9 or 10 hook. We turned to other flies on size 15 and 16 hooks and did less well with them, though still well enough. And we finally went one stage farther still, to upstream nymph fishing with flies as small as size 17. The nymphs were more attractive to the fish than were the small dry flies, but the fishing was actually more exciting and more difficult, because light and water conditions made it hard to tell when a fish had taken the nymph; we were usually wading deep and looking toward the sun across smooth water whose reflecting surface concealed the faint flash of a moving fish that the nymph-fisherman generally depends on.

That seems to show that you can go to almost any refinement of fly-fishing and still find sea-run cutthroats willing to meet you halfway. But in spite of the sport they give in tidal waters, I still prefer to catch them when they have left the estuaries for the fresh-water pools. Tidal waters can be very beautiful. I remember an evening below the falls of Theimar Creek, when the sunset light was blood red on the shiny wet sand of the tide flats and big cutthroats were rising in the narrow channel all down the length of a seaweed-covered log. I remember an August sunrise in the mouth of the Campbell, off the point of the Spit, when big cutthroats in perfect condition came to our flies so fast and hard that we each had a limit within an hour or two; outside the tyee fishermen were passing up and down in their white rowboats, and a little westerly wind came up to scuff the water of Discovery Passage as the full daylight made it blue; behind us the mountains of Vancouver Island were black and white with rock and snow, and across from us the Coast Range was jagged and tall and endless from farthest south to farthest north. Those were good times. But in the comings and goings of the cutthroats in fresh water there is something more than good fishing, something more than any simple beauty of surroundings. Each movement is an outward sign of a change in the year's cycle; more than a sign, it is an actual part of both change and cycle. And knowledge of the movements in any particular river is the seal of one's intimacy with the country at least as much as it is a test of one's knowledge as a fisherman.

In March and April and on into May the cutthroats are there because the salmon fry are coming up from the gravel and moving down; the fishing is often quick and fierce, with a big wet fly quickly cast to a slashing rise and worked back fast. Fish show in unexpected places, in short eddies behind rocks in the rapids, off the mouths of little creeks, and in all the expected places as well. Sometimes the May flies hatch thickly, and not a trout will stir to a wet fly, though fish after fish will come to a dry blue quill or a little iron blue. Then on some hot day in May, the big black ants put out their wings and make their brief mating flight; for a day, or perhaps two days, the river is full of drowned or drowning ants, and the fish feed on them and come to a dry fly that is not too tidily tied and not too well greased, something bedraggled and half-drowned like the ants themselves. After that there is a change, and there seem few cutthroats in the fresh-water pools of the Campbell. I used to say of June and July: it's hardly worth going up—there won't be any fish. But the days are so good and the river is so bright that one goes sometimes just for the pleasure of being out in the sun and the summer, with running water all about one and the trees green on the banks.

I have been surprised so many times now that I am careful

what I say about June and July. It was a June afternoon that I went up to the head of the Sandy Pool, lay on the beach for a while in the sun and at last walked lazily down into the water to make a few casts before going home. Just as soon as my fly reached out into the fast water a trout took hold, a good trout, short and thick and over two pounds. I went on fishing and soon hooked a second fish, the most beautiful cutthroat, I think, that I have ever hooked; he was a two-pounder, like the first one, but shorter still and thicker, splendidly marked with a rich pattern of heavy spots all over the deep and shining green of his back and sides. That was all for that afternoon, but it was enough to leave the short June hour as clear and sharp in my memory as any fishing time.

Two years ago a July day looked good, and I went to the Island Pools, just to look them over. I told myself that the fish wouldn't come in for a couple of weeks yet. So I worked along the bar and floated a Mackenzie River bucktail down the runs, dancing it back to me from wave top to wave top on the upstream wind, lowering my rod to slack the line and let the fly ride the rough water down again. It seldom finished the ride. The big cutthroats, three-pounders, some of them nearly four pounds, came at it like fiercer creatures than any fish, leapt right out of the water with it, fought me for possession of it and yielded only to utter exhaustion and the lift of the net.

So I have no wisdom that will let me write of June and July, even in my own river that I know well. And the wisdom I once had for August and September is shaken a little and likely to grow shakier yet as I grow older and learn to watch more closely. Sometimes in the second week of August the humpback salmon run into the river. With them, I used to say, come the big cutthroats that are maturing to spawn in the following February—magnificent fish that have attained their full weight and strength and a cunning or dourness that makes them hard to catch on bright August days in the Canyon Pool. I argued that they came into the river because of their maturity, following the maturity of the humpbacks rather than in any hope of feeding on salmon eggs that would not be dropped to the gravel for another two months. It was a nice theory, but in the last two or three years I've noticed the cutthroats before the humpbacks. I asked General Money about that, and he had noticed the same thing. So I no longer know why they come in then—I only know that I try to get away to the Canyon Pool as soon as I can after the first of August.

That August fishing in the Canyon Pool is the finest cutthroat fishing I have had anywhere. The fish are very big—I have killed several that weighed within an ounce of four pounds and have lost some that I know were over five pounds —and they can be superlatively difficult. They are not feeding, for only very rarely is there so much as a May-fly nymph in a stomach; they lie in water six or eight feet deep, unrippled by the slightest stir of wind and burnished by the full glare of summer sun. When they rise, they come right up from the bottom, and every cast that covers them is a really long cast. When they feel the hook, they turn and run with a pull that makes every one seem a ten-pounder, and at the end of that first long run, well down at the tail of the pool, they jump with a coho's wildness. That part is easy. Coaxing them back up the pool again, trying to keep them from disturbing the rest of the water, meeting their plunging, boring, heavy resistance and yielding no more than must be yielded to save 2X gut is the hard part, the part that makes fingers clumsy and trembling and the heart quick in the chest when it's time to reach for the net.

After August you may perhaps find cutthroats again in October, when the cohos run up on the first heavy fall rains. They seem less important then, because their season is almost over and you're fishing a big fly and heavy gut for the cohos anyway—tackle too clumsy for a trout—so you turn them back to live and spawn. And again in steelhead time, in December and January and February, they are there, heavy with spawn now, dark, with red gill covers and golden bellies. I hold them hard and bring them in fast, then reach down for the shank of the hook and twist the barb quickly away from them so that they can go back without harm to their important affairs. But recently a few big cutthroats have been caught and killed as steelheads in the Campbell. I saw one two seasons ago that weighed six and a half pounds. This season there was one that weighed well over seven pounds. I hope that next August, or one August soon, in the Canyon Pool . . .

THE BIG SALMON WATER

T<small>HE</small> Columbia River is not, from my point of view, an angler's river. An angler's river is one that can be covered and searched for fish from bank to bank by wading and casting. I don't mean that a single, long cast should reach clear across it, but that by fishing it from both sides and using all his skill and water wisdom, a good fisherman should have at least an outside chance of reaching every lie and holding place. When a river is much larger than that, one is fishing only a part of it, not the whole river. There must be channels and lies and bars and eddies only a little distance away of which one can know nothing; and a really big river, like a lake, has its secret depths.

But a big river has all the beauties and intricacies and delights of a smaller river, and has them on a scale so vast that the imagination is awed and staggered as it is when one turns eyes and mind from the earth on a clear night to look into the infinity of the stars. The Columbia is a big, grand river in this sense, one of the truly great rivers of the world, and the country it drains is immeasurably beautiful, vast and varied and full of the stories of men. The Columbia is also a great salmon river, the greatest of all Chinook salmon rivers, and so when I wanted to write a story of the Chinook run, it was quite obvious that I had to draw my salmon from the Columbia watershed.

When I was ready to start the book, I knew something of the Columbia; I had followed the river in several places and had seen many of its tributaries. I also knew a good deal about Columbia River Chinooks, because so much of scientific research has been directed toward the Columbia runs. But I had never seen the dams at Bonneville and Grand Coulee, I had not seen the Snake River or the Salmon, where thousands upon thousands of Chinooks turn off from the Columbia in each spawning migration, and I had never looked at any part of the watershed with this particular book in mind. I felt I could write a book without going down, but that if I did so, it would be less than the book it should be; and since the Columbia was only three or four hundred miles away, there seemed no slightest excuse for this. So I wrote two chapters and a synopsis and sent them off to New York with the hope that enough money would be advanced to make the trip. The weeks went by and I waited for news. I wrote slowly ahead as far as the end of Chapter 6, then came to a dead stop; thus far my salmon had not left the pool of her birth, but now she had to find her way down to salt water through lengths of river I had never seen. It is one thing in writing to invent when you must, to think into people's thoughts or plan their actions or describe their houses and how they live in them—there is generally enough real knowledge to limit and control the imagination; if not, then to be honest one must go out and search or else find some other way to state one's point. There was no other way to state mine, though I had hoped there might be. And in any case, the difficulties and distances of the search were not such as to justify evasion.

I left the book alone and turned to all the odds and ends of jobs that could be done around the house and the farm. One wet afternoon, because there seemed nothing else to do, I spent in cleaning and polishing Ann's kettles until they shone as the makers had never meant them to. As if that had been a virtuous deed instead of an angry expression of frustration, there was a letter from New York the next day. The money for the trip would be through in a few days.

So Ann and I went down in May, which is a fine month for the purpose, and saw the Columbia and most of its tributaries between Astoria and Grand Coulee Dam. We were in the spirit of the thing as deeply as it is possible to be; we knew the framework of the watershed, we knew the whole essential outline of the Chinook salmon's life history; we had only to fill in the gaps, and we knew where the gaps were and what we must find to fill them; we had only to travel the country, look carefully and see properly.

We started with some of the tributaries on the Washington side, then turned from these down to Astoria. Astoria was not fishing, though the spring run of Chinooks had passed through and the summer run was due to start any day. The scattered piling of the fish traps was gaunt and dreary, but beyond it the river was wide and strong with tide and spring flood—too wide to seem a river. Above Astoria, where the big islands are, we felt it a river; and above the islands it narrows again, though deep-sea ships still climb against it and the little gill-net boats are lonely and lost within sight of the highway.

We stopped in Portland because there were people to see and things to learn about the river there. Portland is a Coast League baseball town too, so we took time out for a double-header on Sunday. I'm for the Seattle Rainiers myself and feel strongly about it, but I can always see virtue in the Hollywood team, and the Portland Beavers were playing to an affectionate crowd and stealing bases in a way that the form sheet said they should not, so the game was fine. On Monday, with slight prickings of conscience, we hurried to Bonneville.

Bonneville is worth any fisherman's time and thought. It is worth any human being's time and thought, for that matter.

Here, where the dam is built, the river has found its way through the Cascade Range, yet the ocean tides run up almost to the foot of the dam, so low is the pass. There is an island at the site of the dam, Bradford Island, and the power dam itself spans Bradford Slough, between the island and the Oregon bank, while the spillway dam closes off the rest of the river between the island and the Washington bank. Being river-minded rather than mechanically minded, I prefer the spillway dam to the power dam. It is a long and noble structure, with many slanting buttresses that gleam white in the sun and dark-steel sluice gates between them. The gates open from the bottom to let the surplus water away in a thunder of foam and spray and great waves that translate into visible form the mighty weight and strength of fifty or sixty solid feet of Columbia River water piled behind the dam.

This race of savage, tumbled water drew the fish when we saw it and wondered at it, for there was only a single turbine turning in the powerhouse. They worked against it, unseen, until tiring muscles turned them toward the sheltered water at either side of the dam, where they found the easier draw of current escaping from the ladders. At Bonneville there are at least three ladders and three sets of elevators, or fish locks, as well as many passes and chutes by which the young fish can find their way to the sea, but the finest of all these is the Bradford Island ladder. A full river of water flows down its curving length, breaking white on the steps, filling the rest pools between them, sending a hidden, twisting flow of current through the gaps in each step which are the main passageway of the fish. We followed the ladder up, walking slowly along it, stopping often to watch. Occasionally we saw a fish, usually a steelhead, jump clear out. Once or twice we saw the shining dark back of a big Chinook curve over, but for the most part they were passing unseen, six or seven feet below the bubbled, white-veined surface of the water.

At the counting fence they had to come up. The water was

smoother and slower here, and the shapes of big fish showed clearly in it, pressing their noses against the feel of the current through the bars of the steel grating, searching along until they came to the counting gap, coming up over the white plate under the counter's box, hesitating, sometimes going back to turn and come again, sometimes going forward to pass over the plate and on into the dark water above. Fish of different kinds came through as we watched—big steelheads, suckers, lampreys and, more numerous than any, the Chinooks. The fish were nervous but not frightened. They passed steadily, almost with an air of knowing the way, and as a matter of fact they did know it, because in spite of dams and ladders it was the same old upstream way, a way that must be made against the current flow clear up from the sea to the spawning bed.

There has been great concern about Bonneville. Thousands upon thousands of words have been written—naturally enough, perhaps, since the dam is so far down the river, well below most of the best spawning areas—to show that the runs will be destroyed or will not be destroyed, that the mature fish would not go up the ladders, that the small downstream migrants could not survive the passage through the ice chutes or through the turbines, that they would fail to find the by-passes especially designed for them. It seems safe to say now that the fishways and by-passes of Bonneville have proved themselves. The fish go up and come down and return again at least as well as they ever did. And from the concept of Bonneville dam, from the first realization that the dam would be a threat to a great fishery, men began to notice properly the other evils, individually small, but collectively greater than any the dam could cause, that had been damaging the runs for years. There was pollution, the effluent of mines and mills and cities that poisoned the spawning streams. There were the hundreds, if not thousands, of petty dams which barred off the acres upon acres of good gravel beds that had built and maintained the runs, dams built without a thought of the passage of fish or with wretched, impossible ladders that filled the letter of some law of man but served the runs not at all. And there were the irrigation ditches, turning the streams out into farmers' fields and orchards and drawing the migrants down to die in mud. These conditions and excessive fishing were the drain. The threat of Bonneville drew attention to them. Now many of the useless little dams have been torn out, and over others there are proper ladders that take the spawning fish to the gravel beds again. Hundreds of irrigation ditches and power intakes have been screened so that the migrants cannot pass down them—though many still remain unscreened. Pollution? Perhaps that has been improved a little, though there is still far to go. Overfishing? They take them as they can get them, and until the fisherman can find no one but himself to blame, he will probably go on trying to catch more fish than he safely should.

I like to think that Bonneville is not the first dam that has helped the salmon runs of the Columbia. A little above Bonneville is a stretch of water, still fast and strong in spite of the dam, which is called the Cascades. The break of the Cascades is caused by a tumbled mass of rock on the river bed—the wreckage of what was once, perhaps, a great natural bridge across the river. F. H. Balch has written of this in a book called *The Bridge of the Gods*. In his preface he says:

Everywhere along the mid-Columbia the Indians tell of a great bridge that once spanned the river where the Cascades now are, but where at that time the placid current flowed under an arch of stone; that this bridge was *tomanowos*, built by the gods; that the Great Spirit shook the earth and the bridge crashed down into the river, forming the present obstruction of the Cascades. . . .

"Ancutta (long time back)," say the Tumwater Indians, "the salmon he no pass Tumwater falls. It too much big leap. Snake Indian he no catch um fish above falls. By and by great *tomanowos* bridge at Cascades he fall in, dam up water, make river higher all way up to Tumwater; then salmon he get over. Then Snake Indian all time catch um plenty."

This is mighty big talk, because it would mean that the whole run of fish to the Columbia above the Cascades is a comparatively new run—that the great runs of the Snake and the Salmon rivers, the run that reaches Rock Island, the runs that used to find their way above the Grand Coulee and into British Columbia, have all grown from the few pioneer fish that first ventured over the newly formed cascades. Even apart from the fish, this conception of the Bridge of the Gods is grandiose, because such a bridge must have been a wonder as great almost as the Grand Canyon or Death Valley. And Balch is very insistent that there actually was such a bridge in almost recent times. He quotes the words of another Indian, a Klikitat, to a pioneer at White Salmon:

"My father talk one time; long time ago liddle boy, him in canoe, his mother paddle, paddle up Columbia, then come to *tomanowos* bridge. Squaw paddle canoe under: all dark under bridge. He look up, all like one big roof, shut out sky, no see um sun. Indian afraid, paddle quick, get past quick, no good. Liddle boy no forget how bridge look!"

Balch continues:

Local proof also is not wanting. In the fall, when the freshets are over and the waters of the Columbia are clear, one going out in a small boat just above the Cascades and looking down into the transparent depths can see submerged forest trees beneath him, still standing upright as they stood before the bridge fell in and the river was raised above them. It is a strange, weird sight, this forest beneath the river; the waters watch over the broken tree-tops, fish swim among the leafless branches; it is desolate, spectre-like, beyond all words.

Such evidence, I suppose, will have rotted away by now, and the water backed up behind Bonneville will have buried it still deeper. Perhaps there never was a bridge of the gods; perhaps the Cascades hide nothing more than a slide from a mountainside; perhaps the salmon always found their way back into Idaho and Montana and British Columbia. I haven't inquired very deeply, because I like Balch's picture and would as soon keep it in error as lose it in truth.

Ann and I crossed the Hood River bridge a few miles above Bonneville and followed the Washington bank back to Portland again. From there we turned up the Willamette Valley—Balch says that should be Wallamet, which is certainly closer to the common pronunciation—because there were things we had to see there and because it is the loveliest valley in the west and we still half wish we lived there. From the Willamette we turned up the Mackenzie, stopping at the Waterville bridge to watch the great panicky Chinooks milling and circling in the shallow water below the weir that holds them from their spawning grounds. The Mackenzie is little more than a stream here, because the Eugene power canal has taken off much of its water; but above Leaburg it is a good-sized river and as wild and white over a bottom of big, round boulders as any river I know. It is also a fine fly-fisherman's river, full of big red-sided rainbows that come nobly to floating deer-hair patterns in the strongest water. We fished a little, because it would have been almost sacrilege not to, but I was more concerned to know the river than the fishing, and we did not catch any really good fish.

From the head of the Mackenzie we followed the Deschutes, another fly-fisherman's river, back down to the Columbia again. From the mouth of the Deschutes we turned briefly back to The Dalles, where the river flows through a deep and narrow lava channel that is as impressive as its broadest reaches. Above The Dalles, all the way to the big bend between Plymouth and Pasco the Columbia is lonely, a wide swift river with gravel bars and rocky islands, flowing among sandy hills made rugged by outcrop of black rock ramparts. Sometimes there are willows near the water, sometimes poplars enclosing a rare farm. Occasionally a heron rises on slow wings, or there are gulls flying, strangely far from salt water. But for the most part the country is sand and sagebrush and rocks, and the flow of so much water through it seems at once tragic and fine.

We turned away at the big bend to follow the Snake and the Salmon back into Idaho, but in a few days we came back to the Columbia again, passed the irrigated lands near the mouth of the Yakima and came into another waste of sagebrush and tumbleweed, rock and sand and gravel. It is a windy desolate country, huge and lonely, with the grotesque and incredible wonders of the Grand Coulee already beginning to grow up out of the ground; but it fitted a mood of breathless wonder already built in us by all we had seen, and we loved it. We found the Columbia's own way through the narrow gap in the Saddle Mountains and knew we were coming near the end, for Rock Island Dam, a little below Wenatchee, is the farthest ascent of the Chinooks since Coulee Dam was finished.

Still below Rock Island we turned away from the river and so came into the Grand Coulee, the dry bed of what was once the greatest river on earth. We stopped at the dry falls and tried, as every dutiful tourist must, to imagine a wall of water four hundred feet high and five miles wide pouring over them. I looked down at the lakes at the foot of the falls and felt that prehistoric monsters might still live in them; I felt for a single quick moment that I knew that fish had run up from the sea to the foot of the falls and perhaps spawned and died in the more sheltered places of the river bed. But the Grand Coulee is death and desolation now, a geologist's delight and a fisherman's hell. Somewhere along the road we picked up an old man who lived and farmed under the shadow of Steamboat Rock. As we went along he showed us the pass he had come down through thirty-three years earlier, then a good spring that came up out of the rock and then a breastwork thrown up by the Indians to serve their last stand in that part of the country. When we came to his farm and stopped, he showed us one more thing, a great yellow cross in the road that marks the place where a car crashed into his haywagon, killing its own two passengers and one of his horses. We were sorry to leave the old man and go back to remembering that the waters of half a continent had once poured over Steamboat Rock in a fall wider than the Dry Falls and twice as high.

We came to Coulee Dam at last and found it almost finished, with the water already pouring over its face. Perhaps I was exhausted by bigness, or perhaps I had expected too much. Coulee Dam is big, but it is not beautiful. It did not seem to me then as impressive as it should have. I tried to feel it impressive, but could not; I saw the fierceness and length of the race below it and understood that no salmon could be drawn from that into a ladder or an elevator, then I felt ready to leave and find the live and free Columbia again.

We found it between Bridgeport and Wenatchee, running with green snow water among orchards and rocky range hills, breaking white in rapids, accepting tributaries that came in beautifully over gravel bars. And at Rock Island it was the real Columbia again, with Chinooks and bluebacks and steelheads using it. Rock Island is the oldest and by far the most beautiful of the three Columbia River dams, a long, low curve, wide and graceful, set among high, steep hills, dry, grassy, hardened by rock outcrop. The two days we spent there were sunny and windy, and the Columbia was in fine spring freshet; the whole main curve of the dam was hidden under a tremendous roll of green water, utterly smooth, brilliant in the sun with an infinite depth of color and light, crashing down into a heavy roar of arching waves and leaping white spray.

The fish turned into ladders on both sides of the dam and were trapped there. We were at the right trap, on the west bank of the river and M. J. Hanavan, the biologist, was with us. Mr. Uber, who is in charge of the fish work at the damsite came down a little later. He raised the brail, a horizontal grating that made the floor of the trap, until the fish were forced up and we could see them.

The work at Rock Island is the solution of the problem made by Coulee Dam. A hundred and twenty miles downstream from Coulee, it is the nearest place at which the fish can be held and saved from wasting themselves in the wild water below the dam. So the ladders that used to pass them over Rock Island are turned into traps and the fish are taken from there in tank trucks to Leavenworth Hatchery or the spawning streams that enter the Columbia between Rock Island and Coulee. No great proportion of the Chinook run reaches Rock Island—some nine or ten thousand compared with a count of three or four hundred thousand at Bonneville in a normal year; but nine thousand big fish are a lot to handle, particularly when you add to them some twenty thousand bluebacks out of a run of a hundred thousand and five or six thousand steelheads. We had followed one fish to a spawning tributary of the lower Columbia, and we had followed others back into Idaho to their spawning places near the Salmon River; now we were to follow others from the Columbia to the farthest spawning tributaries that were still open to them.

Soon after Uber had lifted the brail, a big tank truck came down to pick up its load. The truck backed up to the elevator, shot out a load of stale water and took on a thousand gallons of fresh water. Uber raised the brail a little higher in the trap and turned a strong flow of water through the elevator. This passed into the trap, and the fish turned toward it immediately and began to seek a way through the bars and into the elevator. After a little while Uber opened the gate, and they began to move in, a little nervously, with the same hesitations and turnings they use in crossing the counting plates at Bonneville, but always passing through in the end because their maturity compels them against the current and there is no release until the proper spawning place is found.

About fifty Chinooks swam in, some of them big fish of

thirty pounds or more. There were several steelhead with them and a few jacks, the precociously mature males that follow the Chinook run. Then the gate was closed, the elevator was raised and the fish, with another thousand gallons of water, were shot down from it into the truck. The water already in the tank cushioned their fall, splashing and spilling out over the road-way. The driver closed the hatch, started the auxiliary engine that draws air over the ice compartment and pumps it through the water in the tank, then climbed into his cab and drove off.

Leavenworth was not yet operating, and it was sixty miles to Nason Creek, on the Stevens Pass highway, where the fish were to be dumped to find natural spawning. I was glad of that because I do not care much for hatcheries and I wanted my fish to spawn naturally. The truck stopped once on the way while Hanavan took a water sample and tested it; then we came up into the green timber and the swift streams of the Cascades again. Fish that had climbed five hundred miles of the Columbia were back within a hundred miles of salt water. I wondered how many of those in the truck would have homed to this Wenatchee Valley anyway, Rock Island trap or no. I thought: Not many, because the Wenatchee run had gone far down long before Coulee Dam was built. Yet it may grow again from this freighting of fish by road, and the other runs to the Methow, Entiat and Okanogan rivers may grow, per-haps breeding fish that will home to them as unfailingly as the runs of a hundred years ago. When that time comes, the lad-ders at Rock Island will be opened again perhaps, and the trucks and Leavenworth will have little work to do unless the spawners crowd the streams and there is a surplus to be cared for.

The highway came close to Nason Creek and the truck stopped in a wide space of clear gravel, then backed out on a ramp built over a good pool in the creek. We looked in the tank again (carefully because a fish will sometimes try to jump out) and saw them moving restlessly against the black steel walls. The driver went down and clamped a metal chute under the round rear door of the tank, then tripped the clamp on the door. For a fraction of a second only water came out; then there were fish in it, struggling against it, plunging down into Nason Creek; then there was only a trickle of water from the truck and two or three last fish flopping out and down. We watched and could see many of them in the pool, lying well in the stream, already sheltering behind boulders or close to the bottom. There were six miles of Nason Creek open to them between fences. They had some three months to search their way about it before their spawning time would come.

We climbed the Wenatchee Valley again the next day and stopped for a little while beside the pool in Nason Creek before going on through Stevens Pass to the coast again. I knew the book was all mine now and I could write it as it should be written, with the feel of the Columbia in it.

JUNE

JUNE is the midsummer month,
yet in the temperate latitude of southern England and the
British Columbia coast it is not full summer; growth is still
fresh and young, and the rivers still have the flow of stored-
up winter snow or rain. All the summer months are trout

fisher's months, I suppose, wherever trout swim and feed. Yet June is generally a quiet month on the Campbell, and in most of the lakes near sea level the surface water is almost too warm for good fly-fishing. Some of the mountain streams make good fishing, but it is too early for the really cold ones.

In June, were I near enough to it, I would always go into the Kilipi River, which flows into Nimpkish Lake. Once I had a trap line up the valley, and in the winters I used to catch fine trout for food as they lay behind the late-spawning coho salmon. But in June I fished there for fun and caught, not many fish, but always fish that surprised me.

Generally, I had to go there over a short week end, leaving a logging camp after work on Saturday, walking through to Nimpkish Lake, then rowing six or eight miles up or down the lake to the mouth of the river. That left time to make a quick camp, cook supper and fish through the river's straight swift run from my camp to the lake. Sometimes I caught nothing on that first evening, once I caught two fine cutthroats, each over three pounds, which ran out into the lake so far that I waded almost shoulder deep to hold them and turn them. Once I hooked, on the fly and fairly in the mouth, a five-pound sockeye salmon; this was surprising enough, because properly organized sockeyes are not supposed to take fly or bait of any kind at all readily. It was the more surprising because sockeyes don't run to the Kilipi; but I was reaching well out into the lake at the time, and perhaps a passing school had turned momentarily into the fresh flow of current. I saw no others roll or jump.

On the Sunday I usually fished the canyon and the water below it, but sometimes I walked the five or six miles through to the meadows, to see them in their summer green; the Kilipi meadows are always full of deer as no other place I know, and the deer are bold and calm. It is almost as though, knowing little of the rifle, they place a human being's power of harming them on a par with that of the cougar: they watch cautiously, even suspiciously; they bound away if you come upon them too suddenly or too closely; but generally they stand with heads arrogantly raised, eyes impersonally curious, unless one is within a hundred feet or so—half a dozen easy springs for a hunting cougar. I like the meadows if only for the deer, but there are many birds there too. The snipe nest there, and ruffed grouse drum steadily through the day among the crab apples and cedars. Song sparrows are always there, summer and winter, warblers are quick in the swamp grass, and at different times I have seen goldfinches and vireos, bluebirds, meadow larks, kinglets, red-winged blackbirds, flickers with the lovely flash of orange under their wings, downy woodpeckers and the swooping flight and scarlet crests of pileated woodpeckers.

Bears love the meadows in fall, when the salmon are running, but they come there in summer as well, to roll in cool mud wallows and rub themselves against the trunks of big crab apples. The trout, like the bears, are interested mainly in the salmon runs, but a few of them seem to stay there through the year. A small fork of the river runs through the meadows, deep and slow and very clear. Once I came quietly to the deepest pool of all, ten or twelve feet from smooth surface to pale gravel, and saw three good trout lying quite still on the bottom. It seemed almost foolish to fish for them with anything less interesting than a worm, but I tied on a big dry sedge and cast it well above the nearest fish. Three times I floated it over him, and the third time I thought I saw him move. Perhaps it was less than a movement, simply a stiffening of the body, a tightening of muscles. I cast again, and as the fly touched the water, he started up. He came slowly, his body tilted only a little, with a feathery lightness of flying, up and up and up through brilliant water that seemed lighter and clearer than air. He met the fly perfectly, dropped back under it for a moment, then quietly took it. I fished for the rest of the afternoon but could not move the others.

It is a little like that in the canyon. I have never seen many fish there in June, but the few that are there can be seen; one sees them from above and knows the climb down is worth while. Nearly always they are deep down in the pools, apparently little concerned with feeding, and nearly always they are big cutthroats, beautifully colored. But they do feed there, and they seem to love best of all the bright, blue-green cedar borer beetles. All trout seem to like these beetles, and I made up my own clumsy imitation long ago—a body of emerald green and blue seal's fur, ribbed with bronze peacock herl and gold thread, wings of green peacock and a light blue hackle tied above them. I fish it drowned, with little movement, and in the Kilipi it was often an hour's work to get the fly down to where the trout would take an interest in it. But the take was always worth while, the solemn opening and closing of a great mouth, the twist of a wide body against the strike and a strong run, deep down. Once only I hooked a summer steelhead somewhere far below me in a pool that I had not examined from above. I was standing on a little pinnacle of rock from which I could not move, and it was nearly half an hour before I could bring him back to it. Then, as I reached down to slip a finger in his gills, I fell in. For a few moments I floundered about, trying to climb back on the rock without losing my rod, then I gave up with a good grace and swam to the tail of the pool, praying that the line would not tangle my legs. It did not, and when I climbed out again the fish was still hooked.

But for all its surprises and delights, the Kilipi never gave me really good June fishing, though some northwest rivers have. Almost any stream with a real stock of nonmigratory trout should be at its best in June, when there are plentiful hatches of fly and the water is cool and lively enough to keep the fish active. June is transition from spring to summer, a month when everything has its full vigor, before anything is stale or mature. In June May flies may be thick on the water, stone-fly nymphs may still be crawling up the rocks to split their cases and fly away, midges will be dancing in clouds near the water's edge and falling spent on the water to move fish that the angler finds it difficult to tempt with his larger flies; and on June evenings may come the early sedge hatches.

None of these interest the summer steelhead; yet June is perhaps the best steelhead month of all the year. The fish are not so numerous then as later, in September and early October when the fall run is in. But those that have come up from salt water are perfect, bright and clean, still several months from the full maturity and the slowing bulk of developed ovaries and milt sacs. When a June fish takes, he is into his run before you can move to raise the rod, and that run is fierce and long and dangerous. Almost always a June fish is a jumping fish, a bold, wild, jumping fish, and he is little concerned to keep within the limits of the pool in which he has taken the fly.

Good summer-steel head runs are less common than good winter runs. Oregon rivers and northern California rivers draw fine runs. Some rivers in Washington state have good runs, and the North Fork of the Stillaguamish has been set aside by a wise authority for fly-fishing only. In British Columbia there are many rivers with summer-run fish, but most of them are not easily accessible to anglers. For some reason, the rivers on the east coast of Vancouver Island, accessible from the Island Highway, draw few summer fish. The Campbell has no true summer run; the Oyster, the Courtenay, the Qualicum rivers and all the smaller streams between them, in spite of good winter runs, do not draw summer fish. I believe the Cowichan had a fair run at one time, but Indian fishing killed it. North of Seymour Narrows, rivers such as the Nimpkish have runs, and several of the mainland rivers have really fine runs. There is one in particular that I mean to try out now that the war is over; it comes to a river in Ramsay Arm, near the mouth of Bute Inlet.

Nearly all the rivers on the west coast of Vancouver Island have summer runs, but only one of them is easily reached—the

Stamp River at Alberni. The Stamp is General Money's river and always will be so far as I am concerned. The General lived at Qualicum until he died in 1941, and there he built the big hotel and the golf course. He was the wisest and best fisherman I have ever known in British Columbia, and he was also probably the keenest. A few months before he died, Ann and I stopped at his house on our way up the Island. It was a cold, wet December evening, and we found him just changed after a day of searching for winter fish in one of the Qualicum rivers. All the clothes he had worn during the day were hung to dry in the warmest place in the house. He had been really wet, right to the skin, and his day had given him a move from only a single fish, but the General was happy and satisfied with it and was already making plans for the next day.

When you fished with General Money, you fished as his guest; and never was host more gracious or better informed on the possibilities of his domain. It was a June day when I first went down to the Stamp with him, a sunny day after rain the night before. We drove to the cottage he had built on the high bank above his favorite pool, put up our rods and walked to the edge of the clifflike bank. General Money's Pool is at a good, wide bend of the river; above it there is a straight reach of fast water as far as the mouth of the Ash and below it a broken rapid that gathers itself through two or three hundred yards to a narrow pool under the far bank. From where we were standing we had a clear view of the pool and its bottom, except when a light breeze ruffled the surface, and after looking for a while we knew that there were fish in it—three together, well down the pool and near the middle, and a fourth a little below them and well over to the far side. The General was pleased. "Water's in fine shape," he said. "I'm glad I got you out today."

We walked down the steep trail to the pool, and he settled himself in his favorite place under the big trees near the head.

"Fish this top part through," he told me, "in case there's

something there. You'll cover those three fish from the kidney stones—you'll see them, two light-colored, kidney-shaped stones on this side. When they're under your feet, you ought to be reaching the fish. Then you might reach the other one with a long cast from the flat rock just below the kidney stones. It won't be much good below that."

I fished carefully down, came to the kidney stones, cast well across and felt a good heavy pull as the fly came round in mid-stream. The fish ran without hesitation, hard for the tail of the pool. I put on a heavy strain, and he jumped out twice, still going away, tumbling over himself and splashing the shining water high at each fall. The jumps slowed him a little, and he turned and came back up the pool very fast; opposite me, only thirty or forty feet out, he jumped again beautifully, very high out of the water. For a moment after that he was quiet. The General was beside me now.

"You must get him," he said. "It would be too bad to lose the first fish of the day."

"I'd like to keep him away from the others," I said. "We don't want to disturb the pool too much."

"Don't worry about that, man. Make sure of him."

But the fish ran straight across, and I worked upstream a little so that I had a chance to hold him well above the best part of the pool. After five more good minutes the General gaffed him for me.

"Go and catch another one," he said.

"No, sir. You fish now."

"Go on and fish. I like to watch you."

More than anything, I wanted to watch him, but it seemed too late to say that now. I washed my fly and looked over my gut, then started in again well above the stones. When they were under my feet again, I realized that I was a little breath-less and anxious. It suddenly occurred to me that the General was watching me, closely and critically. I had done well enough with the first fish, but I began to wonder if I might not bungle something now, and I remembered how I hate to put a man in some good favorite place where I know there are fish and see him spoil it. The fly swung round without a touch, and I cast again. Still nothing, and nothing to a third cast. I felt disappointed, but I moved on down and left them then. It seemed better to do that than chance putting them off altogether. At the flat rock I drew more line off the reel and reached well over toward the far side. It was a good cast, but short of the fish, I felt sure, and I wondered if I could handle two or three more yards of line. I took them out, picked up, measured out an ordinary cast, then picked up and cast again with all the drive I could put into the rod. The last loop of line left my hand and I felt the pull of its leaving come cleanly against the reel. The fly curled over, carrying the gut out to its full length, and began fishing. I saw a brown-backed shape come up to meet it, waited a moment, then tightened on him. He began to jump at once, again and again and again, all across the tail of the pool. The General was coming along the bank behind me.

"Lightly hooked," I said. "He won't stay on long."

"I know, I know," he said. "Try and get him though. Bring him into this side, if you can, and I'll go below you and try to put the gaff in him."

The fish had come up the pool a little, but he started down and began jumping again. At the tail of the pool he was right on the surface, working almost gently against me, and I thought for a moment I could swing him across to where the General was waiting. Then the fly came away.

"Rotten luck," the General said. "If anyone had told me you could get over to that fish with only thigh boots and an eleven-foot rod, I'd never have believed him."

That was the most tactful and graceful remark any man has ever made to me after the loss of a good fish. I went back from the pool with a feeling of merit that was completely without justification but extremely pleasant.

We rested the pool for fifteen or twenty minutes, then the General himself started down it. He was a tall slim man, very straight, with a long, brown face, deeply lined, and blue eyes bright and quick to smile against the brownness. He moved out gracefully and easily until he was in water over his hips; then he began to put out line with his doublehanded thirteen-foot rod. He was spey casting, rolling the line out in a long loop that lifted the fly from the water in front of him and carried it over and out in a straight smooth cast that covered the whole water. He worked his fly across, deep and slow, moved down a step or two and cast again, letting the big shining curve of the rod carry the burden of the work. He had fished this pool a thousand times, made each cast he was making now a thousand times before, but his mind was with his fly, working it down to the fish, bringing it easily into the swifter water near his own bank, holding it with the long rod so that it would not cross too quickly, ready to meet the fierce, quick pull of a taking fish with a tightening of the line at the right moment. I watched him cast again, and judged that he was almost at the kidney stones. The fly came in midstream, a shade too quickly, I thought, and the General lowered his rod point. Then the fish took. I saw the rod lift and bend and saw clearly the delayed boil of the fish's deep turn. The big rod dipped to him, met his runs and his jumps, humored him away from the rocks and bad water at the tail of the pool, brought him up and held him at last on his side and ready for the gaff. I set the gaff and brought him ashore, and the General looked at him, his eyes and face alight with the pleasure of it. "I thought we could take another," he said.

It was on one of the last days I fished with him, not much over a year before he died, that he caught a fish in his pool by a new method. It was an August day, and the river was very low—too low, the General said, for someone had closed the gate at the dam and made a drop of a foot or more during the night. I was almost glad because I had planned to fish the greased line anyway; the low water and the hot bright day were perfect for it. The General said he just wanted to sit in the shade and watch; his doctor had warned him a few days earlier that he must show his heart a little consideration.

So I started down with the greased line and a tiny silver-bodied fly that I had tied the night before. I fished carefully, by the book, casting a slack line well across, lifting the belly of the line each time before the current could draw on it, holding the fly right up under the surface in a slow, easy drift all the way across. The fish came again as I reached the kidney stones and came as a good fish sometimes does to the greased line, with a long slashing rise that threw water a foot into the air. For once I did the rest of it right—pointed my rod straight downstream, held it well into my own bank and let the delayed pull on the belly of the line set the hook. When the General gaffed him, he said with something like awe in his voice, "Look at that fly. Right in the back corner of the mouth, exactly the way it's supposed to be."

That was the best of all the days we had together. We ate our lunch in the shade and drank bottles of cool stout. Then I went upstream with the General's big rod and left him to fish his pool with the greased line. Something told me to fish the heavy white water, and I was hardly getting the fly well out before I hooked a fish. He started downstream, and I glanced quickly along the river to pick a place to gaff him, then looked down to the pool where the General was fishing. I saw his rod come up and knew that he was into one as well. Suddenly I was afraid. I thought of the sharp stab of excite-ment that comes with the surface rise to the greased line, of the long strain of the fight with a small fly and light gut, of those last anxious moments as the fish comes within reach of the gaff. I began to run downstream, caring nothing about my own fish, which tumbled on ahead of me. I wondered if I could break in him—it's not always so easy when you want to. Then I saw he was close to shore, and I reached for my gaff almost without thinking. He started out as I came up to him, but I made a lucky stroke and caught him just above the tail. In a moment I had him on the bank, tapped him on the head, dropped the rod and started on again.

As I came down to the big pool, I saw the General was getting his gaff ready. I shouted, "I'll do that, sir," but he looked back and smiled and shook his head. Then I saw him lean forward and gaff his fish with an easy, gentle stroke. He waded ashore and I met him.

"That's wonderful sport," he said. "We should have tried it long ago." He knelt beside his fish and freed the fly from the corner of the jaw. "I'm going to send away for a light rod as soon as we get home. You must help me pick one out of the catalogue."

We took the fish back in the shade and sat down. "That's my day's fishing," the General said. "I'm getting old. But we've found something new for the river after all these years."

LEWINGTON'S CARRIER

For a year after I left school I studied history with Dr. T. H. Davies, rector of the parish of Headbourne Worthy, near Winchester. Attached to the rectory were several scattered fields of glebe; they were strategically placed fields and of good variety, ranging from marsh and meadowland to the high ground near the school and the narrow wood along the Pilgrim's Way. In good partridge country, where the landowners also preserved pheasants and ducks, this meant fairly important sporting possibilities of which Denis, the rector's son, and I availed ourselves to the full. We even managed to extend them a little by friendly agreements with one or two of the near-by farmers. And occasionally we took casual evening strolls across the stubble fields that marched with our glebe, then stirred out early the next morning with our guns to see if the chance shift of wildlife population had lasted through the night. Acre for acre, there were probably not many properties in the south of England that showed a finer yield of game that year. And we achieved considerable variety too: snipe, teal, mallard, pheasants, partridges, rabbits, pigeons, hares, besides crows, hawks, weasels and other vermin which, we easily persuaded ourselves, more than made up for the few pheasants and partridges that might, with some logic, have been considered poached.

Within a mile of the rectory flowed the Itchen, one of the finest trout streams in England. Unfortunately there was very little we could do about that. In the winter we managed to get very occasional permission to try for grayling, but in the trout season we were without privilege and could only admire the gliding water and the fine fish that lay between the trailing weed beds. There were some really big fish in the reach, and I watched them a lot at their wise, quiet feeding. The river was of noble proportions there below the rectory, and the best fish were splendidly difficult to approach and seemed to have about them a quiet air of confidence in their own good judgment which implied that they could treat artificial flies with complete contempt in the midst of the most tempting hatch of naturals; but I felt satisfied that I could have found a way to move them. Once or twice, picking days of bad weather, we hid a rod in our long plus fours and went down to a place where head-high sedges hid us. We would put the rod together with eager, trembling hands, watching for rises as we worked. Generally, when the rod was up, there was no good fish in sight, and we made only a few haphazard, frightened casts, then took the rod down and went home. Once I hooked a good fish, tried to hurry him out and lost him in a weed bed. That was excitement of a really high quality. On another evening, after a day of storm, I was down among the high rushes alone. It was a very quiet evening, and for some reason I determined not to be nervous. The rushes hid me from sight, but they served equally to hide the approach of a keeper or a legitimate fisherman, and that, generally, was a worrying thought that stayed right with us. On this evening I felt I could disregard it—no one would come. A good fish was rising well across the stream, on the far side of a weed bed that made a little island above the surface. It was a difficult chance, and I suspected the fish was feeding on nymphs rather than on surface flies, but I gave him the floating fly first. Four or five times I laid it perfectly above him, watched it drift over him and recovered without hooking the weed bed. The next cast hooked the weeds some way below him, but the light gut broke easily, and he went on feeding. I changed to a dark Greenwell nymph, cast once more and saw him bulge. He ran at once, straight up along the weed bed, past the head of it and into the clear. I got him to the bank almost easily and decided that I had tried my luck far enough. That was the only fish we ever had to show for ourselves in daylight fishing.

We tried several times in the dark of hot July nights. I have always thought night fishing an overrated form, both for entertainment and results, and we found it that way on the Itchen, except on one night. We had gone some little way upstream from the rectory to a place where a fine lawn came down to the river from a big house on the far side. There were lights on in the house, and we could hear people talking and laughing. In the river several fish were rising steadily, and after a little while we found most of the rises. I decided to fish a dry coachman, so that we would have some chance of seeing the white wings against the dark water. Three fish were rising quite regularly close under a wall at the foot of the lawn opposite us, and I began to try to cover them. Time after time the fly went down and was disregarded. Denis said at last, "I think you must be short of them." So I pulled off a yard more line and felt the fly hit the brick wall. It fell back, came over

a fish and disappeared in a good ring. I tightened, felt I had
him, then forgot fish and rod and everything in sudden terror.
I heard Denis gasp in the dark beside me. From somewhere
within fifty or a hundred yards of us had come the sharp quick
sound of a running reel.

When I felt my rod again the fish was gone. Denis and I lay
down and waited, a little way back from the bank.

"Somebody's fishing," I whispered.

"Yes," Denis said. "Pulling line off his reel."

"Sounded too long for that. I think he had a fish on."

We waited and listened. I could still see two fish rising
steadily over by the wall. The sound did not come again, and
we grew bolder. I cast for the second fish, rose him, hooked
him and lost him. The sound of the other fisherman's reel
came again, from a little farther away.

"What do you think he's doing?" Denis asked.

"Catching fish," I said, but I wasn't convinced. There was
something wrong about the sound, it was a tearing off of line
that started and stopped abruptly and seemed to fit no natural
circumstance of fishing.

"Have you got that light?" I asked. "I want to look at the
fly."

The barb was broken from the hook, as I had thought it
might be. Crouching well down in the grass and shielding the
light, we tied on a new fly. The sound came again, from about
where it had been the first time. We strained our eyes toward
it and listened hard. It came again, exactly as before, lasting
the same four or five seconds, starting and stopping abruptly.
It seemed mysterious and frightening because one could not
picture the man's actions from hearing it. "I'm going to get
that other fish anyway," I said. I did, first cast. The other
fisherman must have hooked a fish at the same moment, because
his reel started to run again; time after time it whirred out, and
all the while he seemed to be coming closer to us. I hurried
my fish all I could. The moon was coming up, and in a few

minutes the meadows would be almost as light as in daytime. The screeching of the reel went on, and I began to wonder if he would hear my own much lighter check. The fish was on his side now. We scooped him out somehow and ran back from the bank. Still the other reel gave tongue to the intermittent runs of its fish. Then Denis began to laugh.

"Shut up," I said. "And let's get out of here."

He still laughed.

"Do you know what that is?" he asked.

"No," I said irritably. "I'm damned if I do."

"It's a screech owl," Denis said. "Listen."

We didn't always have to poach. Besides the glebe and the few farmers' fields we could walk through with good right, there was Lewington's meadow, just below the church. And there was the churchyard itself for that matter, which was bordered by the same little stream that flowed along Lewington's meadow. Mr. Lewington was the village baker, a baker second to none in the world for fresh currant bread and half a dozen other good things. He was also a small but very intensive livestock farmer, drawn into it by a deep love of animals rather than by any simple economic reason. His rich little meadow supported, and his low, many-roomed barn sheltered, besides the bakery horse, a herd of goats, many turkeys, big white ducks, guinea hens, chickens and several cats.

Mr. Lewington was well disposed toward us for a number of reasons, and he gave us free range of his meadow and full rights on the little stream that we called Lewington's Carrier. In return for this we undertook to control the surplus of rats that plagued his buildings in spite of all his cats could do. Denis and I did a lot of ratting and were well equipped for it with traps and snares and ferrets and terriers. But Lewington's rats were difficult because the barn and some of the other buildings offered them so many hiding places. We kept traps set there all the time, and the necessity of baiting and resetting brought us often to the meadow.

The carrier was a good clear little stream, varying in width from a yard or so to twelve feet or more. It flowed into the Itchen two or three fields below Lewington's, so there were nearly always good trout in it, and besides the trout many small pike, most of them fish of a pound or less, but some as large as two or three pounds. We found the trout generally impossible to catch; they seldom fed really well and they were very nervous in the small water, so we spent a lot of time on the pike. We started out with some vague idea that by clearing out all the pike we might attract more trout to the stream and give ourselves a better chance to catch them. So we went after the pike with nets at first but were not very successful; then we tried shooting them and did little better that way. We filled ink bottles with black powder, corked them tightly and made them into effective little bombs with a length of fuse and a small detonator. They exploded satisfactorily under water, but the pike wouldn't wait to be stunned or killed, and the bombs had no effect at long range. Finally we gave up complicated methods and went out with trout rods and small treble hooks and snagged them. It wasn't by any means an easy sport, but we grew really skillful after a while and learned to spot the fish quickly, stalk them cunningly, drop the hooks lightly just beyond them, allowing for the drift of the current, then set them in side or back with a single swift draw. Even a one-pound pike, hooked in that way, put up a really good little fight, and several times we came back from the meadow or the churchyard with three or four of them. But they never seemed much fewer, and the trout remained scarce and wary as ever.

Those trout were something of a challenge to me and to my county patriotism. Here was I, a good Dorset trout fisher, completely beaten by a few good Hampshire trout. Denis would remind me of this once in a while, and the thing was no less bitter to me because I knew that the Hampshire trout streams were so greatly superior to ours in Dorset. I liked to think that if we had their trout streams, we could surely do wonderful things. So I walked often along the carrier and hoped to find a feeding fish. Sometimes I found one, and then I used all the skill I had, creeping up on him, setting my best flies out for him in my best manner. Nearly always something went wrong—the fly dragged or hooked a tuft of grass or simply scared the fish and sent him off upstream under a great gliding wave that disturbed everything else in the carrier. When, as happened rarely, I did hook a fish, it was always a small one. The big fish that fed by the mouth of the culvert that brought the stream under the road took my fly once, and I struck too soon. The fish that hung just above the fence at the end of the meadow rose once, far short. The other good ones for the most part disregarded me or swept away and left me at my first preparatory move.

Then, one hot June day, everything was changed. Yet I remember far better than the change in the fish what happened afterward in Mr. Lewington's barn. The day had been very hot, and, with a wisdom I don't always keep about me when there's a chance of going fishing, I told Denis that there might be a good rise of fish in the very late afternoon. We went through Mr. Lewington's barnyard sometime after five-thirty, and he was not yet back with the bakery wagon. The rise was already on when we got down to the carrier; at least the big fish by the fence at the lower end of the meadow was rising. I had a small, dark-hackled olive on, and we had spotted the rising fish from thirty or forty feet out in the meadow. We stayed where we were, and I began to let out line, keeping the fly in the air till I thought I had enough to cover the fish. It was a long chance, because the recovery of the first cast would almost certainly hook the fly firmly in the edge of the bank, and a quiver of a grass tussock was usually all that was necessary to put that particular fish off his feed. But the first cast was right; the fish came up to a natural, took that and broke the surface again to our fly before the little rings of his first rise had spread. He did his best, that fish, running down under the wire of the fence until we thought of jumping into the stream to follow him, but he came back and was netted. Denis took the rod then, and we found another good one rising in the bend. He let the dark-olive float past him twice, but Denis offered it to him once more, setting it on the water a bare two inches above his nose, and that time he had it.

Between there and the road we spoiled two chances at good fish, but we were feeling so good that it hardly mattered. Below the mouth of the culvert there is a miniature pool, and a fish was rising near the tail of this.

"You take him," Denis said.

"No, you," I told him. "I want the other one, the one that rises under the culvert."

"How do you know he's there?"

My fish rose as Denis spoke, a neat tiny rise about a foot below the mouth of the culvert. Denis knelt, ready to cast for the lower fish, and I said, "Hold him from going up if you can. Stand up and walk backward as soon as you hook him."

Denis nodded. We were both excited, and I was afraid it might spoil his cast, but he made it beautifully; the fish came to him, he tightened, started him down, and the hook came away. We both watched the culvert anxiously. One full minute passed, then our fish rose again in the same place, just a foot short of the concrete face of the culvert.

"Do you want to try for him?" I asked.

Denis shook his head, and for a moment I was almost sorry. It didn't look so easy now. I knew it wasn't easy because I had tried it fifty times before and had only put the fly over him properly once or twice. But he was a fraction farther down from the culvert this time than ever before.

"I'm going to throw the fly at the concrete and let it bounce off to him," I said.

I tried it and it worked. The fly dropped perfectly. The fish

pushed his nose under it, backed down with it for six inches, a foot, two feet. Then he turned away and went back to his place. A moment later we saw his tiny rise again.

I let out a great blast of tightly held breath.

"Gosh," Denis said, "I thought he was surely going to take it."

I brought my cast back and broke the fly off.

"What are you going to do?" Denis asked.

"Change," I said. "Orange quill I think. That old boy's particular."

I looked in my box and wondered. The orange quills were there, tiny and neat on No. 17 hooks. Beside them were some beautiful red quills and half a dozen Yorkshire tups I had bought from Chalkley's the day before. For a moment longer I hesitated; then I knew the orange quill was right, if I could put it over him.

I tried the same cast. The fly was short of the concrete and flipped up under the culvert, showing the fish far too much gut. Quite without hope, I watched it ride the smooth current down. Then there was a great sucking rise that echoed up under the culvert, and the fly was gone. I struck, and he took line for his home, somewhere far under the road. But it must have been straight and clear of snags under there because he came back safely, and five minutes later we had him.

"What an evening," Denis said. "We couldn't have done much better on the Test at Longparish."

So we came very happily into Mr. Lewington's barnyard and began to look for him to tell him of our sport and ask after his rats. We found him in the barn, milking a goat, a turkey perched on one shoulder, a big red hen on the other. More goats wandered in and out, the ducks were there, up from the carrier, and a score of chickens and turkeys. One of the cats was drinking out of the pail as the old gentleman milked.

"Scat," said Mr. Lewington as we came to the door, and he brushed the cat away. A moment later he was contrite.

" 'Tis all my fault. I allus gives 'em milk out of the fust bucket and tonight I didn't do it. Dunno what's come over me."

He got up and poured some milk out of the pail into a pan.

"There," he said. "Do 'ee drink it up now." The cats clustered round the pan and began to lap.

"How're the rats, Mr. Lewington," I asked. "We thought of changing the traps round, because they haven't caught anything the last couple of nights."

Mr. Lewington set the pail down with a thump. "Do 'ee come along and I'll show 'ee." He stood up and bustled out of the barn. We followed.

"Every night I see 'un. Durnedest gert big old buck you ever did see. In t' stable he is, every night. He's got t' mare so nervous she won't 'ardly eat 'er hoats."

He opened the stable door and there was the rat, every bit as big as two big rats, sitting up a foot or so behind the mare's hoofs. Mr. Lewington whooped and charged forward, the mare started violently, the rat disappeared.

"He's gone," Denis said sensibly. "You won't see him again tonight."

But Mr. Lewington was busy at the mare's manger, crouching his short body and striking a match to look for something.

"I see 'un go in there," he was saying. "That's where 'e always do go. There's three on us here tonight, and we'll 'ave un this time."

Denis and I moved up and saw that he was trying to look through the narrow triangular tunnel made by a slanting board nailed behind the manger. "That's where 'ee always do go, and that's where 'e's gone tonight. Do 'ee look through other end while I 'old up a light this end for 'ee to zee."

I went round and looked through. The match flared, and

170

I saw outlined against it a huge curved back, ugly and almost hairless.

"He's there," I said. "Shall I get a stick and poke him out?"

"No," Mr. Lewington said. "Do 'ee keep un there, both on 'ee. Don't let un get out." And he bustled out of the barn.

"What's he gone for?" I asked Denis.

"I don't know. Something lethal I imagine."

Mr. Lewington came back. In one hand he had a candle in a lantern and in the other a .410 shotgun.

"You can't shoot him in there," I said.

"Can't I?" said Mr. Lewington.

He set the lantern up on a bale of straw opposite one end of the rat's hiding place.

"You'll frighten the mare," Denis said.

"You'll burn the stable down," I said.

"She'll be all right," Mr. Lewington said. "Out t' way now while I finish un."

"Take the mare out," I said.

Mr. Lewington was at the far end of the tunnel, sighting along his gun. "Move t' lantern up a mite," he said. "I can't see un."

I moved the lantern up and stepped back quickly. There was a roar and a flash. The mare plunged, reared and wheeled out of the stable. The lantern shattered to pieces. I saw a glow of red on the bale of straw and crushed it out with my coat sleeve.

"I got un," Mr. Lewington said. "Couldn't not have. Light that 'ere candle again so's we can see un."

I found the candle, lighted it and held it near the mouth of the tunnel.

"See him?" I asked.

There was a long pause from Mr. Lewington's end.

"No," he said at last. " 'Ee ain't there."

Denis came back with the mare. "Did you find him?"

171

"Oh, he's dead, all right," I said confidently. "Just crawled away somewhere."

"Couldn't not be," Mr. Lewington said. "Could 'ee?"

"No," Denis said. "We'll find him tomorrow."

We found him two days later in a trap we had set in the stable, without a mark on him. We took him away and put shotgun pellets in him, then brought him back for Mr. Lewington.

PACIFIC SALMON

THE word salmon is practically synonymous with game fish. The manifold virtues of the Atlantic salmon established this, but his Pacific cousins do a lot for anglers too. What is more, they are in many ways the most spectacular natural resource available to mankind and a major item of the world's food supply. One need not be an angler to be very much interested in them; but anglers have many special reasons for interest, and most men who have fished on the Pacific coast have a healthy curiosity, not only about the salmon runs themselves, but about the industry that depends on them.

Pacific salmon are confusing chiefly because so very much confusing stuff has been written about them. There is confusion, to start with, about their relationship to Atlantic salmon. They are related, but that is about all. They differ widely from the Atlantic salmon in both habits and physical characteristics, and for this sufficient reason they are classed by biologists as a separate genus: *Oncorhynchus* instead of *Salmo*.

The next confusion comes from the several species of Pacific salmon. There are five completely separate species, and each species is physically different from the others, different in life history, different in feeding and other habits. All five species are commercially important: at least two are directly important to anglers, and the other three are indirectly important.

As though five species were not enough, there is further confusion in that each species has several common names: the Chinook salmon of the Columbia, for instance, becomes the king salmon in Puget Sound, the spring salmon, and also the tyee, of British Columbia, and king salmon again in Alaska. These are local names, of course, but they are the only names that ordinary people know and use, and the locality where each has its meaning is no little county or bailiwick, but an area measured in tens of thousands of square miles and populated by hundreds of thousands. The Chinook has a right to the title "king" or "tyee," because he is by far the largest of Pacific salmon, commonly weighing between twenty and fifty pounds at maturity and occasionally as much as a hundred pounds. Just why my fellow British Columbians and I call him "spring salmon" I am not sure, but probably because many rivers have two quite distinct runs of Chinooks, one in the spring, which is earlier than all the other salmon runs, and the other in late summer or fall. But the Columbia River is the great and famous home of this salmon, and for the purposes of this book it is as well to keep to the Columbia name Chinook.

Because of his size, the Chinook is probably the best known of all the Pacific salmon. But the coho, or silver, salmon deserves equally well of anglers because he is a great fighter, a jumping fool who takes the fly readily in salt or fresh water. Cohos are much smaller than Chinooks, averaging about eight pounds and rarely weighing more than twenty, but they bear at least an equal part with the Chinooks in supporting the commercial troll fishery.

The sockeye is as definitely a fish of the Fraser River as the Chinook is of the Columbia. On the Columbia they call the sockeye the "blueback," which is a pity, because that is the name given to immature cohos by British Columbia fishermen.

Commercially the sockeye is also known as the "red salmon," from the bright-red color of his flesh. This redness holds up well in canning and makes the sockeye, pound for pound, commercially the most valuable of the five species.

The humpback is a little fish, averaging about four pounds. The commercial name, more widely used all the time, is "pink salmon," but most fishermen still use the affectionate "humpie," which seems to fit better and mean more than pink. The humpback takes fly or spoon in salt water but is important chiefly to net fishermen.

The dog salmon also has been given an approved commercial name, "chum salmon," but I haven't heard it used very much by fishermen. Dogs are fine fish, but until recently the industry paid little attention to them. I like to think that when I first watched the big dog salmon runs fifteen or sixteen years ago, they were a true picture of the abundant wealth of all the salmon runs before the coming of the white fishermen; but intensive fishing since then has done much to cut them down to size.

These, then, are the five salmon that make millions of dollars a year for the industry in Alaska, British Columbia, Washington and Oregon. Around the Kamchatka Peninsula, in the Okhotsk Sea and the Bering Sea, the Russians and Japanese take another hundred million or so of the same fish for their canneries and salteries. And so the world eats salmon.

But we are not yet out of all the confusions. There is a favorite misconception, greatly encouraged by the newspapers, that all Pacific salmon go down to the sea soon after hatching from the egg, live and grow there for exactly four years, then return to spawn. The truth is somewhat less simple. If we were to take the life histories of all five species, lump them together and strike an average, an approximate four-year cycle might be the answer. But there are wide variations from this average, not only between species but within species. The little humpback is the only one of the five with an invariable life history:

he goes down to salt water just as soon as he can swim freely and returns to spawn exactly two years after his parents made the same journey. The coho is almost as constant: he spends a full year in the river, then goes to sea and returns to spawn just three years after his parents. But a few cohos return in the fourth year, and a good number of males mature precociously and return after a single year in salt water.

The dog salmon is a fairly good example of a four-year fish. Like the humpbacks, they seem to go to sea as soon as they are free-swimming fry, and they return at the end of the three, four or five years—the great majority at the end of four years. The sockeye and the Chinook have the least predictable life histories. Most sockeyes go to sea after one year of feeding in a fresh-water lake, but some go down almost at once, and a few spend two full years in fresh water. Most of them return after three or four years in salt water, at four or five years of age, that is; but some individuals mature at three, six, seven and eight years. There is a great variation between the runs of different rivers: the Fraser River run is chiefly made up of four-year-olds; while nearly half the fish running to Rivers Inlet and the Skeena River are five- or six-year-olds, and more than 80 per cent of the Nass River run are five-years-old or older.

The majority (about four-fifths) of Chinooks go to sea as soon as they are free-swimming, and nearly all return after four or five years in salt water. This means, of course, that fish will be fairly often returning at four, five, six and seven years of age, though there will be more four- and five-year-olds than anything else. Again with Chinooks, there is some variation between the runs of different rivers: in the Yukon River, for instance, which has a big run of Chinooks, most of the fish spend at least one year in fresh water and six in salt water before maturing; a fair proportion spend two years in fresh water and do not return to spawn until they are eight years old.

There is a fairly well-supported theory that this delay is due to the slower growth rate in waters farther north.

The seaward movement of Pacific salmon is essentially a feeding movement. The young fish go down from the rivers when they have reached a certain stage of development, and they find there the abundance they need to grow them to full maturity. Generally speaking, this feeding migration is a northward movement, made so partly by the set of the current along the Pacific coast and partly by other factors. The extent of the movement varies considerably, for some fish travel little, if at all, beyond the influence of their own rivers, while others may go as far as seven or eight hundred miles northward before they turn back in the spawning migration. The seaward limit of the migration is somewhere near the hundred-fathom line, which is usually about thirty or forty miles offshore; beyond the hundred-fathom line the bottom drops off quite steeply toward the extreme depths of the ocean proper, and the abundance of feed is not so great as it is in the shallower water of the continental shelf.

Since the feeding migration is generally a northward movement, the spawning migration must be generally a southward movement. As the sexual organs of the fish mature, certain stimulations are released in them, and one response is a tendency to swim against the current. The eddies of the Japan Current make a fairly constant northward current along the coast of British Columbia, and by swimming against this with a steadily growing determination, the maturing fish draw gradually southward until they find their own rivers again and ascend them.

The feeding habits of the various Pacific salmon, like most of their other habits, vary considerably. All species feed very heavily on crustaceans, chiefly euphausiid shrimps, but the sockeye is the only species that keeps closely to this feed throughout its life history. Humpbacks, toward the end of their second and last year in salt water, feed a good deal on herring and launce fish. Dog salmon, though they certainly feed on both shrimps and herrings, are probably less selective than any of the other species. Cohos feed on crustaceans almost exclusively until their second summer in salt water, when they turn to herrings and launce fish with a voracity that grows them from silvery three-pounders into mature fish of ten pounds in a short six months. Young Chinooks, like young cohos, feed largely on crustaceans, but they turn to smelts and squid and launce fish as they grow larger, then to herrings and pilchards. Both cohos and Chinooks may turn back to feeding on shrimps whenever they come upon them in their ranging.

The abundance of the Pacific salmon runs produces a fishery whose yield no local market can absorb in fresh form. This was true before the white man reached the coast at all, and the Indians of the Columbia River and other parts of the coast ran what was undoubtedly a commercial fishery in the fullest sense of the term. They fished primarily for their own use, and they certainly ate fresh fish as they fished. But they smoked fish and dried fish for winter use, and they pounded dried fish into pemmican, a powdery meal which they packed into primitive sacks lined with fish skins and used in trade with other Indians.

Their fishing methods were fairly primitive but quite good enough to take big catches from the superabundance of fish that ran to every river and creek and stream along the coast. The Indians of Puget Sound used an ingenious reef net made of willow bark, which they set and worked over the kelp-covered reefs on flood tide so effectively that they could kill as many as three thousand salmon on a single run of tide. In other places, generally in rivers and the spawning tributaries, they used nets much like the modern haul or drag seines, floating or fixed traps, weirs, dip nets, spears, gaffs and even the bow and arrow. Occasionally they trolled with bone hooks and strips of herring for bait.

Almost all these methods have their counterparts in the modern industry, larger and more efficient, but essentially the same. The Indian fishery was limited by the fishing population, by the materials available and by the consuming population within reach. The white fishery was limited at first in the same way, but it overcame the limitations one by one until the sole limitation became the number of fish available.

The modern industry produces fresh, salt and even smoked fish, but the bulk of the product is canned fish; efficient canneries have wholly solved the problem of limited local markets, and now the whole world is a market. Up and down the coast there are between two and three hundred salmon canneries normally operating, half of them in Alaska, thirty or forty in British Columbia, perhaps twenty in the Columbia River and the others wherever the fish run well. Together they pack some ten million cases of salmon a year. Since it takes on the average about twelve sockeyes to make up a case, or ten cohos, or four Chinooks, or sixteen humpbacks, or nine dog salmon, it seems fairly safe to say that the canning industry uses at least a hundred million salmon a year. But there are big variations in all these figures from year to year, because the runs are not steady: the run of humpbacks to Puget Sound, for instance, yielded nearly six million fish in 1935 and less than a quarter of a million in 1936. This was a regular and expected variation, and it is repeated in greater or lesser degree in all humpback runs—one year is good and the next year is bad. Annual variations in the runs of the other species are less marked, but there are variations, and, unless man interferes by closing off spawning areas or by fishing too hard, they perpetuate themselves. A big year always yields, in due course of the cycle, a big year, and a small year always yields a small year.

Gill nets, traps, purse seines and trolling are the principal methods of fishing. Except in the really big rivers, such as the Fraser and the Columbia, few fish are taken in fresh water; the boats go out to sea and meet the fish as they are coming in on their spawning migration. Gill-net boats are probably the most numerous; these are small boats, about thirty feet long and powered by eight- or ten-horsepower gas engines. They are usually run by one or two men and carry some three hundred fathom of a net which is made of fine twine in a mesh just wide enough to allow the fish to slide his gills and pectoral fins through; as the thick part of his body comes against the mesh he is held, and when he tries to draw out, his fins or gills tangle in the mesh.

Most gill nets are drift nets; that is, the fisherman runs out the full length of his net between a small floating buoy and his boat, then kills his engine and lets the boat, buoy and net drift through a stretch of channel where the fish should be running. The net is kept at stretch vertically by a cork line at the surface and a lead line below, so that it makes a great curtain that fish are bound to strike. In clean water gill-netters can fish only at night, when the mesh is more or less invisible to the fish, but many of the coast rivers carry glacial silt well down into the inlets and channels where the fish pass, and in those waters the boats often fish night and day.

Traps are still used in Oregon and Alaska, though Washington prohibited their use in 1935, and the only traps in British Columbia are two or three which operate at the southern end of Vancouver Island. Most traps are made of heavy netting stretched on piles driven into the bottom. In the usual design there is a lead, a straight line of piling which carries a solid wall of web and extends for a thousand feet or more across the normal course of the migrating fish. As the fish turn along this lead they come through a narrow recurved entrance into a semicircular enclosure known as the "big heart." Trying to find a way out of this, they come into the small heart, which leads them through a funnel-shaped entrance into the pot; from there they come through a still narrower entrance of the same type into the spiller, a small enclosure, from which they are easily brailed when it is time for the trap to be emptied. Strategically placed traps are most efficient means of catching fish—too efficient, many people think and public opinion is strongly against their use both in Washington and British Columbia. Yet no type of gear is more easily controlled and regulated than are traps, for the simple reason that they are fixed. A single fishery officer can keep close watch and order the trap closed or opened as the escapement of spawning fish beyond the trap demands. Traps also do much to reduce the hardships and hazards of fishing, and they permit fishermen to live a home life in permanent settlements. Two questions about traps have not been satisfactorily answered: Do they destroy and waste more immature fish than other types of gear? Do they employ fewer men than other types of gear? Without really good answers to these questions, it is impossible to say whether the pros or the cons are right.

Purse seiners are big boats, forty to seventy feet long with fifty or a hundred Diesel horsepower. They have a crew of eight or ten men who fish, not for wages, but for shares of the catch. The boats are broad in the beam, with wide round sterns to carry the big nets, and they roll mightily in the trough of a heavy sea. The nets are usually about three hundred fathoms long and ten fathoms deep, of heavy twine in a four-inch mesh. They have the usual cork line and lead line to spread them in the water, except that the lead line has a number of iron rings attached to it. The purse line, heavy rope, passes through these rings, and by taking it in during a set, the net is pursed—that is, the lead line is drawn up on the rings until the depth of the net comes into a bag that prevents the fish from diving down and escaping.

Making a purse seine set, like most types of fishing, can be pretty hard work. When the fish are running thinly and the crew is making several sets a day to catch enough fish to pay for their grub, it is a depressing business. But when there is a real run of sockeyes or humps going through and every set means a chance of big money, there is a fine, keen excitement in the work. When the dog salmon are running late in the year and the winter southeasters have started, the work is harder than ever, cold, wet work and often dangerous. But the dog salmon run is the one that makes up for bad seasons, and the boats go out and make sets that often circle four thousand fish or more. Sometimes several boats are needed to carry the fish of a single haul, and sometimes ambitious skippers load their boats until the net table is level with the water; then, if a little slop comes up, boat and load may go down together. Men take big chances when the stakes are big.

Humpbacks and sockeyes are the purse-seiner's real gold though, and a purse seiner's real time is a summer dawn when the inside waters are still except for the creases and whirls of the tide. A good skipper knows the fish and the waters he fishes, and his crew gives him its whole faith. The boat cruises along, hunting fish. Fish show, perhaps jumping, perhaps finning, perhaps only by bubbles that wobble to the surface from three or four fathoms down. The set is made with swift and eager efficiency. The big skiff slides into the water from its place on top of the net, the skiff man is at the oars almost as it touches. He rows, steadily and strongly, holding one end of the net while the big boat circles the school of fish, paying the long net out, cork line, web, lead line and purse line, smoothly over the roller on the stern. The long circle is closed in a few short minutes, the winch brings the purse line in until there is webbing all around the fish and under them. The crew brings in the net over the live roller on the turntable, slowly closing the great circle of cork line. The fish show rarely at first, then more frequently, until the circle is close against the boat and only a few feet in diameter. Then the brail, a huge dip net hung on blocks from the boom, goes down and brings up load after load of bright silver fish until the net is empty. The boat and its crew may be richer by fifty dollars—or five thousand.

The trollers are, of all commercial fishermen, most nearly anglers; their problems are angler's problems, with feeding fish, but multiplied and magnified. Trollers hook bottom and lose gear; trollers change spoons as anglers change flies; trollers argue and theorize and think and wonder as anglers do; they play their hunches and gauge their luck as all fishermen do. A good troller, like a good angler or a good purse-seine captain, has some indefinite advantage compounded of knowledge and experience and thoroughness that his fellows have not.

Trollers are little men and very independent. They own their own boats and their own gear, and they go their own way to find their own fish. Their boats are of every shape and size and kind, from rowboats up to fifty-foot, Diesel-powered, deep-sea craft that would make a yachtsman jealous. The little boats, and some of the big ones, fish inside waters. In the Gulf of Georgia big catches of young cohos are made during the early part of the summer, a wasteful slaughter of fish that would double or triple their weight within a few months; but for the most part the inside trollers everywhere have to depend on the spasmodic movements of cohos and Chinooks. Sometimes a run of feeding cohos makes good fishing, and sometimes a movement of herring draws schools of young and hungry Chinooks; but the main runs of spawning fish are no longer feeding freely when they reach the inside waters but are fed to full development, intent on the business ahead. The bright spoons of the inside trollers draw only the careless or quick-tempered or unlucky ones. But for all that, inside trolling is a fine, free, easy way of life for many men, and inside trollers are often good and wise fishermen.

Probably the greatest trolling grounds in the world are the banks off the west coast of Vancouver Island, where a great proportion of the Columbia River Chinooks go to feed. The Columbia fish run farther north than that, as far as the north coast of the Queen Charlotte Islands, and the fishermen follow them all the way, the Americans fishing offshore, beyond the three-mile limit, Canadians fishing with them and also in their own territorial waters. The Americans fish chiefly for Chinooks, because they are a long way from their home ports and the cohos do not keep well on ice. But the Canadians fish heavily for cohos also, as the Americans do in their own territorial waters. American trollers land yearly in Washington, Oregon and California some fifteen or twenty million pounds of salmon, and the cohos make up perhaps as much as one-third of this total. The British Columbia trollers land about a million Chinooks—fish, not pounds—and anywhere from one to three million or more cohos each year.

A troller carries two slender cedar poles some forty to sixty feet long, which stand upright against his mast. When he starts to fish, he lowers his poles until they project horizontally from each side of the boat, to spread his lines. Usually a big troller fishes six or eight stainless-steel lines, two on each main pole, two out over the stern and two more from bow poles which project ahead of and out from the boat. Each line is held almost straight down in the water by a thirty- or forty-pound ball of lead and carries several spoons, perhaps two or three for Chinooks, occasionally as many as seven or eight for cohos, which trail out from the main line on shorter lines of their own. This is modern and highly efficient gear, made possible only recently by the wide use of power reels, called "gurdies," which are driven by shaft and clutch from the main engine, to bring in the lines when a fish is hooked.

The outside trollers fish from dawn till dark, in all weathers, often riding the great Pacific swells for a week or more at a time before turning back with their catch. Good trollers make big money in years when the run is right and the price is right; but the money they make is usually a straight return on skill and investment—to stay out where the fish are a boat must be big enough to carry fish and ice, and seaworthy to stand whatever weather comes. To handle such a boat and fish her properly, a troller needs not only fishing knowledge but seamanship and mechanical skill and a fair share of courage.

I have said that the Pacific salmon runs are probably the most spectacular natural resource on the face of the earth.

Their greatness is less than it once was, but even today this annual movement of millions upon millions of great gleaming fish through the length and breadth of the continental shelf toward their spawning in the high tributaries is a tremendous thing. The salmon runs, more surely and easily than almost any other resource, can be made to last and serve indefinitely, can even be grown back to, or beyond, their full glory. The base of the resource is the sea, which gives life to myriads of diatoms. So long as there are euphausiid shrimps to feed on the diatoms, so long as there are herrings to feed on the euphausiids, so long as there are salmon to feed on the herrings and so turn the diatoms at last to man's use, the ocean base of the resource is solid. And there will be salmon and more salmon to complete this cycle so long as they are allowed to enter the rivers to their spawning in sufficient numbers, so long as the way to the spawning beds is kept clear and easy and open and so long as the rivers are kept clean and fresh and pure. It is as simple as that.

JULY

SOMETIME in July, when the
last of the winter's snow has melted out of the mountains, a
clear river comes down to summer level. This is not the extreme low water of a late, dry fall, when waterworn rocks are
high and dry on either side of the last narrow channel, but a

good, normal sweeping flow of water against which the bars show clearly and the known rocks stand out with the current folding gently on their shoulders. It is a good time to see the river and really learn it; it is a pleasant time to know the river, because the water is mild on the hands, warm enough to wade without boots if one chooses, shallow and clear to reveal itself and very full of life. July is not a good fishing month in the lower part of the Campbell, except perhaps in the tidal part, but it is an expectant month. Very soon the big cutthroats will be up, very soon the salmon will be running; always there may be a fish somewhere, at the head of the Sandy Pool perhaps, off the mouth of the Quinsam, in the Quinsam pool at dusk, under the break at the Island Pools, certainly in the Canyon Pool if you can find him.

But trout or no, a July day is never wasted. Too many things are going on in July. The yearling spring salmon, five or six inches long now, are busy in the little, quick runs below the bar of the Island Pools; coho fry, lively and sure of themselves, feed busily in every quiet eddy—their orange tails flutter brightly behind their trim, beautifully marked bodies—and make me remember the fly I dress to look like them: orange feather of Indian crow for the tail, silver for their bright bellies, tail of golden pheasant for their handsome backs and a few strands of orange bear fur inside the strips, to cover up the feeling that such a simple dressing cannot duplicate all there is of so much light and life.

In July the big gray caddis larvae are thick on the round rocks, dragging their sand cases slowly on six black legs; the trout deal with them ably, case and all, as the current washes them down from a rock they have climbed too recklessly and that is why I often fish a big, dark Greenwell glory at the head of the fastest runs in the summer months. The trout catch them, too, as they leave their cases and swim surfaceward to break out their wings and again when, as sedge flies, they sit the water in weariness after the mating flight; but far more sedges grow trout while they are still in their cases than any other way, and many a good trout learns to twist his body over and scrape them from the rocks with the side of his jaws.

July is a good rock-turning month, if you like rock turning. Medium-sized boulders, six inches or eight inches in diameter, are quite big enough; in a good stream every one has something on the underside of it. Little, flat, black and brown May-fly nymphs are commonest; to be sure that they are May-fly nymphs, look closely for the quick movement of gills along the sides of their bodies in the drop of water that clings to them. Three tails is another certain sign of a May fly, though there are May flies with only two tails, and then you must look for the gills to make sure they aren't stone-flies. Stone-fly nymphs have two claws on each foot, the May flies only one, and stone-fly gills, if they have them, are near where the legs join the body. Stone-fly nymphs are handsome, often strongly marked with dark brown and light brown or with black and yellow, and they love the fast water. I think of them as early-season flies, of March and April, but there are big full-grown nymphs under the rocks of the Campbell in July and August.

Many caddis larvae and pupae will be under the rocks, some crawling free, some securely fastened. There will be snails, sponges, jelly masses of caddis eggs and hundreds of midges in soft tubes that dissolve into mud at a touch. I have a great respect for midges, because trout like them well. They are very important to small trout and young salmon, but even the largest trout take them freely at times and I have often spotted a big trout by a quiet rise or a slight movement under water, put a fly over him and found his gullet lined with tiny, flattened midge larvae. Along the bar of the Island Pools there are half a dozen big rocks, barely covered by the swift water, that I look for every summer because I know they will be black with the tubes of net-winged midges. I always put in ten or fifteen minutes of good fishing time just looking at them, wondering how such tiny things can cling so firmly against the power of moving water.

Even in summer the Campbell has no weed growth—perhaps two or three trailing stems of pond weed in the quietest eddy of the Sandy Pool or behind the sheltering wall at the mouth of the Canyon. The river itself grows nothing nearer weed than the short waving clumps of rich green algae on the rocks in fast water, a strange growth, tiny but lush, its greenness deep to violence. Thinking of the chalk-stream weeds, long trailing mats of shelter for life of every kind, I wonder at the strange fertility of rocks and gravel and silt and swiftly moving water. It is desert apparently, yet everything necessary to life is there—sunlight, minerals, water. From these the algae can grow, and at once the desert is no longer desert, but begins to support May flies and caddis larvae and midge larvae and snails and many other vegetarian creatures. Then there is life for the carnivores, the stone-fly and dragonfly nymphs, some of the caddis larvae and, at last, the fish—bullheads and sticklebacks, trout and young salmon and steelheads and lampreys. July reminds me of this as no other month does, and sometimes in July I watch the clearest symbol of it I know: a great dragon nymph crawls wetly out onto a dry sun-warm rock. I watch and see the split of the nymphal case, then perhaps look away at something else. When I look back, the case is a dry shuck and beside it is a new insect, the body long and fresh and still soft, the wings crumpled and olive green. Slowly the sun stiffens the wings and straightens them, hardens the body and sets its colors. The four wings are straight out now, strong and quivering; suddenly the perfect dragonfly is gone in swift hunting flight. And all that grew from rocks and water.

Very often in July the spring salmon come in well to the mouth of the Campbell. These are not the famous tyees, the big mature spawners of the Campbell run that lie off the river in August and draw fishermen from all over the world, but smaller fish of ten or twelve pounds—a big one might be as much as twenty pounds—that feed hungrily before dark. I often wish they would run into the river, where a fly could find them, or even to the shallow water close to shore, so that one could reach them without a boat, for the strong tides of Discovery Passage would make that very like river fishing. One year, for some reason, the bluebacks did come in, feeding and swirling for days on end all along the tide-flooded beaches. I was busy and could only get out once, for a short hour, but a big fly cast over a swirl in less than two feet of water brought a strong take from a fish of five pounds. There's a lot to be said for a blueback caught that way, and I hope they'll come in again in a year when I'm free to pay them proper attention.

July has thunderstorms. Most anglers seem to worry about thunderstorms, and I think it is true that fish are sensitive to them. In the hot, heavy stillness that comes before a big storm anything may happen. I started out fishing one thundery day in England, and George Godden, one of the gardeners, told me his mother was sick. The old lady was awful fond of eels and did I think I could get her some? They'd do her a power of good.

There were plenty of eels in the river and eels are not hard to catch—that is, you can get them in traps or on night lines easily enough—but I didn't see just how I should be able to pick any up in broad daylight with 4X gut and small dry flies. So I went about my fishing rather thoughtfully, watching the few eels I saw with a new interest and stopping at all the deep pools to look carefully for them. I noticed almost at once that they were not in the pools where I usually saw them, but out on the shallows. That seemed to make things even more difficult, so I decided to follow the river up to a small carrier. The carrier was dry, I knew, but there would be small pools in it, and there might be an eel in one of them that I could chase into the mud and perhaps, if I were very lucky, dig out with my landing net.

A heavy thunderstorm broke just as I came to the long reach of shallow water above Black Hole. For a few minutes heavy rain spattered the surface of the shallow, then the sun came out and the trout started to rise, though there was still thunder about. It was too good a chance to miss. I marked a good trout well ahead of me, slipped into the water and waded up until I could reach him. Just as I began to let out line, I noticed an eel in the water four or five feet away from me. He was lying well down on the bottom, but his body was moving to hold him against the current and he seemed very much awake. I reached for my landing net, not because I expected to get him —I had tried that way a thousand times before and had never had a single eel to show for it—but because he was close and there was no harm in trying. I reached the net forward, over him, put it down into the water above his head. He didn't move away. I got the net well down and scooped back toward me, over the gravel. A silly trick, I thought; you couldn't net him that way even if he had a hook in him. But the net came up and the eel was in it.

I looked him over carefully. He wasn't blind. There was nothing wrong with him that I could see. But I was satisfied there was something wrong and I made up my mind Mrs. Godden would be better off without him. I killed him, hung him up and went back into the water. My trout was down now, but I found another, got ready to cast to him, then saw two more eels. Again I tried the net, and again I scooped up an eel. I knew it must be the thunder then, so I began eel fishing in dead earnest. The spell lasted half an hour and in that time I caught six fine fat eels, all by wading up to them and raking them out with the landing net. Thunderstorm or dispensation from on high, it was a wonderful thing; eels mean a lot to some of the country people in England, and George told me that this catch made Mrs. Godden very happy indeed. He even went so far as to give them credit for the fact that she was out of bed within a week, but it seems probable that there were other factors operating to that end.

On another July day I was fishing a length of difficult club water in England when a heavy thunderstorm broke. Through the whole morning I had found only two or three rising fish to cast for. Now I was starting on a long, wide, straight reach that rippled over golden gravel and thick weed beds. The far bank was lined with tall, heavy elms, and as the storm broke fish began to rise close under the roots of the elms. Nearly all the fish were good ones for the stream, a pound or more in weight, and I simply walked up my own bank and cast across to them. Within an hour I had my limit of eight good fish.

There was another day, a Canadian day, with heavy, dull, vicious blue storm clouds in half the sky and light, pretty, playtime clouds in the other half. The storm had passed over once with bright, violent lightning and great thunder, but it seemed to be still hovering, and everything was very green and very frightened. It was deeply silent. The leaves moved a little on the trees, in an aimless, eddying breeze, but there was no rustle from them. The birds were silent, hidden in the thickest trees, except that one or two spoke occasionally and very clearly in the silence with trembling notes that had in them nothing of movement. The note of the river was subdued, and the stream seemed to creep darkly and slowly seaward, as though unwilling to attract attention. The lightning began to play again and the thunder rumbled distantly. I had been watching, feeling the fear myself without being afraid, but now I made a cast and hooked a good two-pound trout at once. I cast again and hooked another, then a third one, a bigger fish. Three others I hooked and lost, then landed a fourth. When I opened them, they were full of bees, beautiful brown honey bees that I supposed the storm had beaten to the water.

BUTTLE LAKE

THE map shows Buttle Lake at 725 feet above sea level; but it is a mountain lake, deep in the mountains, cradled in mountains, with only the narrow valley of the Buttle River to make an easy way into it. For a mountain lake, Buttle is big, twenty miles long and about a mile wide on the average, and this makes it a broad smooth highway to all the utterly undeveloped perfections of Strathcona Park.

Strathcona Park was created by wise statute of the Province of British Columbia in 1911, and very little has been done about it since. The greater part of the park lies to the west of Buttle Lake, several hundred square miles of fierce and ragged Vancouver Island mountains, gouged and furrowed by creeks and streams, hiding a hundred lakes. Probably this country could stand a little development: a thorough exploration by one or two good fishermen and mountaineers, trails cut to the best lakes and the best peaks, cabins built where they will do most good. The country challenges the imagination; it is virgin, untouched by anyone except surveyors and a few prospectors. There are glaciers and meadows and canyons, slopes of heather and the strange cool growth of a thousand flowers in the mountains. Most of the lakes hold fish, but very few of them have been touched by a line, and no one can say which are the good ones and why. Some of them drain back through the valleys to Buttle Lake, some drain westward to Muchalat Arm on the west coast. One of these, Donner Lake, is a big lake only 1750 feet above sea level, and I often wonder if the summer steelhead climb that far. There are so many questions to be asked about those lakes and the streams that drain them: What insects have they? What hatches of fly to bring the trout up? Might not one or two of them in all that country of diverse rock have the alkalinity that most coast lakes lack and so a growth of weed and insect life that would make really big fish? One thing is quite certain: all the lakes are beautiful, most of them spectacularly beautiful, close under the hard, sharp, snow-covered mountain peaks, rock bordered, decorated by stunted pine and fir and hemlock and all the loveliness of alpine flowers.

Buttle Lake is Strathcona Park's highway, and an easily accessible highway. You can ride to it by logging company speeder from the end of the road or walk the eight or nine miles or even fly a plane in. And most of these unknown mountain lakes are within ten or twelve miles of Buttle. But ten or twelve miles through what? Sometimes through an easy, gentle valley, sometimes through thick brush and blowdown, over rock and by difficult mountain passes. They remain lost and unknown to most people on a short holiday because of these uncertain qualities of the journey. The young and energetic could go and be happy in what they found; the rich man could plan a wise expedition and be sure that his holiday would remain a holiday instead of becoming a formidable task; but most people do not care to take the long chance, and so the lakes remain unknown, a challenge to the adventurous, a faithful promise of unspoiled beauty, invitingly close at hand on the map but distant as the stars for most practical purposes.

Perhaps it doesn't matter very much, perhaps it is even a good thing, that the meadows and heather fields and little lakes, the snow fields and waterfalls and natural bridges, the marble peaks and the limitless rivers should be lost in the difficulty of the country for a few more years. Even though they remain invisible for the most part, the imagination places them in the magnificent mountains that climb from Buttle Lake; and the knowledge that they are there somewhere, hidden in the timber of the deep valleys, just concealed behind the peaks or over the shoulders of the passes, cut from sight by the climb of the ground or simply by distance, gives far stronger meaning to the loveliness that can be seen. Buttle Lake itself is joy and pleasure and beauty enough.

For all its length and size and in spite of the mountains round it, Buttle is a gentle lake, seldom stirred by the fierce sudden winds that come down upon most long mountain lakes. Its shores are sometimes steep and rocky, but there are many friendly beaches and many sheltered bays. Best of all, it is fed by many streams, little rivers really, and each one of them has something for a fisherman.

When I first went in to Buttle Lake, I was disappointed in the fish I caught there, as I have been very often when following up popular reports of good fishing, especially in lakes. Most popular reports, I have learned at last, follow much the same line: "Boy! That's real fishing in there. Why, a three-pound trout's a small one. They'll average three pounds, and all on the fly too." It's always three-pounders they talk about—three, not four or five or two—and I have never been able to understand why. A three-pounder is a fine big trout almost anywhere, a fish well worth talking about, worth going after and worth catching. But he's not nearly such a common fish as most people seem to think, and I've learned to listen to reports of three-pounders with fingers crossed on both hands and the blackest doubts in my heart. Buttle Lake, "they" told me, was a lake of three-pounders hungry for a fly. Well, it isn't. The trout you catch there on a fly don't average three quarters of a pound most of the time. But once you've forgotten your original disappointment and got used to them, they're fine little fish that can show you a lot of fun.

There are big trout in Buttle, very big trout, eight- and ten-pounders anyway, both cutthroat and rainbow. There are also trout of all weights up to eight pounds, including three-pounders, but the chance of catching anything over two pounds on the fly is fairly remote. That doesn't mean that the big fish haven't their effect on the character of Buttle Lake fly-fishing.

They are a little like the beautiful things hidden in the mountains, a rich invisible backdrop for the beautiful things within sight. It is always possible to leave the lake, climb a valley and come upon the hidden splendors; and it is always possible that one of the really big fish will have come up out of the depths of the lake and will be cruising his slow way forward over the bar at the mouth of the creek just as your fly lights. That is all the measure of chance a fisherman needs to keep him happy. It keeps me happy, year after year when I go in there, and it fills those evenings of gentle fly-fishing for little fish with an almost subconscious tenseness of hope and excitement that makes every rise, every strange ripple of the sunset water something to be closely watched. I know that one day I shall set the hook, see a boiling turn and a great smooth shoulder of water running fast out toward the lake.

I don't know why I should write of Buttle as though it were a lake of splendid, but unfulfilled, promises, unless it is because the lake has some breathless quality far beyond any mere sum of trees and mountains and water and snow. The rewards that one finds there are so rich that it seems necessary to reach beyond the tangible and visible for their source. One does not commonly see a great deal of wild life near the lake in the summer months—perhaps deer on a mossy bluff, using the gentle breeze to keep the flies away from them, perhaps humming birds in the salmonberries at Cross's cabin, certainly the sleek, sharp-billed loons swimming low in the water; by great good fortune, perhaps a beaver working in the slough at the head of the lake or a black bear hunting berries along one of the streams. Yet there is the feeling that creatures are moving freely up and down the wide, timbered valleys that bring the larger streams down, and there is the sure knowledge that they have been little disturbed and not at all changed in their habits since the trees first grew on the slopes.

There are few places anywhere, even in the noble inlets of

the British Columbia coast, that the mountains are closer to water or better open to view. At the foot of the lake they are rounded, almost gentle at first sight, with dark timber climbing to their four- or five-thousand-foot summits. But even these mountains have great, precipitous bluffs of bare rock and climb very sharply from the lake. Only five or six miles farther up one comes into the high mountains, not giants by Rocky or even Coast Range standards, but six- or seven-thousand-foot peaks, impressive because they climb sharply to their full height from the lake instead of merely crowning some already high plateau. Timberline on the coast is somewhere a little below 5000 feet, so the heads of these mountains are snow fields and bare rock; and the shape and color of the different mountains vary with the different rocks that make them, from pure smooth marble, through limestone, to rugged, weathered granite.

One is seldom out of sight of mountains, never wholly unconscious of them, while fishing. They are there, a frame and a setting and an atmosphere, and they have their effect: the feeling of the fishing is different. That is why it is so good to fish the mouths of the many streams that enter the lake—Price and Myra and Henshaw, Shepherd's and Phillips and Marble and Wolf—particularly at dusk, when the lake is calm in the long-slanting light of the late sun. One stands at the mouth of Shepherd's Creek, perhaps, loose gravel underfoot, swift water racing past, flattening out into smooth current lines that lose themselves well out on the still, shining surface of the lake. The sound of moving water is strong and cool, quick and lively and close at hand; everything else is silent and vast and still, yet almost oppressively living, vibrant with life and growth and change in superficial sameness. The lake was blue and white with the light touch of a westerly only a few hours ago. The mountains were clear in the sunlight; they are clear still, yet somehow veiled by the lesser light of the sinking sun. Soon the snow slides will be colored with sunset, not pink, though pink is the word that means some part of the color, but flushed and glowing with the reflection of clean, bright flame.

The light and reflections of light are there long after the sun has gone down under the mountaintops. The water is darker and calmer than before; even the chatter of the current is quieter now and the current seems to pull less strongly against the legs. Fish are rising along the edges of the several runs, flies are coming down while others still dance above the surface of the water. A fish takes the fly and jumps, and there is still color enough in the sky to touch his sides with the same glow that is on the snow fields.

All the creek mouths are beautiful. Each has its own special quality. Shepherd's has its several runs over the gravel; Myra, its single, wide, even flow far out to the steep drop-off; Henshaw, its exposed position so that one seems to be standing securely far out in the lake. Wolf River comes out in a long, smooth glide, deceptively deep, fanning out at the drop-off into a dance of quick ripples like wind ripples but never quite still even when the lake itself is utterly smooth. Mount McBride stands high and near on the south bank, and the timber on both banks becomes tall and big only a little way up from the lake. I was with my friend Bill Reid, of Long Beach, on the last evening I fished Wolf. Bill fishes the river often because his pleasant Nootka Lodge is just around the point, only a mile or so away, and at least once he has found a big fish willing to take his fly up on the bar. There was a good rise on this particular evening; flies were drifting steadily down, and fish were breaking the smooth surface almost as steadily to intercept them. I noticed carelessly that the flies were duns, a smoky-blue color, not large, but I fished on calmly enough with a gray-bodied sedge because it had always been a good fly for me during the hatches of July and August evenings on Vancouver Island mountain streams.

It seemed to me at first that the fish must be moving a good deal between rises. I covered rise after rise, generally without result, sometimes drawing the fish into a short take, only once or twice managing to set the hook firmly. I had worked well up from the lake and was just coming to the awkward corner that nearly always means two or three cupfulls of ice water in each boot before I thought of the fly on the water again. Perhaps they didn't like the sedge; ridiculous, I told myself, they always like it; they aren't chalk-stream fish or even fish near a city; they'll come if it looks like food. A good fish was rising about fifteen yards away, and a chance light showed me his body clearly against the pale gravel. He was rising beautifully, taking fly after fly with tiny, easy dimples, holding himself just below the smooth swift surface current between each rise. I put the sedge over him. He turned to it, looked closely at it, turned away and took a natural fly. I changed then, unwillingly because the light was going fast, to a Mackenzie River blue upright, a heavy, bushy, deer-hair fly two or three times the size of the natural that was coming down. I hadn't much faith in the change and wanted a fly that I could still see when the light became really difficult.

My fish was still rising, a clean, pale, round-bodied fish of at least a pound, and I realized that I wanted him badly now. I put the fly over him; he took it at once, confidently and easily, and the hook set firmly when I raised the rod point. In two or three minutes he was safe in the net. I covered two more rises and hooked two twelve-inchers, which I turned back. It was clear that the change had done something, and I began to pick the fish I cast to more carefully. Every fish I covered took the blue fly cleanly and well, until I came to a run of heavy current that battered itself against a log which slanted out on an angle from the bank. I saw a quick rise near the end of the log, where the current shot from it, then another and another. I knew that the fish was a good one—the shape of the rise, the place he was feeding in, the steady ease with which he picked the flies from the swift current all seemed to show that —and I dropped a fly over him at once. It swept past him, untouched; I tried again, half a dozen times, and the same thing happened. Yet he was rising steadily, always in the same place, within an inch of the log and about two feet from the end of it. He never turned out for a fly, and that was what I had been trying to make him do. I couldn't get a drift of any length right up against the log because the throw of current would drag the fly out almost immediately. The cast had to be exact, within an inch one way, within two or three inches the other way, and it was a long cast. I tried it twice, dropping the fly behind him, then tried the one I really wanted. The fly almost touched his nose as he broke the surface to take a natural, and I thought my luck was exhausted. It was too much to expect to do that again without hooking the log or getting a drag that would frighten him. But the next cast did it perfectly—cast, rise, strike, all in a moment of time—and he was securely hooked. It was one of those perfectly satisfying things that happen in fly-fishing and stick in the memory forever; yet the fish was no three-pounder, simply a good little Wolf River cutthroat of a pound and a quarter. I stopped fishing as soon as he came to the net and waded back down to where Bill was waiting on the bar.

I had to go out from the lake next day, so Bill took me down in the speedboat. It was a calm day of bright sun. Bill and I had talked a little of Harry's Flats, sometimes called the Northeast Shoal, and we decided to stop and fish there. The flats are near the foot of the lake, a good area of water, nowhere much over twenty feet deep, where the cutthroats nearly always come well to the fly. It looked hopeless as Con killed the big outboard and the boat drifted—glass-still water, hot bright sun, nothing moving anywhere. But Bill rose a fish before he had made half a dozen casts. For the next hour they came to us quite steadily. We stood as high as we could in the boat, once we had found it did not matter, and cast dry flies well out. Then we watched as the fish came up, sometimes two or three at once, right from the bottom in the clear, still water.

That is the sort of thing Buttle does for you, even though really big fish on the fly are little more than a dream. There is a strong need of pleasure in watching even a three-quarter-pounder swim up and up to a fly through twenty feet of bright water. A fish in a really difficult place or in a beautiful place need not be large to make fishing interesting and good. I have caught fish in Myra Creek that I could watch without interruption from the moment I first marked them until the moment they were ready for the net, and sometimes after that, when I had turned them loose and they were finding themselves in the stream again. I have fished an evening at Shepherd's Creek, caught nothing and loved every moment of the time. But I still would like to know more and see more. I should like to fish the lake regularly through a long full season from March to October. I am sure that somewhere in that time I should meet big fish, really big fish of five, six, perhaps ten pounds, cruising the bars at the mouths of the creeks.

DARK ON THE WATER

Early morning and late evening are supposed to be great times for the fisherman. Generally, I have not found them so. There are exceptions: maturing Pacific salmon, for instance, are very likely to take best in salt water toward change of light; there may be rare circumstances, such as the movements of Corethra and other light-hating creatures, which make early-morning trout fishing not only profitable but almost essential; and after a hot, bright summer day the gentle evening light is reassuring to almost any creature. Dawn can be a beautiful time on the water, and I am glad I have tried early-morning fishing as often as I have and in as many different places; but I am glad, too, that I know

it is seldom necessary for a fly-fisherman to get up early to catch fish, because early rising tends to make work out of pleasure. I like to start comfortably after a good breakfast and that, perhaps, is why I can make the broad generalization that the best fishing hours are likely to come between 10:30 A.M. and 4:30 P.M.; certainly a fisherman will be doing his own best work then, and that is at least as important as the mood of the fish; moods are changeable and skillful fishing can sometimes change them.

Evening fishing is important, though, traditionally, aesthetically and actually. The hot summer months are the time for it, July, August and early September, and it is no effort then to stay out until the last light is gone. The hours of a summer evening from seven o'clock onward are an exciting time; the day's work is done and man's world is very peaceful, but other creatures begin to move. I have seen many things at that stealthy time. Once a family of coons, working their way in playful hunting along the river's edge, came past where I was standing, less than half the river away from them, and went on round the upstream bend without noticing me. Once a cougar came silently from heavy timber onto a railroad track that I was following toward a good pool; he saw me, stopped for a moment, then went on across the track and disappeared to his hunting. Several times I have seen beaver, out in the quiet hour before their night's work of harvesting willow and alder; several times otters, sleek bodies sliding from rock or dirt into the water, little quick-eyed heads held low in swimming; and many times bear and deer moving with a calmness and a sense of right that forsake them in full daylight.

If land creatures move to their feeding at that time, perhaps it is not unreasonable to suppose that trout also will move then. Sometimes they do; often the dusk of a hot day brings flies down to the water, spent after their mating flight, and the trout move up to take them. Nearly always the quiet light of dusk brings fish into the shallows and stirs them to greater activity than during the day. Again and again one sees the still surface of a lake, scarcely broken by movement all through the day, marked by a thousand rings at sunset.

A fisherman is always hopeful—nearly always more hopeful than he has any good cause to be. He is probably most hopeful of all when he goes out in the early dawn, feeling that he has stolen an hour on his brothers and earned himself a reward by sheer virtue and fortitude. But the hope of the evening rise is a darker, more powerful hope; it is a mysterious time, when miracles may happen: a big fish, stirred from the hidden depths of a dark pool, may be under that tiny rise in the shallows; heavy gut and a clumsily cast fly may not matter; perhaps the sedges will be out and the fish will forget all caution to come to them. At worst it is a different time, quiet and strange, and it may well be that something stirs in a fisherman to give him a kinship with the time, just as something in the slant of the sun and the length of the shadows moves the cougars and coons to their hunting.

Generally the great hopes one has of evening fishing are not fulfilled, the imagined shapes of huge fish do not materialize. But it scarcely matters. Whatever affinity with the time may stir in a man, it is not hunting lust, but something far gentler. I remember the good evenings I have fished, even the ones that realized material hopes, not by the fish that came to the fly, but by the color and movement of water and sky, by the sounds and scents and gentle stirrings that were all about me.

There was a strange and beautiful evening once, below Theimar Falls, when the creek poured over into the slack of a small full tide. It must have been late in the year, for the coho salmon were running, but it was a warm evening and the sun went down red and the clouds grew mauve and gold behind it, as they often do over Johnstone Strait. I was not expecting much, a cutthroat or two, perhaps, and possibly a coho if a school chanced to turn in. I reached a fly across the foot of the falls, well into the eddy on the far side, felt the current draw the line tight, then knew I was hooked to a twenty-inch length of silver that leaped in brightness from the eddy. In six casts I had hooked six of them, precocious male cohos, coming in a year early to spawn with the rest of the run. They were larger than any I have seen before or since, the smallest of them over two pounds, and they were so clean and bright that I knew they must have found the creek only that day.

By the time I had landed the last of them, the light was only a reflection from the pale sky, but it was reflected again from the smooth water of the strait and I could see well enough to keep fishing. I had worked well down and was dropping my fly where the fresh water spread invisibly into the open strait when I felt the solid, heavy stop of a big fish taking. He ran out and fought without showing, except when the stir of his tail broke and made the light strike from oily swirls on the surface; he fought slowly and sulkily, and the lights came gleaming on in the bay across the strait. He took out my poor little forty yards of backing till there were only a few turns left on the reel; and I heard the solemn, throaty diesel of a purse seiner very clear and close across the silent water. My fish began to give a little, to come back, and I heard the heavy splash of another fish jumping far out of the water. The moon was up when I slid mine to the beach, and I heard a dog barking in the woods behind me and knew that Ed and Scraps were coming down to look for me. I took the fly out gently, turned him and slid him back, for we had no need of a fish like him, a great cock coho, clear silver still, broad sided, heavy shouldered with a strength that would surely take him to his spawning.

I have fished many evenings on lakes and had great pleasure from them, but a lake is not so good as a river unless one is waiting on some known shoal for some known monster to come up to his feeding. Evening salt-water fishing has its peaceful beauty, the quiet fading of the distant mountains, the blackening of the nearer hills, and distant sounds clear across the water. Once or twice I have caught feeding spring salmon until nearly midnight, when the full moon was the only light. But sea fishing is not river fishing, and night fishing is not evening fishing at all. I remember that I used to think that as evening fishing might yield stranger miracles than day fishing, so night fishing would be yet more powerful than evening fishing. We used to try this theory on the Frome, poaching the deep dry-fly pools with silver-bodied salmon flies in black darkness, but we caught only half-pounders and grew discontented in the darkness as one seldom does while there is still light in the western sky.

There is a little river that flows down Elk Valley from Summit Lake to Upper Campbell Lake. It is a beautiful river, or was while the heavy timber still stood along it, very clear and very cold, cold enough to make your legs ache after a long spell of fishing even on a summer day. The fish do not spread through it until late July or August, and Buckie and I went there in 1937, at what should have been just the right time. The first afternoon we fished was hot and sunny, too bright really, but we covered a lot of water and saw very few fish. I wondered a little if it might be a late year and hoped not, because Buckie had come a long way to fish with me.

We went back to camp for supper and afterward went down to the big pool just below camp. It is a very fine pool, the head of it a smooth, swift run on a sixty- or seventy-degree curve, good current sliding beyond the curve, past the narrow entrance of a little slough, spreading wide at the tail, but still three or four feet deep and deeper than that under the bushes on the far side. There was nothing moving in the pool when we came to it, so we sat with our rods on the gravel bar on the inside of the curve and watched the water. A few flies were coming down and many were playing above the water. "We ought to see a few rises," I told Buckie. "It's a perfect place and a perfect evening."

Then I saw a single quiet rise right under the bushes on the far side. Buckie hadn't seen it, so I went down to try the fish, wondering if I could reach him well enough to bring the fly over without drag. The pool was even wider than I thought, and I dropped the first cast well short; but the second reached him, and he took the sedge gently as it slid along just short of the bushes. Elk River fish fight well for their size, and he did his best; but there was little to help him in the open water at the tail of the pool, so I led him to the net fairly quickly.

The sun was almost gone behind the mountains, but there was still a warm light on the pool and the flies still danced in it. Then a fish rose at the end of the curving run, another rose above him, one rose at the head of the run, and suddenly they were rising all along it, beyond it in the mouth of the slough and below it in the tail, where I had hooked the first fish.

Buckie started in to work up the run with a dry sedge, and it was all so peaceful and lovely that I simply stayed to watch. He waded well out and fished steadily up the center of the run. He was fishing a short line, covering the rises as they came, and the fish took him well, accepting the sedge as calmly as they were accepting every natural that drifted down. Once or twice I helped Buckie with the net, but after that I left him on his own and just lay back on the gravel while he caught six or eight good fish one after another. It was quick and almost automatic—certainly rhythmic: a rise, a cast, the float of the brown-hackled fly against the light water, its sharp disappearance in the confident swirl of a solid rise, the strike, and then the quick active fight of a good little trout in perfect condition.

There were two or three fish cruising in the slack water at the mouth of the slough, rising steadily, and another, taking everything that came to him, on the far side of a broken tree branch just below the slough. I had been watching them for some time when the fever of evening fishing came suddenly upon me. It was getting dark, but I wanted those fish. I had a feeling that they might be big; watching the rises in the half light, considering the places they had chosen, I felt sure they were big.

So I went down into the water and cast for the fish behind the branch. He had to take it the first time, to save my fly from the branch, and he did. I tightened on him and saw that my line bent around the branch, as I had known it was bound to unless he chose to run upstream immediately he felt the hook. Perhaps it's foolish to try for fish in places like that. Some good fishermen think so, I know, and leave them alone unless they can come at them from some other angle. But I always do try for them and only begin to worry about getting them out when the hook is set. This time, as nearly always happens, the fish solved the problem for me by running hard for the far bank. I worked upstream a little, keeping the line tight on him and my rod high in the air, held by the butt at the full extent of my arm. Nothing happened, so I slacked the strain, gave the line a flip, tightened again and saw it slide easily over the backward curve of the branch and come free.

The fish didn't weigh quite a pound, but I still thought the others in the mouth of the slough were good ones, and I waded over as far as I could to try for them. My first cast reached the slack water, but the fly was well short of the nearest rise. I waded a step farther and felt the icy water pouring in over my boots; I could reach the fish then and I did, dropping a slack line across the current so that the fly held for a moment without drag. The next rise came within an inch of it, but left it floating. I knew the drag was coming, held my rod far downstream to delay it, then there was another rise and this time the fly went down. I caught three fish from the slough before it was too dark to see the fly, not one of them over a pound.

The evening rise is very often like that, many fish, feeding well and taking well, but the big ones are not always up, or else one does not happen to find them, in spite of high hopes. But it is still a magic time, even on western rivers, where big trout are reckless enough in broad daylight. On the English chalk streams it is almost a holy time, not only because there is a real chance of finding a big fish in a foolish mood, but because a summer evening in English water meadows has a rich and gentle loveliness that is quite different from the quality of our own newer, harder country.

It was a July evening in 1930 when I last went up to Stratton Mill. The day had been very hot, not oppressively hot but with a pouring-on of heat from a hard, bright scorching sun. During the late afternoon I had worked my way slowly and rather carelessly along a small and difficult carrier, finding few fish moving and fewer still that I could approach and cover. When I came to the mill, I had risen only two good fish; one of them had come short and gone off upstream from my strike, throwing a startled bow wave that put down two more feeding fish, and the other had buried himself in a weed bed and, in the mysterious way that chalk-stream trout seem to understand so well, left my fly holding nothing livelier than a strand of milfoil.

Stratton Mill is not an especially attractive or pretty building, but it settles comfortably enough into the meadows, and its red brick is mellowing to a good color that is soft and pleasant even now in an evening light. The meadows are not very wide here; the little river, the Wrackle, runs past Chick's Farm some two hundred yards from the mill and the ground climbs quickly from its far bank to the churchyard and the center of the village. On the other side, the Frome is only thirty or forty yards away, and beyond the river the ground climbs again. The millstream is cut away from the Frome at a big hatch pool above the mill, runs down past the wheel and curves on to join the river again some way farther down. This leaves a long oval island of meadow between the Frome and the millstream, and it was from that island I meant to fish the evening rise.

There were very few fish moving when I first came there, and I felt it was the pause between the sparse hatch I had fished in the carrier during the afternoon and what Hills calls the "casual rise" at six or seven o'clock; so I went on up to the hatch pool and sat there, looking upstream and across to the wider meadows where Farmer Chick's beautiful Devon cattle were feeding. There is no pasture land in the world richer than the Dorset water meadows; even in July they are knee-deep to cattle in heavy, dark-green grass, scented and full of moisture. Chick's animals showed the quality of it, straight-backed, slow-moving, rich-red creatures, sleek with well-being, yet proud and almost light with the grace of their long curving horns. Man has developed no creature more beautiful than the dairy cow, building her deep-bellied and heavy-uddered, calm-eyed and with a slow wisdom for her own deep business of production. I have felt a powerful admiration in me for many handsome cows, Holstein, Jersey and Guernsey, but for none more than the red Devon.

A fish rose in the deep, smooth water above the hatches, where I did not mean to fish, and I turned to look below me at the pool. There was a good run of water through the hatches, and two or three small fish were rising where the run of it spread in the pool, but there were no fish up on the bar yet and none moving in the slower water along the sides. It seemed time to go down, since I meant to fish all the way up, and I picked up my rod and went. There was little water passing through the milltail, but I stopped there and found a good fish cruising slowly in the shallow water five or six yards below the wheel. I watched until I thought I knew his line, then dropped a hackle olive near him, somehow too clumsily, because he turned at once and went down into the depths of the pool, leaving me to feel ashamed and awkward.

I went straight down then, a little angrily, right to the downstream tip of the island. Just below is a beautiful strip of wide, clear water that runs between weed beds over pale-golden gravel. I looked down over it, wishing I could fish it, and saw a big, wide-backed trout rise gracefully a long cast below me.

July

As he hovered there, waiting for the next fly, the evening light seemed to slide under him, pick him up and hold him invisibly suspended, so that I knew everything about him—his size, his shape, his depth and thickness, his very spots. He rose again and I wanted more than anything to see him rise to a fly of mine. I could have one cast, I knew. It must fall just short of him, with two feet or so of slack in twenty yards of line. I should probably put him down with the cast or, if not, then with the drag as the line came tight in the current; and if all went well I should miss him on the strike. A really respectable dry-fly fisherman would have left him in peace. I didn't. The fly dropped perfectly, drifted, drifted—and a moment before the drag came, he took it. I tightened slowly, my hand quivering on the rod, and came solidly into him. He jumped once in shocked surprise. Then the light showed him to me, every run, every twist, every struggle toward every weed bed, through a long five minutes while I brought him up to the net. I measured him against the handle of the landing net, fifteen inches, light-backed, golden-bellied, the deep-red spots sharp and clear on his sides.

I became orthodox then, working upstream, waiting for my rises, considering them, covering them if I judged the fish worth while. The light began to fade, so I broke off the olive after a fish had let it drift past him twice and tied on a ginger quill. He took that at the first cast and made the fourth fish in the bag. I was pleased with them because they were a level lot, all within an inch of the length of that first one.

It was some little while before I found another good one rising, and then I spoiled the chance he gave me by striking too hard and breaking off the fly. It was too dark to think of threading another ginger quill, so I mounted the heavier cast I had ready with a silver sedge tied on it. There were sedges on the grass and in the air, and I felt that the fish would be coming to them on the water very soon. I was opposite the mill again now, at a sharp bend in the river where strong

current ran against the low branches of an alder tree. A fish
rose close to the branches, and I felt certain that he was a good
one. I made the first cast well outside him and found I could
see the big fly perfectly against the water. I cast for him and
hooked an alder branch. A gentle pull showed that the fly was
fast. Then the fish rose again, and I still thought he was big.
I pulled hard and knew that the gut had broken. It took me a
long, agitated five minutes to tie on a new sedge, but my fish
was still rising, and I covered him, rose him, hooked him—and
found he was barely ten inches long.

I followed the river through two bends, hoping for a rise
that I could know was a big fish. But the light was wrong, and
the water was dark until I came to the short stretch that runs
east and west just below the curve from the hatch pool. Two
mallards rose from the hatch pool, climbing almost straight in
the air on short quick beats of their strong wings, bodies and
stretched necks black against the light sky. The water reflected the lightness of the sky almost perfectly now, and I
could see the dark dots of the sedges against it and fish rising
to them everywhere. One fish showed head and tail as he rose,
and I thought for a moment he was big, then remembered how
deceptive the show of a trout's tail can be in half-darkness.
There was a tiny quiet rise, steadily repeated, close against a
long island of weeds near the head of the stretch. I liked the
look of that one, went up to fish it, then was sorry. Another
ten-incher, I told myself. But I wasn't sure and I made the
cast. Something went wrong, and the fly hooked weed just
below the fish. I pulled and it came free, dragging horribly.
Something splashed fiercely and heavily near it. I struck
blindly, and the fly whipped back, caught in the grass at my
feet. As I freed it, the little rises began again, a quiet nose pok-
ing the surface softly almost against the weed. I didn't know,
I told myself; he could be big; he might have turned to make
that heavy splash at the dragging fly and the surging boil that
cut away from it. The next cast was right, and the fly slid

along so close to the weed bed that I could scarcely judge
where it was in the short shadow. The little rise came again.
I tightened to it and the reel screamed like torn cloth. Foolishly
I checked him, held him at last and turned him. He came back
toward me, swimming slowly and dangerously, then ran again,
straight for the weed bed. This time I had to turn him and I
did, just enough to force his run straight upstream instead of
across. He came to the tail of the hatch pool, rode over the
shallows in a great sweeping wave and went down into deep
water. I went down into the river myself, wading the shallows
right out to the center of the stream. He was boring up into
the deep water, still strongly, swinging over to the bank I had
just left. There was an alder tree there and behind that the
stakes of rotten cribbing against the bank. He hadn't quite the
strength to reach them and in a little while I netted him, gratefully. The poplars on the far side of the pool were dark against
a dark sky now and it was time to go home. But I had my limit
of six fish, all of them good fish for the water and the last one,
the only one that had come on the sedge hatch, nearer two
pounds than anything else.

AUGUST

I LEARNED to fish in August, which is a natural enough time for a boy to learn in England since the summer holidays do not start there until the last days of July. I learned late because of the 1914-1918 war. Before the war started I knew something of fishing tackle from the hours spent in my father's study, helping him dress lines or change them from one reel to another; occasionally I had been out with him and held the net while a beaten fish was drawn over it. Once I had held my hand lightly on the rod through cast, rise and strike and then been left on my own at the mercy of a ten-inch trout. But my father was too wise a teacher to hurry things, and when he put on a uniform in 1914 I was still only six, so I knew little more than that fishing was a serious and important business in which I should be entered in due time.

During the war, until he was killed in 1918, my father was seldom home, and when he did come it was only for a short leave. My Mother's many brothers came on leave from time to time, and I carried the net for my kindly, but ferocious, Uncle Alec through a full week of exciting fishing one summer. Uncle Alec was a big man, with a fine black mustache and red cheeks; he was a good fisherman and quick-tempered, so I really began to learn something then about landing fish.

Of course, I tried to catch fish in that time. There were rods and reels and lines available, gut casts and flies, a river and trout. But I had no idea of how to cast and I had a thin thread of a line that wouldn't have done much for me if I had been a champion caster. So the trout remained in the river, feeding and visible, utterly desirable, but completely protected from me. I set night lines for them and caught only eels, except once when a kingfisher flew under a bridge and tangled his wings so that I found him next day and had to free him while he tried to peck blood out of my fingers. I remember the black beak, the rusty breast and lovely blue-green back and wings with a twinge of conscience even now, and I cried when he flew away with something less than the arrowlike speed I felt he should have had. At times I stooped to things lower even than night lines. I tried bread for the tame trout under the billiard-room window. They would rise to bread with great bold splashes, two or three at a time rushing in fierce competition upon a single floating piece; but though I buried hooks cunningly and hid myself and tried to float my captive bread naturally down to them, I can't remember that I ever hooked one. In fact I only remember hooking one sizable trout by any means during the war and the years just after it. That was on the first evening of a brand-new summer holiday, when my two sisters, having seen only an hour or two of me, were still ready to follow and admire. We went up the long walk to the head of the garden, I, no doubt, boasting suitably of what I would do to any and every trout we saw, and I began to fish in the deep pool behind the laurels. Trout were rising in the pool, well beyond reach of any cast of mine, but they were rising also far up under the single arch of the brick bridge that divided the garden from the meadows. Before I had lost too much prestige in clumsy efforts to catch fish I could not possibly catch, we all came away from the pool, climbed the iron fence and went round to the upper side of the bridge.

The trout were still doing nicely there, coming up in handsome rises whose rich sound echoed from the arch. I waded out a little, keeping well behind the shoulder of the bridge, dropped the little dry fly on the surface and began to pay out line to keep it floating down the current. Peering round the brickwork, I could see it floating, floating beautifully toward those enormous rises. Then there was one more rise, more enormous than any of the others, and the fly was gone. My poor little reel screeched hoarsely, frantically trying to keep up with his plunge for the pool. The end of the line came, and I felt him there, pulling and kicking and struggling, almost dragging the rod out of my hands. Then the gut broke. I looked round into Joan's pale face and wide eyes.

"I had him on, didn't I?" My voice was urgent with anxiety. I have never had greater need of a witness. "You saw him. He took a proper dry fly and everything, didn't he?"

"Yes," Joan said slowly, still pale. "Did he get off?"

"He broke me, when he came to the end of the line. But

that's nothing. We know how to do it now. We can get lots more. We'll have to go fishing often these holidays."

So we all three sat on the bridge and discussed it solemnly and sadly, comforting ourselves with the thought of eight long weeks ahead in which we would perform a thousand more successful deeds. But the magic was gone next day and I couldn't do it again. By the day after that my brief prestige was finished and I was fishing alone; one day more and I was setting night lines again.

But that August did give me my first real fishing. A favorite aunt and uncle took me up to the Lake District. We stayed at Grasmere Lake, and I saw mountains for the first time and sheepdog trials and Cumberland-Westmorland style wrestling and Wordsworth's seat and Kirkstone Pass and many other wonders which impressed me deeply. But none of them was greater than the bobbing of a green and red float near the reeds of Grasmere as a perch came to the worm, or my first pike, fierce jawed and fully three pounds, flopping fearsomely on the floorboards of the boat. The perch were beautiful fish, with high, spiked, scarlet fins on their backs and dark bars across their deep, golden-olive sides; some of those we caught must have weighed well over a pound, and they fought quite well enough to teach me a lot. There were big pike in the lake, and we set out trimmers—night lines on wooden floats—again and again in high hopes, but the largest I cought, by rod or by trimmer, was only six pounds. Once or twice we climbed to Easdale Tarn, and there I caught a few little trout on the wet fly, but there was nothing in the catching of them that persuaded me I should be better able to deal with Dorset trout from then on.

I never doubted that I had to learn sooner or later. My father, as I was often told, had been a very fine fisherman. Besides, I had my father's book, *My Game Book*, dedicated to myself at five years of age and as beautifully written a piece of tradition as any that ever sought to mold a boy. *My Game*

Book has always delighted me and still does. It tells in clear and simple words of a vigorous man's love of shooting and fishing, of a hundred happenings, defeats, rewards and triumphs, by stream and meadow and hill, in Dorset and Sussex and Norfolk and Scotland. But it was a lot to live up to, and I began to be afraid I should never fulfill the hopes that I knew were written into it for me.

Then, in the summer of 1922, my Uncle Decie, tenth of my grandfather's eleven sons and the gentlest man and best fisherman of them all, came home from the Rhineland. He put his own tapered fly line on my rod, took me out on the lawn and in one short hour opened the essential secrets of casting to me.

"No one can fish with a line like you had there," he told me. "It's got to be heavy enough to work the rod."

Then: "The back cast is just as important as the forward cast. You lift it, wait until it comes straight out behind you, bring it forward, and there you are. It's got to go back straight if it's going to come forward straight."

So I practiced while he watched, and after a little while I had the timing of it. At the end of the hour I could lay out ten or twelve yards of line quite straight and with a decent measure of accuracy.

Decie said, "You'll have to practice on the lawn every day for half an hour if you ever want to be any good. But you've got the idea now. Go on and catch a fish."

So I went across the fields to the Frome. I tried for a fish in Hatch-Hole, tried for others along the shallow reach above it until I came to the Trough Bridge. Many fish were rising there, both trout and dace, but there was one little fish I wanted. He was rising over deep water just below the bridge, very active and busy in the sunlight. I had a Tup's indispensable tied on 4X gut, and I dried it carefully and cast for him. He came to it slowly while my heart almost burst with pounding the blood to my wrists. He backed down with it, backed down with it— and took! I handled him somehow in my frantic, flushed excitement, got the net under him at last and lifted him out. I went straight home with him then, a half-pounder but my first, honestly and fairly caught by a skill I had not had when I climbed out of bed that morning.

Decie fished with him once or twice, watched my practices and taught me new things, then had to go away. Two days later he sent from London a double-tapered fly line and a copy of Halford's *Dry Fly Man's Handbook*. That settled everything. I caught about thirty sizable trout that summer, and by the start of the next season I had enough confidence to have thrown a No. 17 fly at a whale if one had found his way into the river. What was more, my years of hopeless wandering about the rivers had taught me where the good trout lay and how they rose.

It was a queer cycle that brought me to a uniform in another war when my own yearling, Alan Roderick, bearing his grandfather's name, was lying on his back in the study and playing with a fly reel. I hope he will fish and I hope I shall be able to teach him as quickly and effectively as Decie taught me. I hope he will be a competent, and not a jealous, fisherman, so that fish will come to him without too much straining and he will have time to learn about rivers and water and other things about fish than simply how to fish for them. And I hope he will find along the rivers all the thoughts and sounds and scenes and scents and movement that have made me happy, and others of his own besides.

SALT WATER I

THE earliest memory I have of sea fishing goes back to a misty morning on the shore of the English Channel when my Father took me down to watch the fishermen set for mackerel. It was a wonderful morning for me, a morning of mysterious small hours that I had always, until then, spent in deepest sleep. We went out in a rowboat into the mist and rowed along the great circle of bobbing corks; then we came back to shore and watched the men haul in the net, saw the lovely massed green and silver of the catch and took a basketful away for our own—a prize which my Father undoubtedly paid for, but which seemed to me a wonderful reward that made us part of the fishing.

A mackerel, just out of the water, is one of the most beautiful fish there is. Small head, round slender body, arched tail spreading widely from slim wrist, purest silver belly and the unbelievably blue-green back that changes so quickly in the dry air, with darker, irregular markings briefly emphasizing the iridescent color—all these are intense loveliness enclosing a few inches of life.

Mackerel are fast surface fish, busy feeders and free takers under the right conditions. I think of them sometimes as fly-fisherman's fish, though they are not really that. From a rowboat one can catch them on a light fly rod and have really good fun doing it. They fight at least as well as any trout and have an erratic way of running that makes them exciting to handle. For this reason they almost deserve to be caught with a rod. But they have another good quality—they like a fast-traveling bait, and this changes the picture completely because it means they can be caught from a sailboat. No one wants to use a trout rod or any other rod under the boom of a mainsail, and even if one chose to make the attempt, the business of hauling in a two-pound mackerel against the five-knot speed of the boat would not be very fair to rod or fish. So, one fishes instead with a hand line, and though the quality of the mackerel's fight is lost, there are many compensations. I used to go out often in Weymouth Bay, usually with a sober-minded professional named Jewel, who considered that the purpose of fishing was to catch fish. Nearly always things started slowly, and we

sailed peacefully among the whitecaps with two or three lines
trailing astern. Then, perhaps, there would be a few little
knocks against the line in one's hand, then a good pull. For
some reason I seemed to make a fairly steady habit of hooking
the first few fish that we caught, and I would bring them in
slowly, watching Jewel's face as I did so. His jaw would be
grimly locked, his eyes hard on the two lines trailing from his
hands, his ruddy skin redder with a flush of anger, dozens of
tiny blue veins showing close under the tough surface of the
skin. As I brought in the second or third fish, he would say,
"You don't deserve to catch them, ahauling them in slow like
that. Move your hands fast, like I showed you last time."

"Hell, I'm not fishing," I would tell him. "I'm handling the
boat. What's the matter with you, anyway? You haven't
brought in a darn thing yet."

Jewel would clamp his jaw down tighter than ever and say
nothing. Then the fish would start taking, and we would be
hauling them in as fast as we could. I never learned to match
his amazing proficiency; he would run a line in with quick
short movements of his hands, swing the fish out over the
basket in the cockpit, jerk sharply and flick his baited hook
back into the water; in the same moment his hands would be
on the other line and seconds later another fish would be kicking in the basket. So we fished in businesslike silence until the
basket had twenty or thirty mackerel in it, then Jewel would
break down and say something, probably "They're biting tonight," or, if his mood were really good, "We're doing all right
for ourselves." As the evening drew on and we came about to
run through the schools for the last time, Jewel's face would
be relaxed and smiling. "I'll bet there's none of them others got
what we got. We can show 'em up when we want to, you
and I."

He was always like that over mackerel. But when we went
out for other fish, he was calm and almost patient, except when
one or the other of us lost a fish, and then he would swear pas-

sionately and handsomely. We put in many days in search of
bass, fishing with live prawns, light tackle and all the cunning
we had. The bass of the English Channel are high in the aris-
tocracy of salt-water game fish, handsome silver creatures and
fine fighters, but often hard to catch. I never knew much about
fishing for them and I am not too sure that Jewel did either,
but we were always hearing of new and secret grounds and we
would go hopefully to find them and try them, lining the
fourth chimney of the Coast Guard Station with haystacks on
the hill or some entrance of Portland Breakwater with a head-
land across the bay or a bathing hut on the beach. Once or
twice we caught bass. More often we did not and then, after
an honest try, we would change our fishing and make sure of
a good catch of white-bellied, green-backed pollack, inferior
fish, no doubt, but good just the same. In this, as I realized
later when I worked as a guide for anglers, was the explanation
of Jewel's stern concentration on the mackerel: he had a professional reputation to guard; when we went out for fish, we
had to come in with fish, more fish, preferably, than any other
boat, and in spite of my hedonistic tendency to be lazy about
my sea fishing, we generally did.

In Weymouth Bay also I learned how a trawl net fishes.
With one or two other young and energetic Dorset boys I
sailed as crew in Major Eddie Foster's yawl *Heroine*. The
Heroine was an old boat, red sailed, black hulled and seemingly heavy alongside the smooth, white-winged sloops, but on
a rough day she could outsail anything in Weymouth Harbor,
even under a heavy handicap, and we were mighty proud of
her, belligerently proud of her seaworthiness, contemptuous of
all the fine arts of the gentler sailing days. Those gentler days
were not for us we decided eventually, and when Major Eddie
invested in a big trawl net, we were glad because it gave us a
reason to be out when the sloops were reaching for capfuls
of breeze to carry them round the racing course.

A trawl is a diver net, dredging bottom with the lead line

while the cork line simply serves to spread it upward in the water. The rings of the net are spread wide on either side by otter boards, heavy, iron-shod boards bridled with rope to pull outward as the pressure of the water comes against them with the boat's movement. From its wings the net tapers to a purse and finally to the narrow cod end where the catch collects; there is a release at the cod end so that when the net is brought in and hauled up to the mast, the catch can be dropped on the deck for sorting.

Probably we worked the net amateurishly, and certainly we were interested in sailing rather than fishing, but it was fun and hard work too. It was pleasant to be sailing easily along, watching the throb of the heavy rope as the otter boards rode the bottom, and it was always exciting to start the net in and wonder what might be there. If it was still heavy after the otter boards came up over the side, we were hopeful; if it was light, we were still hopeful, convinced that for once we had escaped our usual share of rocks and seaweed.

Sorting was a big job. Nearly always there were forty or fifty big, horny, long-legged spider crabs to be picked out and thrown overboard. Hundreds of smaller crabs would be there and were sure to crawl down into the cockpit or find their way into the bilge unless we watched them closely. Sometimes we caught beautiful squids, colored like green mother-of-pearl, big skates and rays with their strangely human-looking mouths, spotted dogfish, round, flat-sided, queer-looking John Dorys, sad-mouthed, huge-eyed, with fantastic fins and deep lines of sadness, wisdom, oppression or what-you-will on gill covers that seemed like heavy cheeks. Many of these were edible fish, worthy of the net and more than worthy of our limited skill, but we searched eagerly among them for the true flatfish, the red-spotted plaice, the lovely lemon sole with paler spots marking its rich brown upper side, little sand dabs, the royal turbot, common soles and flounders. And we found them, two or three buckets full perhaps, fish from the unbelievable plenty of England's offshore sands, slow, quiet creatures but nobler on the table than any trout or salmon.

I often wish I had spent more time with trawl nets and among sea fish. Again and again my own ignorance of almost everything that swims, except salmon and trout, shocks me. It seems to argue the narrowest sort of specialization, and it grows, of course, from excessive love of rivers and fly-fishing. Yet I can never see any new fish without a surge of curiosity and interest or hear sea fishermen's tales without hanging onto every word of them. I have promised myself many times that I will set out to learn more and to learn properly, but I turn back at the edge and never do learn, somewhat as I turn away at the edge of entomology, almost at first thought of the thousands of species of sedges and May flies because the thing is so huge that a lifetime of specialization wouldn't be enough. And if one has to specialize anyway, why not in rivers and salmon and trout?

I suppose the greatest wealth of the sea is in the tropics. I have twice traveled through the Panama Canal by slow freighter and would gladly go the same way again if only to see flying fish against the rich blue of the Caribbean. Even apart from the fish and the seething life in them, those seas are beautiful with an intense luxury of beauty that reaches down into one's most imaginative depths to build thoughts and sensations of matching intensity. There is a breathless expectancy in crossing the mouth of the Gulf of California, in leaving the storms of the Atlantic for the northeast trades of the Caribbean. Some night one comes from a hot room out onto the cool deck to find that the ship is passing through the Indies. A bright moon, clear as the clearest mountain stream, is high in the center of the sky, straight above the ship, and the stars seem scattered, each as bright and clear as the moon. The sea reflects all the light of the sky, breaking it and throwing it in tiny dancing swells. Southward is Puerto Rico, a line of land perhaps four or five miles away, bounded at either end by a winking light and set beneath a great puff of silver cloud that flashes occasional lightning. To the north a little, round, lightless island, standing high out of the water, is lonely under the moon. For some reason, passing it so, one yearns toward the land; it is so close, within swimming distance in the warm, soft water, but tomorrow forever away. Perhaps there would have been nothing there that one wanted to see or do, but it seems ungrateful and unappreciative to pass it and leave it so easily.

Everything in the tropics is intense to the northern mind, sometimes so dramatic in effect as to seem unreal and so, in spite of scale and color, tame. The sharp sunsets, starting as the sun touches the edge of some cloud on the horizon and breaks everything into color—puffs of crimson and orange, long streaks of shining gold, flecks and wavelets and wisps of color hovering motionless, yet always changing shape, forming and reforming, massing and breaking up; to turn from these eastward into instant, silver night—shining white clouds, bright stars, silver light on rippled water—is breathtaking, yet still theatrical and somehow unconvincing. Only the noon sun is real and the clean touch of the trade winds, breaking whitecaps on blue water; these and the scorch of sun and dry wind on bare skin as one stands on the fo'c'sle head to look down at the ship's creaming bow wave.

The fo'c'sle head is the best place in the ship through those sparkling days along the Pacific coast of Panama, Costa Rica, Nicaragua, El Salvador, Guatemala and southern Mexico. I went up there the morning after we left the canal, and at once there were things to watch: flying fish, of course, and little brown and white sandpipers that flew ahead to pitch on the water again almost as the flying fish pitched into it; other birds, much larger, but also brown and white, that flew in determined, menacing formations just above the water; bright orange and black sea snakes swimming just below the surface, tuna leaping clear of the water, their smooth, firm, white bellies flashing in the sun. We were heading for Puerto Armuelles, a little banana port in Panama, no more, really, than a wharf in a big bay sheltered from the west but from nowhere else. We reached the bay in darkness, and the captain shut off his engines and let the ship drift until daylight. We tried to fish in the darkness, but could move nothing more tangible than an occasional great flash of phosphorescence.

Before breakfast next morning we looked at the town, a clutter of untidy stores and tumbled shacks, with lovely black children everywhere among vultures and dogs and tethered fighting cocks. There was a stream at the far end of the main street, a trickle of water across tide flats with storks wading in it and a black dog eating offal on the far side and daring the vultures to take it from him. A white bitch came down, and the black dog slunk away while she in her turn defied the vultures; then a naked black baby tottered down to the stream, carrying a coal oil can of rubbish, dumped the can and scolded the bitch competently. We crossed the suspension bridge and came upon happier shacks walled with bamboo poles and thatched with banana leaves, bananas and melons growing around them. On the beach and along the stream men worked on their dugout canoes or just sat quietly with long banana knives in their hands. The jungle was cool and fresh and clean behind, a rich contrast to the hot, dark-gray sand that made the beach and the village streets.

Back aboard the ship, I looked over the stern and saw three narrow, olive-green swordfish, four or five feet long, hanging just under the surface of the water. They looked like pike in an English lake. Then there were flashes of red and swirls in the water—red snappers, great, deep-crimson-barred fish, beautifully shaped, and under them or among them an occasional flash of green or the silver of a broad side and a long, wide, forked tail—green jacks that were lightning fast in every move. We fished a long while and caught nothing; then at last we got a green jack, which the snappers tore off the hook in a moment, and another, which dropped off as we hauled him up the side of the ship, and then one that we managed to bring aboard. But there was nothing we could do about the snappers. We tried them with dough and meat and bread, with frozen herring and fresh green jack. They would take anything without a hook in it, but they were as perfectly gut-shy as the wisest Test trout. I kept at it for two or three hours, sweating with excitement as they played around my hook but failing utterly to convince them.

North of Armuelles I went to the fo'c'sle head again and watched great handsome flying fish, brilliant blue with black pectorals, start up from the foaming bow wave. Once a great brown bird swooped down to the water and snapped one up in mid-air. And the roll of white water was so beautiful that the porpoises came to play in it, huge, long-snouted porpoises that rolled and splashed, then rushed suddenly ahead to leap six or eight feet out into the air and twenty feet or more along the water; they kept ahead of the ship's $12\frac{1}{2}$ knots with hardly a visible move of their slim-wristed tails, jumping lazily, sliding back with a fierce slap of their tails, breaking the surface in rushing white bow waves of their own, darting off to play somewhere far beyond sight, swimming lazily back from hundreds of yards ahead to take up their places again.

Off the Gulf of Tehuantepec I saw, dead ahead of the ship, what seemed to be the fins of two sharks swimming in slow, narrow circles. I wondered if they were mating or fighting or feeding on some dead carcass, then realized that the fins were keeping their distance from one another with an impossible regularity—they were the fins of one fish, not two, the pectorals of a giant ray. The ship kept on and on toward them, and I leaned eagerly forward, hoping to get a perfect view of the ray a few feet to one side or other of the bow stem. Instead, we hit him squarely, and I could feel a tremor clear up through the heavy steel stem. For several minutes he hung there, breaking the bow wave to different shape and sound, then slid away and I could not see him again. A whale blew three times, not far away, between us and the land.

Later we passed among hundreds of little queer-shaped scarlet crabs drifting near the surface, and for several hours, while we were within sight of the surf breaking against the foot of rounded blue islands, the water was full of the orange and black snakes. For a long while there were turtles, sodden lazy with sun and fine weather, sometimes bothering to flap once or twice when they realized the ship was near them or even, when the steel hull was very close, rolling to turn a shell back of matching strength toward it. One little one only a foot or so across, swam down and down for all he was worth just to one side of the bow wave. I saw swordfish of some kind, slim and graceful and violet finned, very beautiful; great sharks and a hundred other mysterious, sharp, sleek black fins; and thousands upon thousands of tuna, great schools of them, jumping and rolling and feeding. It was impossible not to wish for a small boat of some kind, one of the ship's lifeboats, perhaps, amply provisioned and well supplied with tackle, from which to try one's chances there for a week or a month. Perhaps there would have been a good camping place on one of the islands and a bay well sheltered from the surf.

There are things almost equally wonderful here in the inside waters of British Columbia. In a thirty-two-foot gas boat in Baronet Pass we once passed close enough to a big sperm whale to see his barnacles clearly, and the fisherman in me heaved a pike pole at him, but it bounced away as though his skin were armor plate. Again, in a still smaller, open gas boat, we met and passed schools of blackfish for at least half an hour one morning in Johnstone Strait, schools rolling ahead of us, behind us, alongside us and clear across the channel from side to side of its three-mile width. Blackfish are the true killer whales, fierce, predacious and swift; they are twenty feet or more in length, heavy bodied, strong and bold. That gray and stormy morning in Johnstone Strait it seemed that the law of averages must sooner or later bring one rolling to the surface right under the boat, yet none came nearer than twenty feet.

I find that I like blackfish, as I like all whales. Salmon fishermen are supposed to hate them because they come fiercely to the fishing grounds and for hours or even days afterward the salmon hug the bottom and will not feed. After blackfish have passed, I have seen the backs of salmon motionless on the floor of a kelp bed; but I have also caught salmon at the surface while blackfish were still in sight. I once saw blackfish rolling and playing in a bay where salmon were feeding and thought I saw the bodies of salmon thrown high in the air by their tails, but I know now that the curved shapes I watched were not salmon at all, but the tails of the blackfish themselves, throwing over in their heavy, powerful roll. I am not even sure that blackfish feed on salmon. It is probable that they do, but I know of no record that salmon have been taken from their stomachs. All records that I can find point to larger prey: they attack the largest whales, wearing them down and killing them, and Beddard quotes a record of thirteen porpoises and fourteen seals taken from the stomach of a single blackfish and describes the blackfish's method of hunting young walruses. It seems more than possible that blackfish are the salmon fisher's friends rather than his enemies.

To watch a school of them passing down a narrow channel is a strong experience. One hears first, with the delay of distance, the sharp, strange sound of their blowing and perhaps traces from this the roll of their great black backs and tall, curved dorsal fins as they dive. They come down quickly, deep in the channel, to show again in the slow dignified roll, perhaps twenty or thirty of them, in a procession of backs, of high fins, of spouting.

The blowing or spouting of any whale is a fine thing. It is a great exhalation of fine vapor, a lusty sound, almost an explosion, and the vapor shoots up like a burst of steam, sometimes hanging on the still air, sometimes swept back by the

wind like spray torn from wave tops. Blackfish show little
fear of boats; I have seen a whole school all among the boats
of tyee fishermen off the mouth of the Campbell, some of
the fish actually inside, between the boats and shore, and this
at low tide. Yet for all their boldness and for all their ferocity
in attacking whales far larger than themselves, I know of
no case where a blackfish attacked a boat. I feel comfortably
certain that they will not attack, except perhaps under some
extraordinary circumstance of mating anger or in protection
of their young, but it is still intensely exciting to be near them
in a small boat. Rather rarely I have seen them jumping, clear
out of the water, tail-free, and that is awe-inspiring. Once I
saw three of a school jumping, close in to shore, off Orange
Point in Discovery Passage. They might have been half a mile
away when I looked up at the first great splashes, and I supposed at first that they were simply coming down on the water
from an exaggerated roll. But they came on toward me, close
to the edge of the kelp, and I was sure they were jumping. I
pulled the boat into the kelp and through to the other side of it,
then turned back to watch. One of the blackfish jumped at
that moment, almost straight up, only a little forward, and for
an instant I could see the shore of Maud Island below his wide,
horizontal tail flukes; his belly was pure, gleaming white, curving back in a white coil on his black side; he crashed down on
the water and the other two jumped just outside his splash, one
clear out as he had, the other in a half roll. Three or four more
times they jumped, straight out and little more than the width
of the kelp bed away from me the last time; then they seemed
to go back to the school. The whole school held on southward.
Then I heard the crack of a rifle as someone shot at them, and
they sounded, one of them with a last angry slap of his great
tail on the water. They were off Cape Mudge before the sound
of their distant spouts came back to me again across the still
evening water.

SALT WATER II

I<small>N</small> a literal sense British Columbia's most famous tyee salmon fishing, at Campbell River, is
salt-water fishing. Nearly all the fish are caught in the tides of
Discovery Passage, within half a mile or so of the river mouth.
But the tyees have, in effect, reached fresh water by this time.
They are resting and waiting within three or four short river
miles of where they will spawn, having already finished and
left their sea-feeding years. All urge to roam and search and
slash at the herring schools is gone from them, and they are as
much fresh-water fish as are Atlantic salmon or steelhead that
take the fly forty or fifty miles from salt water.

Fishing Discovery Passage is a little like fishing a huge river.
The passage is for the most part between one and two miles
wide, and the tides run strongly through it, breaking whirls
and rips and eddies at least as plainly marked as those of a big
river. The mouth of the Campbell, where the tyees lie to win
for anglers the bronze and gold and silver and diamond buttons
of the Tyee Club, is only six or seven miles south of Seymour
Narrows; and at Seymour Narrows, which is on the marine
highway to Alaska, the tides build up to twelve knots or more
in boils and waves and overfalls to match those of the fiercest
river rapids.

August is a great month at Campbell River. Our dusty
gravel roads play host to handsome cars whose widely varied
license plates prove the powerful attraction of the big fish—
New York plates, many from California, Oregon, Washington,
others from Florida, Alberta, Montana, even from Hawaii and
the Canal Zone. Yet the tyees are not really co-operative; dour
brutes they are, sulky and little heeding beneath twenty or

thirty feet of water. Dusk stirs them a little, and earliest dawn and the change of the tides swinging a fresh flow of current into their sheltered lying places. At dawn and dusk and through most of the August days, except when the tides are running their hardest, forty or fifty of Painter's white boats ply up and down, through the rest pools and along the bar, each with its guide and its fisherman, each with its rod throbbing to the beat of a six-inch spoon bait or marking the less rhythmic wobble of a plug. On a good day ten or fifteen fish may come to boat—thirty- and forty- and fifty-pounders; on a quiet day, perhaps one or two.

Between strikes the fishermen lean back in their chairs, watch the water and the mountains, talk a little from boat to boat—and hope. It is a quiet form of fishing, perhaps too quiet for anyone used to the activity of fly-fishing, but it is all done in expectation of action, and a forty-pound tyee, when he makes up his mind to take, is a worthy and powerful fish. What is more important still, a good strike off the mouth of the Campbell in August may mean, not merely a thirty- or forty-pounder, but quite possibly a fifty- or sixty-pounder and just possibly something even larger, for salmon over a hundred pounds in weight have been caught on the Pacific coast, and no angler needs more than that to stir hopes in his breast.

All fishermen have the big-fish complex—we want one bigger than we have caught before, something just a little bigger than it's reasonable to hope for, the mysterious, exceptional fish that has been able to make better use of his opportunities than have his brothers all around him. To salmon fishers everywhere thirty- and forty-pounders are big fish; the chances of a sixty-pounder is a dream of dreams, a hope of distant hopes. That, I think, is why my Uncle Decie comes back to Campbell River and why he will come back again. Decie is all fly-fisherman, skillful with wet fly or greased line for salmon as he is with the dry fly for trout, but he will sit out the hours in a boat at Campbell River with all the grim determination of a still fisherman. He tried first in 1927, for ten days or two weeks, and caught nothing larger than a feeding spring salmon of twenty pounds or so. That's a fairly unlucky stretch, as Campbell River fishing goes. In 1936, he fished with me for three days. I can't remember that we hooked a fish on the first two days, though we worked along the bar for every hour that the tides would let us, holding there sometimes long after the other boats had gone in. On the third day I said, "Let's forget this and go and fish properly somewhere. There'll be steelhead over in the Stamp."

"No," Decie said. "I've got to have one; just one. After that I don't care if I never troll again."

The evening of that last day was very rough, with a hard wind from the southeast breaking waves that would slap uncomfortably over the side of the boat. There were no other boats out, but I knew we could fish and we went out. We were backing down with the wind when the fish took, and Decie came up into him with a good solid strike. The fish ran at once, straight away from us and near the top of the water, so that his broad, bronze body showed for a moment on the side of a wave. Then the line broke, right at the rod top. Decie looked at his straightened rod and the broken line that dropped back into his lap.

"Your damned line's no good," he said.

"It's brand-new," I said defensively.

But that didn't change the fact that the line had broken without any good reason. We went ashore and tested it, found no weak places at all and went out again. But our luck was used up for that time and Decie went away, still without his big fish. He says he will be back, looking for another one, and I tell myself that this time things will go right and we shall be free to put away trolling rods and take out fly rods after only a day or two of working along the bar with the big spoon.

It is not that I don't think tyees are worth catching; there are very few fish I would rather catch. But I have been lucky enough to catch plenty of them by more active means than trolling, and I do not want now to catch by trolling even a bigger one than I have ever caught. I don't dislike trolling, but I like fly-fishing so much better that I would rather search for a two-pound trout in a river than troll for a sixty-pound salmon in salt water. Casting a minnow or spoon and fishing it round the current is only a little less pleasant than casting and working a fly, and it is a method that will catch tyees very satisfactorily. So I hope that is how I will catch my sixty-pounder when I do catch him and I'm ready to wait until the chance comes again.

In British Columbia the salt-water rod fisherman bothers himself with little else than salmon—tyee salmon (call them "springs," if they are less than thirty pounds, or kings or Chinooks if you would match them with the same fish in Alaska and Washington and Oregon) and cohos, which are quick and active feeders even when they are coming near their spawning. These and the trout in the streams and lakes are enough to keep a sparse population of anglers and a good supply of visitors well satisfied. If the salmon fisher occasionally catches a rock cod or cultus cod, a skate or a dogfish, he is likely to be annoyed rather than pleased. I have never felt any great desire to go after our salt-water fish for sport. Halibut are big and can be difficult to handle if you let them turn away instead of hurrying them right in toward the boat; rock cod are fine fish to eat; the cultus cod is a fierce brute, but not a game fish; big sharks can be caught in some places, but catching one is merely an experience, desirable once, perhaps; the occasional runs of tuna are too uncertain and generally too distant. None of these offers possibilities of sport even nearly equal to that given by the salmon. Yet they, with nearly everything else that swims or even drifts in salt or fresh water, are interesting to a confirmed fisherman. One may not care to fish for them, but it is mighty hard not to peer into the hold and ask questions when a commercial boat brings them in.

One of the best places to see and catch feeding fish in salt water is where two currents meet. The line of such meeting is generally marked by little, pointed, dancing waves, by flecks of foam and a gathering of drift on the surface; below the surface there is more drift, broken strands of kelp and seaweed that are the outward and visible signs of invisible drift—a mass of plankton, diatoms, rotifers, flagellates and the rest, copepods, jellyfish, shellfish larvae and a thousand other tiny forms of life with little or no power of resistant movement. Each current brings its own burden of drift to the meeting, adding constantly to the collection held along the line of the rip. Other sea creatures come to the rip as deer come to a meadow or bees to blossom, small ones because the plankton is their feed, the larger ones attracted by the movement and flashing bodies of the plankton feeders.

Rips form off the mouths of all rivers that flow into channels with strong tides and from all confusions and changes and breaks of simple tidal flow. The river rips are roughly semicircular, constantly moving and changing as the true salt water strikes more or less strongly against the river's flow. Rips form from the jut of headlands and across the mouths of bays, wherever a straight run of tide slides along an eddy; they form in the lee of islands, where two tides come together again, and they are everywhere about rapids, in the narrow places where tides force through. Wise salmon fishermen search the rips when they are looking for cohos or feeding springs, and there is a great satisfaction in finding fish this way. Sometimes a rip is soupy with plankton, alive with launce fish or herrings, even marked through half its length by the rolling olive backs of porpoises, yet there are no salmon. Then the gulls and terns come to it and little grebes and murrelets collect along it, bobbing on the sharp waves, diving down, chasing up launce fish for the gulls and for themselves. Perhaps a cormorant comes, and the gulls and terns follow his dives, hovering watchfully over every twist of his underwater hunting until a shower of needlefish flips into the air ahead of his pursuit to summon them, flapping and screaming, down to the water. Then, perhaps, there are sudden fierce slashes through the broken water of the rip, fierce boils where no grebe or murrelet has dived, showers of needlefish where no cormorant is swimming, a crying and fluttering and diving of gulls and terns, a newer, stronger excitement among them that brings others flying from far away across the water. That is how you know that the salmon are in, and you work up toward them until you are casting at the feeding slashes; your fly lights and sinks, you work it, a great wave follows, cuts off in a boil and a pull, and you strike. Then the reel runs and runs, you brake until the tips of your fingers burn, and a coho jumps for you once, twice, three times, straight out and over, tumbled by the drag of the drowned line.

Watching porpoises and catching cohos along the line of a rip is only the surface of the thing. Deep down the tides are moving too, and on the bottom rock reefs and sandbars break up the currents again. Opposite Campbell River the passage between Vancouver Island and the mainland of British Columbia is broken into a dozen narrow channels by several large islands. The tides force their way among the islands with a fierce struggle that is shown in the names of the channels—Seymour Narrows, Yuculta Rapids, Arran Rapids, Green Point Rapids, Hole-in-the-Wall, Surge Narrows, Whirlpool Rapids.

Seymour Narrows is the most famous of these because it is on the main steamer channel. The tides run at ten or twelve knots through Seymour, building three or four big broken waves below Ripple Rock and heavy rips clear across the channel from Race Point on the flood. Big whirlpools form in many places, and great fierce boils burst up without warning through water that seems glass still. Feed collects in the rips and eddies, and salmon come to it. Some of the Indians know the place well and fish it cunningly from dugouts. White fishermen also have learned it and fish there, though anglers go up less often now that the grounds off Campbell River are so well known. There is, inevitably, some danger in fishing such a place—three lives were lost at Ripple Rock only a year or two ago. It is essential to study time and the tide book and to allow a generous safety factor which must never be cut just because the fishing is good or the water looks easy. Given this elementary measure of respect, Seymour Narrows is safe enough, and the fishing is both good and exciting. Big fish feed there almost all year round, and big fish pass by there, eighty- and ninety-pounders, almost certainly, every year, because the narrows is the main southward gateway to many fine rivers. If one hooked such a fish just as the tide began to run, it might not be easy to remember the necessary safety factor.

Next in importance to Seymour are the Yuculta Rapids. The awkward name has several spellings—Yuculta, Yaculta, Yuclataw, the last of which is nearest to the common pronunciation —and applies primarily to the narrows between Stuart and Sonora Islands, though it comfortably fits the whole four-mile length of twisting channel from Stuart Island to the Dent Islands and is generally used that way. The Yucultas are a splendid confusion of six- or seven-knot tides broken many times by islands and bays and by the nine-knot run of Arran Rapids from Bute Inlet around the north end of Stuart Island. Salmon feed along the Yucultas much as they feed around Seymour Narrows, and in the summer months many handsome yachts and smaller power boats put in at Stuart Island while their owners fish. One local settler has built a concrete abutment on a point that juts out into the swift water from Stuart Island and on this he has rigged a heavy pole that slants out over the water and trails a spoon bait. The action of the tides gives the spoon a good lively wobble, and passing salmon see its flash, strike at it and are hooked. I can never pass this contraption without feeling that I live in a country whose generosity is in a class with that of the better South Sea Islands.

Yuculta cod fishermen catch numerous big Sebastodes which

are known locally as "red cod." I think they must be almost identical with a European fish known as the Norway haddock, and certainly they are among the handsomest fish imaginable and are fine table fish as well. They are large-scale fish that live in fifty or sixty fathoms of water and come to the surface with their eyes popping at the change of pressure; but the bright scarlet back and deep, full sides of a fifteen- or twenty-pounder seem to belong in daylight rather than the unlit depths. So far as I know, red cod are always caught at a considerable depth, and presumably that is why they are not more adaptable to pressure changes. Many fish come to the surface from much greater depths still alive and apparently unharmed, but these probably make the change habitually and voluntarily at dusk of each day when the light-hating plankton come up from the depths.

One generally thinks of a hundred fathoms or thereabouts as the limit of useful fishing depth; I know that salmon have been caught at ninety fathoms and the sablefish, which is still too often called the "black cod," is commonly found at 250 fathoms. But depths beyond a hundred fathoms (six hundred feet of crushing sea water) seem too deep to be useful; for there is little light below a hundred feet, and true plant life, dependent on sunlight, cannot grow there. The deeps are very cold and, one imagines, almost sterile in their cold darkness and under the burden of the pressure. Yet there is life, varied and active life on parts of the ocean floor at a thousand fathoms, and I heard only the other day of commercial fishermen who put out their set lines for dogfish in 350 fathoms—this is Toba Inlet, only a few miles from Yuculta Rapids. Large-scale dog-fishing is fairly new in British Columbia, a fishery built on the recently discovered value of the dogfish's vitamin-bearing liver, and so the fishermen experiment as they probably would not in an older fishery. I asked eagerly what came up on the lines from 350 fathoms in Toba Inlet: dogfish, of course, and sable-fish; ratfish, which render a fine machine oil and look like their name; red coral, a little shark, an eellike creature (no, not with a sucking mouth like a lamprey's), cultus cod, and a fleshy growth that looked like ivory canes. Many of these creatures one might find as easily at five fathoms on a brightly lighted sandbar, yet all come up from that tremendous depth and pressure without even showing the signs of violent change that a red cod shows in coming from fifty fathoms. How do they live there and why should they choose to live there? Nearly everyone has seen dogfish by the hundred playing right at the surface, seeing with their eyes, rolling their backs out in free air. What do they find on the floor of Toba Inlet to make them drag their bellies over the scarlet coral? They had pink feed in their stomachs, my informant said, pink shrimps, the euphausiid shrimps that one also sees often at the surface.

The mysteries of salt water, deep or shallow, leave me shocked, afraid, overwhelmed, yet urgently curious, filled with desire to know more and understand at least a little. Sometime soon I shall drift again over a kelp bed on a hot still day, looking down between the wide smooth brown ribbons, past the slender dark bodies of massed launce fish, to an uneven hazy bottom covered with sea cucumbers and sea eggs, starfish and devilfish; perhaps I shall see again, as I once saw, a brilliant scarlet squid swimming swiftly, fiercely, purposefully, a headless, deadly body with angry eyes that fear nothing, not even the strange white shadow of the boat's hull above them. Almost certainly I shall still be ignorant, unable to name him properly, doubtful of his life history, groping to name the purpose of his swift movement. But I shall feel again that I have seen something which, for all its namelessness, is strong and vivid with meaning and pleasure quite unconnected with the exactitudes of natural history.

SEPTEMBER

Sᴇᴘᴛᴇᴍʙᴇʀ has a touch of the year's death in it—one notices that a little more sadly and fearfully as one grows older. Even five years ago I welcomed September, hoped for its early frosts, accepted gladly its promise of the strong demands of winter days. The softness of summer

239

was over and done with; ahead, I felt, was a time for doing. Now I shrink a little from the implication of the first cool nights, remembering the dark days of last winter, the cold that cut back the laurels, the snow that buried the pastures, and the long slow waiting for a spring whose coming seemed delayed on into months that really should be summer.

But that is only a brief mood, passing quickly away, because September is one of the loveliest months of the year and I shall have to be really decrepit, past caring much for living life, before I carry my old bones south to California's sun at the spattering roar of a winter's first southeaster. September is as good a fishing month as one could hope for, and if the fall frosts come early they can do no more than clear away the heavy heat of summer and color the leaves of maple and willow and poplar to make the river banks more beautiful. In September the lakes, too hot at the surface for trout to move freely in July and August, grow cool again, and a fly-fisherman can go to them hopefully; the big fish he failed to find in April may be cruising in the right place now, and the long dark spawner he turned back may have grown clean and respectably fat through a summer's feeding. All the streams and rivers are full of fish in September and there is an abundance of fly to move the trout. A September evening, with a cool dusk descending on the day's warmth, can be a busy time on one of the mountain streams where sedges hatch thickly, and an exciting time too because the big trout will be stirring from the deep pools; and there is always a chance that the change of season may have moved something very big to leave the lake's security for a smooth glide over clear shallows or a strategic holt under the shade of alder branches.

Here, in the four miles of the Campbell below Elk Falls, there are humpbacks and cutthroats that ran up in August. A touch of squaw winter, a three-day southeaster and heavy rain over Labor Day, will have brought the tyees through to the Canyon Pool. One sees them there a few days later, in the sunlight of Indian summer, perhaps two or three hundred great, dark fish, square-tailed and thick-bodied, holding calmly midway between surface and bottom in ten or twenty feet of transparent green water. I always look among them for a real giant, but I have not seen him yet; and I look too for the flash of a spoon left in an angry jaw by some fisherman's clumsiness, but I have not seen that yet either, though many spoons are lost and I have several times found spoons or flies in the jaws of the cohos that run up in October. I think the tyees too often break the line somewhere above the four- or six-ounce lead that the trollers use and are tangled and held in the weed by lead and line until they die or tear the hook away from them.

Nothing is more impressive than the sight of a big school of tyees under the smooth surface of the Canyon Pool in September. They are so big and calm and dignified, so clearly visible, so solidly set in their still-distant spawning purpose, so utterly contemptuous of a fly or spoon drawn across them or among them. And they have lost none of their ocean perfection. They are dark, it is true, but their bodies are perfect, unscarred, thick across the back, tremendously powerful. What is the immediate purpose of this schooling in the Canyon Pool, at what must be almost the end of their journey, I do not know. They simply hold in midwater for hours on end, like gigantic brown trout waiting for a hatch of flies to come down over them. Occasionally half a dozen fish turn away, drift down as the weight of the current comes against their sides, then turn and swim back into place again. It is strange to see all that so clearly, not more than twenty or thirty feet away, confined in a little pool of fresh water. Only a few days ago they had all the breadth and depth and security of the sea to play in; even when they jumped and rolled their backs out over the bar in the evening light they were immeasurably beyond reach. Tomorrow they may be out there again; that is something else I am not sure of, but I know that you can go to the Canyon Pool one day and see them there, go again the next day and search the whole pool with the sun clear and strong behind you and fail to see a single one. Then, perhaps weeks later, I will see them again, the females turning on their sides to dig out nests in the gravel, the males waiting behind them. I once heard a Campbell River guide describing this movement of the tyees to an angling bishop whom he had been rowing on the early morning tide.

"Yes, sir," he was saying, "they pair off in the salt chuck, male and female, and go up the river to pick out their nests. Then they come back down here and wait till they're ready to spawn—maybe go up two or three more times to make sure the nest is all right."

"Remarkable," said the bishop. "Most interesting."

No doubt the guide had inferred a good deal more than he had ever seen, and the bishop probably was merely being polite, but the fish do move strangely in the river. In August the Campbell is no big stream for the ascent of thirty- and forty-pounders; I have seen them many times, flashing their broad red sides right out in the sunlight to work up over the bar in the Island Pool, rolling out in the fast run under the north bank, even jumping high in the air and crashing back on their bellies within three or four feet of my trout rod. All these were fish moving upstream, showing their progress plainly by successive jumps or rolls or the wave of their passing on shallows. Yet I have gone up to look in the Canyon Pool after seeing them pass and have been unable to find anything there that looked larger than a four-pound humpback or cut-throat. Perhaps they go on through the Canyon itself, right up to the foot of the falls. I have seen salmon jump there, but it is hard to believe that they find good spawning ground between the steep, dark walls.

September is a hunting month as well as a fishing month. The sharp smell of smoke in the air, the crackle of an early-fallen leaf underfoot, morning mist along the river bottoms and heavy dew in the meadows all make one think of dogs and shotgun or rifle and hunting knife. The early days of the season are far too good to miss altogether, but no fly-fisherman should put his rod aside just because September is a hunting month. Even here on Vancouver Island the two sports fit well together—a hot morning on the dry hills while the dogs flush blue grouse from short salal is the better for an evening spent waist deep in the cool river. In England my father had a September ritual which I have dutifully tried to follow whenever I have been in a position to do so: on September first one must serve the gods of three sports by killing a duck, a trout and a partridge. Theoretically it is not too difficult to do this, for one can find mallard at their feeding along the river in the early dawn, and even if an official partridge shoot takes up the whole day, there is still the evening rise for a trout. But things can go wrong.

I think I was sixteen when the Important Relation came to dinner on September first. It had been a good day. I had found my ducks in the early dawn; and all through the blazing hot morning and afternoon we had walked stubble and root field and downland for partridges. There was only the trout to be found, and I was confident I could take care of that. But when we came home from the hills, there was the Important Relation. Grandfather had ordered that everyone must pay homage by appearing at the dinner table clean and brushed in black and white. Grandfather's dinners were slow and calm. I sat through this one somehow, slipped away after it, found my rod and dived out into the growing dusk. I thought I knew of a fish that would be rising where a strong current swept round a sharp bend some thirty or forty yards above a barbed-wire cattle fence that stretched clear across the river. I came to the place, saw his rise and put a fly over. It passed him, went down in a clumsy rise and I knew I had hooked an eight-inch sprat. I turned him back, but my good fish was no longer rising, though I tried him several times. It was almost dark and I felt that the day was done and faith was broken. Then I heard a rise somewhere below me. The fish rose again, and I cast to him without moving, right across the river and eight or ten yards downstream. I couldn't see my fly, but something rose near where it should have been and I struck—late, I knew. The reel ran fiercely, I tried to check it, knew that I dared not and knew too that the line was down to the barbed wire. A moment later it caught. I plunged in the river, waist deep, cursing the luck that had hooked me to a two-pounder at this of all possible times. The line seemed hopelessly tangled in the wire, and I was sure that the fish had broken the gut and gone on his way. Then I saw the shine of his body, hanging in the stream straight below the wire. I ducked under the wire and came up on the lower side with water streaming from my hair and the stiff shirt front sodden flat against my chest. The fish still hung there, and I slipped the net under him easily—thirteen inches, hooked in the dorsal fin.

Years later, when I was last in England, I tried to keep faith again. I knew it wouldn't be easy because I had to stay in London until late on the night of August thirty-first. I drove down to Dorset in time for breakfast on September first, too late for early morning ducks and with a date to play cricket for the village in the afternoon. There was no official partridge shoot that day, but I went out by myself and found a covey quickly enough to be back at the house soon after eleven-thirty. Cricket was to start at two, so I had just two and a half hours of sweltering midday heat to find my trout. Village cricket is important business, and if you are at home or within reach of home on a match day, you play—without argument, no matter what else may seem important. You arrive on the field in time to help take down the fence that keeps the cows off the pitch and you stay after the game to see the visiting team on their way and put the fence up again.

For some foolish reason I thought of the old black trout that cruised the shallow eddy below Gaston Bridge and decided to make him my fish for the day. I could not have made a worse choice. He was a wise and level-headed fish, the eddy he cruised in was slow, wide and perfectly smooth, as well as shallow, and one could reach him only by a long cast across a run of strong current.

I came to the bridge and crept across, keeping well down below the solid parapet and setting my feet down lightly. Gaston Bridge is built of brick, in two arches, and the deck is wide enough only to carry cattle and foot traffic. Ten or fifteen yards below it is a ford through which carts and wagons pass, and just below the ford the river makes a sharp turn to pass along a willow bed and on beneath a single strand of barbed wire that prevents cattle wading up from the meadow and out onto the road that comes down to the ford. The water below the bridge fishes properly only from the south side, which is on the inside of the curve, and almost the whole force of the river's current comes through the south arch of the bridge in a good straight flow until it strikes the willow bed, sending an eddy back into the shallows of the north side of the ford, and dancing on its way close under the willows to spread again before it reaches the barbed wire.

I saw the black shape of my fish almost at once, quite still against the golden gravel of the eddy. For a moment I thought he was not feeding at all, then I was not so sure; he seemed poised and expectant, even though he was not moving, and his body was not resting right on the bottom, but was raised a few inches from it. Then he began to move. He swam a few feet upstream, turned almost sharply and swam back against the eddy. Before he reached the willow bed he had risen three times, very gently and quietly, hardly breaking the surface, taking something that was quite invisible to me. He disappeared when he reached the shade of the overhanging willows, but I knew he had turned north along the bed and would soon come out again over the sunlit gravel. As I was wondering what to offer him I saw the second rise, a quick competent rise exactly where the current struck the withy bed and swung along it. It was a good place, I knew, and a fairly easy place, because I had hooked several good-sized fish there in other years. The fish rose again, close against a little triangular pile of drift that was caught between the main current, the eddy and the willow bed.

My black fish came out from the shadows and cruised very slowly across the ford, rising several times and holding his course to within five or six feet of the bridge. I had tied on a small iron-blue dun, but I felt doubtful about it; if the first fly failed and was pulled away by drag, he would almost certainly go down. The fish in the current rose again and I saw him, a shadow just below the surface of the water; he was big, bigger than the black fish, wide-backed and in fine condition. I floated the iron blue past him, saw him turn to it, turn away. Twice more I put it near him, but he would not even turn to it. I changed to a pale watery dun, still doubtful because I could see nothing on the water. The pale dun looked pretty to me as it rode buoyantly past the drift on the quick current, but the fish rose to something else. Then I thought of a nymph; a nymph would be safest anyway for the black fish, and if drag whipped it away from him, he might not mind. I put on a tup, tiny and lightly dressed; I knew my fish by the patch of drift was rising, not nymphing, but I felt sure he was feeding too well to let such a tempting, sunken thing pass him—our Frome trout are suckers for a nymph. But he did let it pass. His superior ways were destroying my confidence now, and I dared show it to him only twice for fear he would thumb his nose at me for a blundering, ignorant fool and stop rising altogether. I opened my fly box and sat down to look through it. Olives looked up at me, tups, halfstones, sedges, quills of all colors—blue, red, ginger, orange and olive—alders, my pet iron blues, hare's-ears, pheasant tails, flies of Dunne and flies of Halford, flies of Chalkley and Jeffery and Hardy, my own clumsier creatures; and I could not, for the life of me, tell which to use.

I went to my own in the end—a glint of black on a No. 17 hook and two visible turns of fine gold tinsel. I felt better as soon as I picked it out from among its fellows; I tied it on, let out line, dropped it on the current. The fish came to it so matter-of-factly, so calmly in the rhythm of his feeding, that for a moment I wouldn't believe it was my fly he had come to. But he still had it when I tightened. He went up and I turned him hard to keep him away from the black fish. That was a mistake. He hadn't been thinking of the eddy at all but of the big weed bed behind the shelter of the bridge pier. Swung over from that in the current, he turned down and ran on and on, far down under the single strand of wire that fenced the meadow. I didn't deserve him. There were weeds down there and a good strong current as well as the threatening barbs on the wire, but he came back, swimming quietly of his own free will past all the dangers, and I netted him at last. He was a pale-gold color on sides and belly, with a lovely green in the deeper color of his back and he carried the pointer of the spring balance handsomely past one and a half pounds.

I looked at my watch and figured I had an hour's fishing time left. I had my trout, but not the black fish, and the black fish was still rising. By the time my fly was dry again he was coming back against the soft flow of the eddy, so slowly that he was hardly moving. I dropped the fly six inches ahead of him, with yards of slack on the fast water. He was interested at once, but he speeded up not at all. Slowly and slowly and slowly he came, his body tilted just a little toward the fly, his nose pushing up to it. The slack was almost used up. I moved downstream as far as I could, held the rod point down, watched and prayed. His nose touched the fly, took it down in the tiniest end to the slowest rise I had ever seen. I think the drag set the hook in him, because my line was not tight until he had almost reached the shelter of the willows. But he hadn't the condition to fight hard or dangerously. He was a shade longer than the first fish, a quarter of a pound lighter; but he pleased me because he was the one I had wanted.

I almost went home then. I had folded my net, reeled in my line, hooked my fly to the reel seat. A fish rose below the bridge, and I saw another poised in the water beside him. Flies were coming down, quite a lot of them, there was one almost at my feet at the edge of the ford—a blue-winged olive. I still thought I'd go home. Then there was the deep, echoing sound of a huge rise under the far arch of the bridge. It was a sound of ponderous weight, of awe-inspiring dignity, magnificently musical. I tried to tell myself that a bridge arch always magnifies the sound of a rise to those proportions, that it was probably a small fish, that the current was running at least two miles an hour through the near arch, probably less than a mile a day through the far arch, that the rise was over halfway up under the bridge, where I couldn't possibly reach it. But it was no use; I had to change to a blue-winged olive—I hesitated long between that and an orange quill—and see what could be done.

I slammed in an underhand cast so that the line struck the bridge pier and threw gut and fly well up under the arch. Very slowly the gut came back in sight; four or five feet of it were showing when the enormous sound of the rise came again. I jerked the rod nervously and dragged the fly out into the open; certainly the rise had been at least two or three feet above the fly, but who was I to remain calm at such a sound? I cast again, and this time the fly bounced on the water and shot well up under the far side of the arch. The line was too straight across the current and brought it dragging back almost immediately. That had finished it, I thought; true, the fish seemed to be under the near side of the arch; but he surely must have seen the drag even from there. If he were any size at all, he would already have left for a less disturbed place.

One point I had missed: that arch of the bridge, difficult to reach across the fast water and with a slow current flowing

through it, was probably the quietest, safest place in the whole river for a fish to grow up. This fish had almost certainly not seen an artificial fly in the whole time he had lived there. He saw one just a moment later.

The cast did exactly what it was supposed to—brought the line hard against the pier, whipped fly and leader far up under the arch, almost through to the other side, I thought. The full length of the gut was still out of sight when the rise came, louder than ever before, spanging from arch to water to arch again. I struck to it and the reel howled. The line dragged against the brickwork, and I moved downstream and out into the water, trying to keep it clear. From somewhere far above the arch two great splashes told me the fish was jumping. He'll hit for the current and come back through the wrong arch, I told myself; it's been fun while it lasted. Then I felt the sinister vibration on the line that means weed. He went in and stopped. I waited a moment, then put a smooth, heavy strain on. I felt him. That was good, but there was no reason why he should come out. I had 4X gut, and anything that was done to move him had to be done by the spring of the rod alone. For one reason, and one only, that was enough—he didn't feel safe out in the daylight, even under the shadows of the weeds. He made up his mind to that point quite suddenly and came back with a rush to his dark holt under the far arch, dragging the gut free of the weed. I tightened on him by hand-lining, kept him coming until he was below the arch, then he turned and drove back. It went on like that for quite a while, and every so often he jumped with a splash, out of sight, under the arch.

Once I brought him back almost to the net, and what I saw of him made my knees shake. He saw the net and ran up under the near arch, against the current. I knew I had him then; he tired almost quickly and came in quietly, on his side, until I lifted and the net had him. I carried him up on the grass, well back from the stream, knelt beside him, and looked and looked.

He was the most beautiful brown trout I have ever seen. Not quite two pounds, but hugely thick and short and deep, with a tiny head and a huge tail. His back was a rich, deep olive, his belly pale golden, his red spots were big and vivid, and over his whole side was a sheen of red, a diffusion rather than an overlaid color, the golden redness of sunset light. I packed him away with the others at last and went home.

The cricket and the ducks? Village cricket is a fine game. Unexpected things happen, funny things happen, everything happens quickly—man up, man down, almost with the speed of baseball. Everyone laughs, but everyone takes the game very seriously. The umpire is not too sacred; anyone can give him a dirty look and most of us go a little farther on occasion, and our best slow bowler was often darkly threatening, emitting thundery mutterings from the corner of his mouth and glowering fiercely from under heavy black brows. In village cricket no one has ever asked of me the subtle and difficult things; I am expected to go out there, hit the ball hard, make runs fast or get out. I generally do something of both, and this day was no exception. Between two-thirty and six-thirty we played through four innings—something a pair of international sides seldom manage in a full week of playing—and we took time out for a good heavy tea with lots of bread and butter and fruit cake. By seven o'clock the fence was back in place around the pitch, and everyone was happily on his way home—a slow way for the visitors, because they had to pass through half a dozen villages, each with at least one pub in it.

I gave dinner a miss and went up the river with a gun. I couldn't find ducks in any of the usual places. As it grew dark I waited by a hatch pool for the evening flight down the valley. Nothing passed within sight or sound of me, and I turned away for home at last. I hadn't walked more than a dozen steps when I heard them, quacking nervously on the water. I crouched down and ran toward the sound, heard the splash-

ing as they rose, saw the gleam of the light underside of a wing
and fired. While the flash of the gun was still in my eyes, I
heard the heavy, satisfying thud of a big duck's fall on the far
bank.

SACHEM RIVER

I HAVE told this story before
in different ways, but it is the best fishing story I know and it
touches one of the loveliest rivers I know.

In the summer of 1927 I went up to the northern end of
Vancouver Island to work for the Wood and English Logging
Company on Nimpkish Lake. I had heard, before I went, that
the Nimpkish River had a run of tyee salmon probably at least
the equal of the Campbell River run, and I made up my mind
that I was going to get some fishing out of it. In 1927 I was
away at the head of the lake all through September and missed
the run, but in 1928 I was ready for it, with a brand-new Mur-
doch spinning rod, a good line and plenty of spoons that were
supposed to be of the right kind.

My knowledge of the fishing was wretchedly slight. The
tyees ran in September—that seemed fairly definite. Someone, a
few years earlier, had caught a sixty-seven-pounder by trolling
with a hand line inside the river. But, so the boys in camp
told me, it was the height of folly to expect to catch such fish
on rod and line: in the first place, no such fancy gear could
possibly deceive them into taking hold; and if by some obscure
chance an especially foolish fish were to impale itself on the
hook, no possible good could come of it; rod, reel, line and
everything else would be irreparably smashed or else taken
right away in the first run.

Fishing for trout in the river and waiting for ducks on the
tide flats at the mouth of the river during the previous year,

I had learned a little about the water; but I didn't really know where to start in. Not too far above tidewater, I thought; perhaps the first pool above. And that was where I went with my new rod and a big bright spoon on the last Sunday of August.

The pool I had chosen was very big, deep and fairly slow between high, steep banks. I found it difficult to fish and discouraging because I could not wade to cover it properly, and no fish showed to convince me that I was not wasting my time. As a matter of fact, I doubted if any were yet in the river, and my main purpose in coming down had been to size up the water before the fish came in rather than to catch fish. So in a little while I left the big pool and followed the river on down.

I came almost at once to a much more promising pool, one at the head of tidewater which I later named Lansdowne Pool. It was separated from the other pool by a wooded island and a short rapid. The main body of the river flowed on the east side of the island, under the bank that I was following, and stretching back from the pool on this side were several acres of cleared land with a primrose-yellow farmhouse set in a small orchard in the middle of them—something altogether unique in the Nimpkish watershed, but I knew the farm belonged to the Lansdowne family and I had met the two sons once or twice when I had been trout fishing up the river. I tried a few casts in the pool, but there was a deep eddy under my bank which made it difficult to reach the water properly, and I strongly suspected that the best lying place in the pool was under the steep rock bank on the far side. So once again, and very fortunately, I told myself, I was exploring rather than fishing and went on my way.

I had great hopes of the estuary of the river. I knew that at Campbell River the tyees were caught only in salt water and that, generally speaking, Pacific salmon were supposed to be impossible to catch once they had left salt water, though I knew also, from Cobb's *Pacific Salmon Fisheries*, that they were caught by anglers in the Willamette River. I supposed vaguely that my best hope might be to find some tidal pool where the fish rested before committing themselves to fresh water. On this Sunday of exploration the tide was fairly well in over the flats, and I could not follow the river channel as closely as I had hoped. But I could see that there was a short and narrow pool under the far bank some two hundred yards below Lansdowne Pool and a larger pool under a high-cut bank of blue clay a hundred yards down from that. Opposite this Blue Clay Pool was a small grassy islet, Sachem Island, then a shallow channel about forty yards wide, then a much more considerable island, the Indian Island, with several Indian smokehouses standing on it, separated from the bank I was following by a deep backwater.

A little below the Indian Island I met Ed Lansdowne. He was sixteen years old then and looked younger, dressed in a shirt and a pair of blue shorts, without shoes or stockings, his hair a tight cap of red curls above his sunburned face. I liked what I had seen of Ed up the river and I felt sure at once that he would prove a valuable conspirator in this salmon-fishing project. He was not talkative or much given to asking questions, but the new rod caught his admiring eye and I told him what I was looking for. He was doubtful, but not discouraging.

"There was a policeman used to come over from the Bay and troll in the river with a hand line. He caught a few. Pete and some other guys come once in a while, but they fish outside."

He pointed downstream to where the Fishing Island, a low triangular island with more fishing shacks and net racks, split the tide and held the river in its channel.

"Beyond the Fishing Island—between there and Green Island —you can see the fish finning out there when the run's in. You see them all the way up the river too, past Sachem Island and as far up as our place."

"Do they seem to lie much in the pool opposite your place?" I asked.

"Sure, they lie there pretty good. We see them jumping and

rolling—you can hear them all night sometimes. But I don't think there's any in yet this year." He grinned. "Gee, I'd sure like to see you get one."

I told him I wanted to fish the pool the next Sunday. Did he think the fish would be in and could he get hold of a boat from somewhere? He thought that the fish would surely be in and he knew of a boat he could probably get. So we made it a date.

I was down at the side of the pool well ahead of the appointed time, in spite of a five-mile walk from camp, and Ed was soon with me. He had not been able to get a boat, but he had a raft, a heavy thing of logs with planks spiked across them, which would float when the tide came in and which he thought we could maneuver enough to cover at least some of the good water. The fish were in all right. A big one jumped soon after I arrived, and others jumped at intervals all through the morning while we waited for the tide. From time to time I waded out and tried to cast to where they were lying, but I had not yet learned to handle the big six-inch spoon very well and I knew I wasn't reaching them. So at last I sat down to wait with Ed and plan what we would do when the raft floated. Every five or ten minutes a fish jumped and the splash echoed back from the timbered hill opposite. They were huge fish, cleaner and brighter than I had dared hope, though some were bronze rather than silver; I tried to guess weights—thirty, I would say, forty-five. Then a great pig of a fish would come over in a short-bodied arc, and I would realize that if the last one had been forty-five this one must be seventy at least. And perhaps he was; the Nimpkish had yielded her ninety-pounders to the nets.

The tide came in at last, the raft floated and we pushed off. The surface of the pool was still and dark now, with only an easy current through it and a little ripple close under the foot of the rapids, which still ran white and strong and broken against the big boulders. I fished carefully and thoroughly and expectantly, working the big spoon very deep and slow; we covered the whole pool several times, but nothing touched the spoon. It wasn't easy to handle the heavy raft with only a paddle and pole over the deep water, but Ed did really well with it and worked at least as hard and enthusiastically as I did for a long while. We went up behind the island and found a deep still backwater fed by only a light riffle of water from the Canyon Pool, and once or twice we saw the shadows of big fish moving or lying near bottom. Ed, whose brother was a commercial troller, began to wonder if my spoon was working just right, and knowing little of how a spoon should work, I began to feel doubtful myself. Then Ed suggested that we might do better when the tide started to ebb, so we ran the raft back to the beach and waited. Ed went up to the house and came back with huckleberry wine and sandwiches.

"Do you really think we've got a chance to catch something?" he asked.

"Sure," I said, and I was sure. "The hand trollers catch fish, don't they? There's no difference in what we're doing."

"They mostly catch them out in the salt chuck."

"I know that. But there's no reason a fish should change so much just for coming up a mile or so on the tide. And anyway, they fish mostly in the salt chuck. You said so yourself."

The tide began to ebb at last, and we started to fish again. This time we took the raft straight across to the low rock face of the far bank and held there, for it seemed that we might have disturbed the pool too much by moving about in our first attempts. I worked the spoon through the water every way I knew, fast and slow, deep and shallow, steadily and in jerks, casting upstream and across and down. Still nothing took. I could see that Ed was getting a little restless and told him about a fisherman's faith in the last cast of the day—if you make enough of them, saying each time "just one more," you're sure to get something.

"You still think there's a chance?" Ed asked. "I don't."

"There's always a chance," I said. "I'm going to try it right through to dark. You stay with me, and if we get a fish, I'll send you up a Hardy trout rod from town next week."

So we kept fishing. I really had plenty of hope left in me. After all, I had fished the Frome with Greenhill every day for a solid week to catch my first Atlantic salmon and I knew something of how dour and moody nonfeeding fish can be. The tide was almost out of the pool now, and a hand troller came up, rowing right through the middle of it. That, I thought, wouldn't help any. I made a cast at a long angle upstream and fished it back to me deep down. I noticed that the sun was gone behind the hill and most of the pool was in shadow. Then the spoon came against something solid and heavy. I struck hard; the line ran out for fifteen or twenty yards, then went slack.

"That was it," I said. "But we'll get another."

We did. Two or three casts later I felt the spoon stop, brought the rod up and was into a fish that ran with wild strength straight up toward the rapids. I checked him as hard as I dared, because I had only sixty or seventy yards of line on the reel. There were about a dozen turns left on the reel when he came out in a beautiful jump not ten feet from the stern of the hand troller's boat.

"Let's get across," I said, "and finish him from the bank. He'll tangle in that guy's line if we don't."

Ed picked up the paddle and drove the raft across. I jumped overboard in three or four feet of water with the fish still on. But we had him. He ran again, several times, almost as strongly as the first time. Then he was swirling and fighting about twenty feet away, unable to tear loose from the strain I held on him, but still too strong to give up. I walked back onto dry land, drawing him in, then went forward again into the water, shortening line. He came close, and I reached for his tail, gripped it and carried him ashore. He was a perfect fish, silver and clean, certainly a spring salmon, but he was hooked just ahead of the dorsal fin and weighed only twenty-one pounds.

"What do you think happened?" Ed asked. "Do you think we just snagged him?"

"No," I said. "He came at it; I'm sure of that. We can't prove it though—not till we get another one."

"Tonight?"

"No, you've earned that trout rod now. Next Sunday."

Ed had a boat the next Sunday. We fished the pool for a while without touching anything, then went down the river to see what we could find. I wanted a thirty-pounder, to meet the British Columbia angler's traditional but arbitrary distinction between tyee and spring salmon, and I wanted him hooked fairly and squarely in the mouth, so that I'd have an answer for the boys in camp who still insisted that there was nothing new about snagging salmon—anyone could do that.

There was some tide in and the water was quite smooth. Below Sachem Island we saw the little arrowhead ripples of a school of fish swimming up the river, and I cast across them from the boat. A big fish turned and had the spoon. I had spliced an extra length of backing onto my line since the previous Sunday, but he had all the old line and backing and a good part of the new out before I could bring him up to break the surface. He didn't exactly jump when he did come up, but for twenty or thirty seconds he stayed right at the surface and thrashed the water white. Suddenly he turned and came hard back for the boat, getting himself some slack line, but I soon picked that up, and he seemed well hooked. For about twenty minutes he fought this way, running close to the surface, turning when I put heavy pressure on him, running again and jumping occasionally. He made one more short run, which I held easily, then I told Ed to head in for the island, where we could tail him—we still had no gaff. Something made him run again, strongly and fiercely for forty or fifty yards. That seemed to finish him. He lay on the surface with little movement. I tried to lead him back to the boat, and he began to roll.

"Quick," I told Ed, "row out to him. I think I can get him right where he is."

Then the spoon came away. The fish was still rolling in the surface, his belly showing white. Ed drove the boat toward him, and I crouched, ready to grab any part of him I could reach. But as we got there, he righted himself and all we saw was his big, pale, shadowy form swimming slowly down through the clear water.

"Gosh," I said, "forty-five pounds anyway. And that's leaning over backward to be fair."

"Yes," Ed said. "Hooked in the mouth too. I could see."

"Seeing like that's no proof though."

"There's no proof he was forty-five pounds either."

We got what we wanted the next Sunday, a thirty-two-pound fish, bright and clean, hooked in the mouth and killed after a good fight in the shallow water between Sachem Island and the Indian Island. That was the last fish we killed that season. I had to go up to work in the camp at the head of the lake, and by the time I got back to the river again, it was October and a high freshet had drawn all the big fish on upstream to their spawning in Woss Lake and the Kla-anche River. But at least we knew the game was worth trying; we had killed two fish, had narrowly missed getting a third, and had run several others, some of them in Lansdowne Pool. Next season, we promised ourselves, we would be really fishing, with proper equipment and at least some knowledge to start on.

It happened that September of 1929 found me with a broken elbow and a very slim bankbook after a bad summer of contract logging. As it turned out, that was a fairly convenient set of circumstances: I couldn't hire out on another job until the elbow was mended and I was within easy reach of the Nimpkish. The logical thing seemed to be to go there and combine business, pleasure and convalescence by catching what tyees I could and selling them.

The season started slowly. A few fish were in the river at

the end of August, but Ed and I were busy cutting a winter's wood for Mrs. Lansdowne. When the wood was all split and piled in the woodshed, we began to fish. This year we were well off for boats. We had a small power boat, a good ten-foot dinghy and a canoe, so we could cover a lot of water in searching for fish. I caught the first tyee in Lansdowne Pool on September first, a fine fish of forty pounds, and after that we picked up fish fairly regularly all the way down the river from the pool and out in the salt water as well. There was a great run of big cohos in early September of that year, so we spent quite a lot of our time on them, using the little power boat to tow the dinghy and canoe over to Race Pass or wherever the fish were feeding. Pound for pound, the cohos outfought the big tyees, and fishing for them was certainly more remunerative than fishing for the tyees because they took so freely. But after the first few days I always stayed in or near the river; in spite of the quick-jumping fight of the cohos, there was something in the solid, heavy take of the tyees and the tremendous power of their first run that I could not resist. Besides that, there was the steady hope of a fifty- or sixty-pounder and all the attraction of fishing a river instead of salt water.

It is difficult to pick out the great days of that month of fishing—almost any day that one has the luck to kill a salmon of thirty or forty pounds is a great day. But there are some days and some fish that I remember more clearly than others. There was an evening at Sachem Island, with a flooding tide and sunset light smoothing the water until it seemed as still as a lake's surface on a windless evening. I had anchored the dinghy a little below the island and about forty yards over toward the right bank of the river. I could see schools of fish finning three or four hundred yards downstream, opposite the Fishing Island, and I knew that they would soon come up to pass me; so I waited, standing in the dinghy ready to cast. In a little while the first school came on, thirty or forty big fish, each one pushing his slender, arrowhead ripple ahead of him on the face of the still water. It was very quiet, and the crash of a great fish jumping somewhere up in the bend seemed to hang over the river long after its last echoes had died away. The fish were very close now, coming steadily but slowly. I swung the spoon back, then sent it out across them; it flew well for once, cutting the air with its edge, and dropped gently ten yards beyond the school and perhaps ten yards upstream of the leaders. I could see the outlines of the big bodies under the finning ripples and the tiny flashes of the spoon as I reeled it in, held only a few inches below the surface by a half-ounce lead. The leader of the school turned toward it and began to follow it, two or three feet behind the hook. I could see him clearly, and he was very big; and muscles tightened all through my arms, making my hands clumsy on the reel. A ripple moved, fast, from the near side of the school, and something hit with a jolt that dipped the rod hard down. I struck, and the still water was heaved by thirty or forty great smooth swirls as the school turned short away. The reel ran wildly, and I checked with all the strength of my fingers until my fish jumped twice about seventy yards away. He turned then and ran hard back for the boat, bored deep down, came out again in another jump, very high and very near the boat. Ten minutes later I gaffed a thirty-five-pounder.

Twice more the same thing happened. Once the fish threw the hook when he was halfway out on his first run; the other time I gaffed another thirty-pounder. The sky was still light, and I could see the colors of trees and grass; but it was almost dusk, and the surface of the water had that clear, dark shine that makes every movement of it seem oily and slow. Another school came up and another fish took. After my strike he was still for perhaps one full second, as fish often are, then he began to take out line, jumped in the first ten yards, jumped again a moment later and kept going. Something warned me to grab for the anchor line. The fish was still running. The anchor

came free of the shallow and hung straight down in deep water. The river current and the start of the ebb carried the
dinghy down, and the fish still ran, straight out for salt water.
He jumped again, high and tumbling over, falling flat, ran a
few yards and jumped again just as high. He was big and very
silver, and I clamped down on the reel until he was towing
the dinghy. Twice he checked, and I picked up on him until
most of the line was back on the reel. But each time he ran
again and jumped in his running with all the abandon of a coho
and all the authority of his own forty-five-pound weight. I was
outside the river mouth when he came alongside at last, completely played out so that I could slip the gaff under his gill
cover and lift him into the dinghy. He was unlike any fish I
had seen in the river before, beautifully clean and with a green-
ish sheen along his back, thick and deep as a good fish should
be, yet gracefully shaped instead of hog fat as so many tyees
are. No other tyee ever fought me that way.

I remember too a leaden-gray morning when the light made
the water seem opaque and palely off-white. I was on the salt
chuck below the river mouth, halfway down to the old breakwater, when a school showed near me, and I made a quick
cast which immediately hooked a fish. He ran a few yards, and
the spoon came back. I cast again, hooked another and fought
him in frantic haste while the school kept showing near the
boat. I killed him, a thirty-three-pounder, in six minutes and
cast again as soon as he was in the boat. Another fish took, ran
and sent the spoon back. Three times that happened, then I
hooked and killed a thirty-nine-pounder. By the time he was
in the boat, I had lost the school, but they, too, were bright,
clean fish, newly arrived from the north and not yet rid of
their salt-water ways.

At dusk salmon crowd into the river channel from all their
near-by lying places. I was there one evening in late September, working the last stage of a long ebb tide. There were
schools all around me in the narrow channel, and I had already

touched several fish without hooking one of them. I made a careless cast that landed right in the middle of a school and saw the great swirls of frightened fish all around the spoon. I began to reel in disgustedly, holding the rod high to hurry the spoon. Thirty feet from the boat a fish took with a slash that broke water, jarring the rod almost to breaking. I saw a great, dark tail roll out in the swirl, let him take line and slipped the anchor. He made a heavy run, deep and strong. I made him work for line and brought him to the surface in a threshing break sixty or seventy yards away. He came in a little—or rather the tide and river drifted the boat up on him—but went away again and went down. He didn't sulk but swam strongly and heavily, and I couldn't lift him at all. Suddenly he came up fast, slashed the water with his great tail and went down again. I told myself that here was the sixty-pounder at last and I could afford to take things slowly, even if it was getting dark. When he came up near the boat, we were within a hundred yards of Green Island, drifting fast for the kelp bed. I reached for the gaff, but he was still swimming strongly three or four feet down in the water and ten or fifteen feet away from the boat. Nothing that I could do would bring him closer, and we drifted into the kelp bed that way. I thought it was all over then; the line would tangle on one of the heavy stems and give him his chance to tear away the hook. But he seemed afraid of the kelp. He turned deliberately away from two plants, tried to turn from a third and the movement let me lift him. On the surface he seemed helpless, floundering among the trailing ribbons while I floundered to bring the boat within gaffing reach. Three times I missed with the gaff, clumsily and inexcusably; then suddenly he was easy, and I had him, not sixty pounds, but forty-eight, a noble bronze color, so deep-bodied and hog-backed that for once I doubted the steelyards.

That was 1929. I missed the next two seasons, but in 1932 and 1933, Ed and I fished again. We were both of us wiser and better fishermen, and we fished carefully and thoroughly, keeping close records not only of every fish we killed but of every day we fished and every fish that moved to us at all. They were fine records, full of details of time and tide and light, of the condition of the fish, of the leads we used and the spoons, even of the angles of the casts that hooked fish—upstream, downstream or straight across. But we stored them in a house that burned down in 1934. There is less now to check my memory of those two seasons than the simple notes I kept of the earlier ones.

But we did learn certain things. We solved, in some measure, the difficulty of catching fish in Lansdowne Pool by finding that the best time in any day comes after the sun has gone behind the hill. Between that time and full darkness we were nearly always able to hook at least two fish. There were exceptions to this for which we could never properly account —September 2, 1932, was one of these. Ed went down to the pool at three-thirty in the afternoon. I followed him an hour later and found him fighting a thirty-five-pounder; he had another already in the canoe and had lost three others after short runs. Between that time and darkness we hooked and fought nine more big fish and lost at least as many more in the first or second run. The fish were almost the start of the run, and the pool was full of them. Time and again they took as the spoon hit the water. It was a No. 6 Superior, copper at first, changed to brass as the light failed, and fished with a ¾-ounce lead. At the head of the pool and just below the rapid there is a fast ripple three or four feet deep between the line of the main current and the light flow that comes in from the backwater behind the island. Holding the canoe in the backwater and dropping the spoon in the shallow ripple, we hooked fish after fish, and many times we saw the flash of their heavy bodies as they turned in striking. Ed hooked the biggest fish of the day, a forty-eight-pounder, in the main run. I knew somehow in the moment the fish took that he was heavier than the others and I drove the canoe hard to follow his run.

He jumped once, still running, turned at the tail of the pool and started back. I had turned the canoe and was holding it well over toward the west bank, but he ran straight for the foot of the rapids, jumped there and swung over into the eddy.

"That's the end of him," I said. "He'll come back to us now."

He circled and did come back, and I put the gaff where I could reach it easily. Ed tried to lift him, but he swirled his great tail once near the surface, then ran again upstream through the strongest current. It was a moment before either of us realized what was happening; then Ed said, "He's going on, straight up for the Canyon Pool."

He jumped then, right among the rocks and the broken water, thirty or forty yards up in the rapid. Then he was quiet, and we couldn't see him or tell exactly where he was because the current held the line down. I pushed the canoe up along the west side of the river to the backwater, then swung out across the foot of the rapid and picked up the pole. Ed got his drowned line up out of the water, and we could see that the fish was at least fifty yards above us and still working slowly upstream.

"Heave the daylights out of him," I said. "It's about the only chance. Pick up your line fast when he comes down through."

Ed lifted with everything the rod had. The strain turned the fish across the current so that it caught the side of his body and threw him down, but as he came back, the line still ran out.

"Round a rock," I said and pushed the canoe in tight against the foot of the rapids.

Ed jumped out and started up, stumbling and slipping on the rocks but making time; he had to find which rock was holding the line and bring the rod round it. He was almost there when I saw the fish, hanging helplessly on his side, bounced by the current waves at the head of the pool. I picked up the gaff and began to edge the canoe toward him; then Ed was round the rock, and the fish was drifting down out of reach. Ed came back, half swimming, and piled into the canoe, and I gaffed the fish for him down at the tail of the pool again.

There were no other days in the pool like that one, but we caught fish often enough in the broad-daylight hours to keep us trying. And we caught fish down below, outside the river, in the channel by the Fishing Island, off Sachem Point, in day-light and dusk, on many different stages of tide. The biggest we killed weighed 52½ pounds, which is not really big for a tyee. We saw many jumping that were much larger and, perhaps once or twice, we hooked larger ones. There was one that I hooked below Sachem Island in the first hour of a big ebb tide. He took deep down in twenty feet of water and made his first run lazily downstream. We followed him almost carelessly in the boat. Suddenly he turned into the stream and really ran, still deep, straight up the main channel. I saw the hundred-yard mark slip away on the line.

"Get after him, Ed," I said. "I can't stop him."

Ed pulled hard on the oars, but for several seconds the line was still going out; then the fish turned and came slowly downstream toward us. I held hard, trying to lift him, but he came back to the boat still two or three fathoms down. Rowing steadily, Ed was little more than holding place against tide and river. The line started out again fast, cutting the water toward the channel between Sachem Island and the Indian Island.

"He'll break this time, sure," I said. "There can't be more than five feet of water in there."

But he didn't break. He took a hundred and twenty yards plus whatever distance Ed's rowing moved the boat and came slowly back near bottom all the way.

"Gosh," I said, "if he doesn't show soon, I'll begin to think he's big."

"You aren't bearing down on him. You never let one get away with that much line before."

"I never had one wanted it so badly."

Then the third run started up the channel between the Indian Island and the bank. It went on and on, stronger and faster than either of the others, yet Ed was rowing up hard in the slack water behind the island. The hundred-yard mark flashed out again; then the reel stopped running. I knew he was off, but neither of us would believe it until we saw the spoon come back to us, wobbling its stupid flashes in the green water.

WHY FISH?

During a Zeppelin raid on London in the 1914-1918 war, my Mother and Father were walking home from the theater. My Father was a colonel then, a biggish man and solidly built. It wasn't more than five or six years since he had given up playing important amateur football. But his military dignity was rumpled and his athletic frame was tested to the full when a little Cockney private came round a corner at full speed and butted into him a fraction above the belt buckle. My Father dragged some air back into his lungs, the private picked himself up and Father asked in stern tones, "Why run?"

The Cockney hardly glanced at him. "To please myself," he said and went on his way rather faster than before.

That's a swell answer to any impertinent question. It can close almost any discussion right at the start; it is almost always rigidly truthful and it is quite complete—an adequate explanation of any type of behavior that isn't positively antisocial. But it is ungenerous, on the curt side for the present purpose.

Why fish? is a question, posed or not, that most fishing writ-

ers have the courtesy to attempt to answer in some detail.
J. W. Hills, in his *History of Fly Fishing*, says that the fashion
was set even before *The Master of Game* was written by Edward Duke of York in the early fifteenth century and has been
followed by sporting writers ever since. Dame Juliana begins
her *Treatise of Fishing with an Angle*, the earliest known fishing book in the English language, with a comparison of angling
with hunting, hawking and fowling, by no means to the advantage of these latter sports. She writes, as have a thousand
angling writers since her time, of "the swete savoure of the
meade floures, the melodyous armony of fowles" that delight
the angler at his sport. "He seeth the yonge swannes: heerons:
duckes: cotes and many other foules wyth theyr brodes . . .
Surely thenne is there noo man merier than he is in his
spyryte." And she concludes with a sketch of the good angler,
implying that the influences of his sport are directly responsible
for his high virtues. And it seems highly significant that
Juliana's good angler possesses all the gentle virtues of Walton's Piscator; Juliana's man is a generalization, his picture
growing rather from cautionary words as to decent behavior
for all anglers than from direct description, and he does not
speak; but had he spoken, it would have been with the soft,
patient yet merry voice of Walton and in his wise, tolerant,
Christian words.

It is an amiable custom, this quiet justification of a sport that
harms no man and needs no justification. It grows, I suspect,
from the ribald comment that surely followed the angler on
his way to his sport in other days, the evasion of which Juliana
no doubt had in mind when she described the building of a
rod with a hollow butt in which the other two pieces could be
carried: "And thus shall ye make you a rodde soo privy that
ye maye walke therwyth: and there shall noo man wyte where
abowte ye goo." It argues a fine sense of responsibility in
anglers toward their fellow men that the fishing writers have
taken such unintelligent criticism seriously enough to answer

it in tolerant words and noble phrases. They say in effect: we spend much of our time in our sport, and our brother man has a right to ask accounting for it, what gain or benefit we find in it, material or spiritual, for ourselves and the rest of mankind.

I have found in fishing all the sweetness of the meadows that pleased Juliana, and pleasure in the sight and sound of all her birds too. Born at the end, instead of the beginning, of five centuries of progressively intense research into the ways and lives of fish and other water creatures, I have been able to understand more clearly and perhaps enjoy more keenly things that happen within rivers as well as about them. I have learned a love of wilder scenery and swifter, more broken rivers than she knew, though I have loved, too, the very ones she fished and loved. I can find, as I know she could, more rest and relaxation, more stimulation for the mind, in an hour of wading a stream than in a full day of any other activity.

I do not fish, as I understand some people do, for fresh air and exercise; no doubt I pick up a share of both when I go fishing, but they are unearned increment—I am not really looking for them. I do not fish for fish to eat; having to eat fish is one of the penalties of having been out fishing and with this penalty in mind I probably fish a little less often and less painstakingly than I otherwise would. I do fish to catch fish—at least, that is an idea not too far in the back of my mind while I am fishing; but I have fished through fishless days that I remember happily and without regret. I want fish from fishing, but I want a great deal more than that, and getting it is not always dependent upon catching fish.

All this brings us back to the original answer—I fish to please myself. And I am pleased, not by one thing but by many things, often unexpected things, that grow out of the sport. I am pleased and interested and held by the problems that grow from it: the problem, for instance, of matching silk and feathers and tinsel to a natural insect or some other creature that reaches

September

a trout's fancy; the problem of how to wade a piece of bad
water with reasonable comfort and safety and so get my fly
to what lies beyond it; the problem of how to bring a fly
through a stretch of uneven current with a motion and speed
of my own choosing; or the endless problems presented by the
movements and feeding caprices of the fish I am concerned
with.

I have found strong and deep pleasure in fishing alone
through a whole day, and I have found richer pleasure in fishing with friends who, whatever their skill, give the sport its
proper measure of quiet concentration and effort. I have even
found pleasure, as have all hunters and fishers and hawkers and
fowlers since the beginning of time, in food and drink at the
end of a day or during a day, pleasure keener and better by far
for the fact that I had been out on the river. Walton writes
of "a good, honest, wholesome, hungry breakfast" on a fishing
day. Cotton, who dallies little over his meals, follows his
"Father Walton" in remembering always to have a meal ready
at the right time and place, and whenever discourse grows long
in the little Fishing-house by Dove, glass and pipe are handy
for relaxation. Of all eating and drinking connected with fishing I remember best the suppers that we came home to after
the evening rise at Wrackleford. They were simple enough—
good Dorset ale in plenty; a salad of lettuce and tomatoes that
one made and dressed oneself with olive oil and vinegar; crisp,
well-flavored celery from the garden, where it grew in banked
rows like steeplechase fences; white bread and golden Jersey
butter with all the richness of the meadows we had walked
in our fishing; and blue vinny cheese. There is no other cheese
to equal blue vinny at a time like that. Stilton is noble, but rich
and clinging for such a late meal; Cheddar is a grand cheese,
mellow and clean and full of flavor. But the Dorset cheese puts
no restraint on the appetite, because it is made from skim milk,
with no soft richness in it; yet the flavor is full and smooth and
satisfying, with a slight dryness that reminds one suitably often

that a glass is waiting to be refilled. After cheese and salad, perhaps a great ripe peach, fresh from the greenhouse, or a bunch of black grapes, Madresfield Court for preference, and currant cake to go with them.

Cheese and beer and the fruits of summer and fall fit naturally into any picture of fishing days. But a winter fisherman has other delights as good: after a January day of hard wading, good Irish whiskey, sparkling by artificial light, and a fire of alder wood or maple leaping up the chimney; five or six hours to talk and a dinner of roast beef or roast saddle of venison somewhere in them, the inward warmth spreading slowly out to meet the surface warmth already built by a bath and the fire.

All these things—fish caught, problems solved, the sights and scents and sounds of woods or meadows, the quiet ease of companionship, good food on a sharpened hunger, comfortable warmth built from cold and a measure of discomfort—are satisfactions. Some are physical, some mental, some, no doubt, spiritual. I count myself lucky that I am a fly-fisherman, because a fly-fisherman has all these things in full measure and in addition he has an active, moving sport. Friends who do not fish ask me where I find the patience for fishing. The answer is that I have none and in fly-fishing none is needed. Waiting around is seldom a productive occupation for a fly-fisherman; if he wants to catch fish, the best thing he can do is keep his fly on or in the water and keep it working for him. Unlike the worm or the bait, dead or alive, of the still-fisherman, a fly will not do much good work by itself. And the business of getting it out where the fish are, of bringing it over them properly, is at least as intense and satisfying as actually hooking and playing fish. If one is fishing in the light of acquired knowledge, with a definite plan in mind, a theory to test or retest—as one should be—there is never a moment when mind and body, eyes and hands are not fully occupied.

Many writers make fly-fishing seem a very difficult and complicated art. Fly-fishing is an art, certainly, which means that it is infinitely flexible in scope; a master of the art attains skill and beauty in performance, subtlety and wisdom of conception, that are both difficult and complicated. But a reasonable proficiency is enough to give the strongest measures of pleasure and satisfaction, and a reasonable proficiency is not in the least hard to attain.

A reasonably proficient fly-fisherman inevitably wants to improve and almost as inevitably does improve as time goes on. He probably does not become a master of the art, but he probably does become a good fisherman. I often wonder about the masters anyway, whether or no they really exist outside books. In a book it is very easy to seem like a master if one writes chiefly of the days that worked out right and the casts that caught fish, and one is likely to do so because the other days and other casts are not generally so interesting. But I have known and watched quite a few really good fly-fishermen, one or two of whom probably are as good as the masters, and I never yet saw one that couldn't get himself into some fancy troubles on occasion.

It is interesting to think about what makes a good fisherman, and any answer to the question should go a long way toward answering the other question of why people fish. I am tempted to make the answer very simple and say that a fisherman is good in proportion to the satisfaction he gets out of his sport. This is obviously a sound answer because it puts Walton and Cotton at once where they belong—right at the top of the tree. It also means that a merry duffer is better than a dour master, and I suspect that is a good point too.

A fisherman is not a professional athlete, to be judged by results only. Walton quotes to his Scholar:

I once heard one say, "I envy not him that eats better meat than I do, nor him that is richer, or that wears better clothes than I do: I envy nobody but him, and him only, that catches more fish than I do." And such a man is likely to prove an Angler; and this noble emulation I wish to you and all young Anglers.

This is distilled wisdom; the words are not Walton's own and he does not fully adopt them; "such a man," he says cautiously, "is likely to prove an Angler." Walton himself had no such competitive envy in his make-up, but he recognizes that a good strong desire to catch fish is a necessary part of a successful fisherman, and so he recommends "emulation" to his Scholar, first qualifying it by the word "noble." A strongly competitive fisherman is a curse to himself and others, but no man can do a good job of fishing unless he really means and expects to catch fish.

A man's quality as a fisherman cannot be measured by the distance he can cast, by the lightness and accuracy with which his fly falls on the water, by his style or even by his knowledge. All these things are part of a really good fisherman, but a fisherman can be very good without excelling in any one of them. Returning to satisfaction achieved as the true measure of a good fisherman, examine the points one by one. Casting a long line, when necessary, is a very satisfying performance; a truly accurate and delicate cast is an achievement in itself, whether or not the fish comes up to crown it. Style, in fishing as in all else, means ease and grace of performance, and there is intense satisfaction in the easy and graceful handling of anything from a manure shovel to an artist's brush. But knowledge, knowledge is the base of true appreciation and so, necessarily, of true satisfaction.

A fly-fisherman's knowledge is compounded of many things. It grows out of imagination, curiosity, bold experiment and intense observation. A fly-fisherman must always be picturing to himself what is going on under the water; he must try to understand what his fly means to the fish and so he must choose it or tie it with meaning, he must try to make it move in or on the water with meaning. He must look for new ideas, try them out when they come to him and watch closely to see their effect and find others.

A mark of all the best fishermen I have known has been

power of concentration, and this, perhaps, is the most important single quality a fisherman can have. This does not mean that fishing must become a strain. I like nothing better than to tempt fate by slinging my rod under my arm with a full line out while I take time to watch some ducks circle or to fill a pipe and light it. But it does mean that every cast should have an idea behind it and should be fished out to the end with the expectation of catching a fish. The men who do this are those who have a close knowledge of fish and water, who know where a fish is likely to be lying, how he will be feeding, what the current will do to the fly, and, not least, who realize that their knowledge is imperfect and that the unexpected can happen. All this knowledge will force concentration on a man almost in spite of himself.

To take proper advantage of his opportunities, a fly-fisherman needs reasonably quick and sure reactions and fair control over his emotions,—many a fish has sampled an artificial fly with impunity because the fisherman was slow to respond to the sight or feel of the rise, and many another has gone off with the fly in his jaws because of a jumpy strike. On this purely physical side of things, a fisherman may sometimes need endurance,—a long day in cold water can test it—and perhaps even courage, for bold wading and climbing often enough put a fly in a place it would not otherwise have reached.

Lastly, there is an intellectual qualification: a knowledge of the traditions and orthodoxy of the sport. There is plenty of enjoyment in fishing without it, but no sport has a longer or closer tradition than has fly-fishing, and it seems a pity not to use it: a pity not to know, for instance, that Dame Juliana tied her flies on hooks as small as 11 or 12 in the fifteenth century and that Cotton fished a single horsehair on occasion, in place of our 4X gut; that Juliana's flies, planned as imitations of natural insects, have come down to us through the centuries with changes of material rather than of intention. Orthodoxy, of itself, has no special merit, but it is a good point of departure, since most fishermen like to develop their own new ways, and most of them like to have a standard for comparing their own accomplishments with those of other fishermen in other times and places. A knowledge of the sport's orthodoxy gives a base for this.

Perhaps such a list of skills and virtues may sound a formidable burden for a man to carry down to the river with him when he wants nothing more than a quiet day's sport. But we are civilized men, not merely fishers for meat. Our tradition is that of the first man who sneaked away to the creek when the tribe did not really need fish, a tradition developed for us through thousands of years and millions of river lovers. We fish for pleasure, and fishing becomes pleasure from within ourselves in proportion to the skill and knowledge, to the imagination and flexibility of soul that we bring to it. Like the hunter, the hawker and the fowler, the fisherman takes life in finding his pleasure. It is reasonable to ask of him that he make it as keen and thorough and satisfying, as productive of growth in himself as he reasonably can. For only then can it be the strong and sensitive pleasure of a civilized man.

OCTOBER

I~N~ October it is more difficult to forget the gun and remember the rod. In September there are only blue grouse, slow starters and so numerous that one holds the dogs back from a broken covey for fear the day may end right there in a limit. It is pleasant on the rocky hills in the heat, with the dogs working low salal brush and big birds thundering out. Occasionally a bird flushed high on the slope above comes past on set wings at his full speed, and it is a great shot to make or to miss. Always there is the smooth eager questing of the dogs until one comes at last to a creek and they wallow in it, cooling heated bellies, panting, restoring the sure keenness of their noses.

But October has the little ruffed grouse, live red-brown among the fallen maple leaves, a crafty woodsman when he is on the ground, leaping instantly into full flight when flushed, turning and twisting among the trees that are almost sure to be all about. For nearly ten seasons now I have hunted ruffed grouse over black Labradors, and they do the work beautifully, working close in and thoroughly, never tiring, steady to shot and wing. One dog I had (and lost at four years old) wanted to point his birds, but I broke him of that because the work is in such thick country that it is too easy to lose a dog who is really stanch. He worked out his own compromise; when he found birds, his body would come to a perfect point, tense, with legs and tail as they should be, his head turned back to watch me. When I had moved into a position that satisfied him, but never before, he would go in and flush, then drop to wing.

This was Southern Pine of Elwha, whom we called Souse, as great on the bench as he was in the field. He loved the ruffed grouse even as I do; but when I went out with a rod instead of the gun, we could kick them up from under our feet and he would not even turn to look at them. When we came to the river, he would stand beside me if the water was shallow or sit on the bank as near to my wading as he could get, ears cocked, legs trembling a little. His eyes would follow the line of every cast, watching the drift of a dry fly or the sweep of a wet fly as closely as I did. If I moved my rod point sharply, he would press forward, his whole body trembling; if a fish jumped free in the river, he would look from the splash to the rod top and back again in puzzled surprise to the splash.

And whenever I hooked a fish, he whined a little and followed
every move of the fight until the fish was beaten and I sent
him in to retrieve, which he always did faultlessly, bringing
the fish to hand without a mark on it to show how he had
held anything so awkward and slippery. He retrieved hundreds
of fish for me, fish of all weights up to ten or twelve pounds,
and I never lost one through him. "How did you teach him?"
people used to ask me. I didn't teach him; he knew, just as he
knew when we were hunting, because he was a dog in a thousand, a dog that had puzzled out for himself the meaning of
the business in hand. If I walked through a willow or poplar
swale, gun in hand, and he flushed a grouse, I would kill and
he would retrieve. If we went up the river with a rod, he knew
that I would wade out and cast and after a while hook a fish;
I wanted the fish or I wouldn't have bothered to work for it,
so it was natural that he should go out to retrieve at the right
command.

The dogs I have now are not as good. Nellie, Souse's kennel
mate, is getting old. Lancer, Souse's successor, is still quick and
excitable, though he seldom breaks shotgun range, and we get
plenty of birds. When I change from the Labs to a setter or a
pointer who will let me flush the birds myself, I shall know
I am getting old. Keeping up with Lancer through a good
warm day in the swamps and brush is no work for a cripple.

Perhaps it is wrong to write of dogs and grouse in a fishing
book, but one is never very far from fish in the ruffed-grouse
season. Ruffed grouse like the low places, the swamps and the
creek beds. In a normal season, when there has been a good
rain early in the month, the creek-loving cohos are nosing up
over the beaver dams in the shade of the willows and alders.
It is strange to see them there, such big fish in such tiny pools,
often shouldering their backs right out of water on the shallows. Some of the males are red and hook-nosed already, and
occasionally, if one comes quietly from downstream, one sees
male and female side by side over the pale gravel and perhaps

two or three grilse, two-year-old males precociously ripe, waiting below them.

The activity of the creeks is only in proportion to their size. In all the streams and little rivers and in many of the lakes there are spawning salmon in October; and the big rivers carry their own tremendous runs, becoming tributary to their own tributary streams. In the Fraser the sockeye salmon pass through Hell's Gate and turn into the South Thompson to Shuswap in runs that have once or twice in recent years seemed large again; in the Columbia watershed, half a million Chinooks are about their spawning; some are already spawned out and dead or dying. So it it from California to Alaska, rivers filled with salmon while nests are dug and billions of eggs are buried deep in the gravel.

Here in the Campbell tyees are spawning, and one sees them easily. Sometimes a great fish, still thick and powerful but dull dark brown even to his belly, jumps startlingly close from heaviest white water, plunges back and jumps again. Out in the October rain he seems a strange creature, half ghost, half monster; the loss of all his silver brightness makes him seem scaleless, and his tattered fins give him a shaggy, unreal look that is utterly different from the clear-cut picture his jump would have left on the mind's eye a short six weeks earlier. The humpbacks, what is left of them, will have chosen their redds in the Canyon Pool or the Island Pool; some will have turned off at the Quinsam, and a few may seek out Coal Creek, pathetic survivors, these, of a run that crowded the creek a few years ago. Far up the Quinsam the cohos will pass under the high, fire-blackened logging trestle while the dogs and I sit there to watch them and their attendant cutthroats.

In the Nimpkish, freshet will have taken the tyees on in their longer journey, through Nimpkish Lake, up the Klaanche River until they turn, just short of the falls, to Woss Lake, and find spawning with the sockeyes on the broad gravel shallows. Hustan River and Willow Creek will have their spawning sockeyes, and the earliest cohos will have come into the Kilipi.

There is not much for the trout fisherman in October. It is not a trout month. True, there are trout in the rivers, trout in their hundreds, following the salmon and picking up rare eggs that escape from the nests or are shed from the bodies of the female salmon by their exertions of digging or swimming against the current. One can catch trout then by tying a fly more or less to the color and shape of a salmon egg and sending it down to them in a slow, deep, rolling drift; but there is little in this of the real joys of fly-fishing, the planning and under-standing and matching and figuring that one can put into a summer day's fishing. It is better to admit the attractions of the ruffed grouse and take the dogs and follow him.

Yet to put the rods away in October would be to miss much that is good. Salmon are still moving in from salt water; cohos are still taking the fly off the mouth of the Nimpkish, taking it well in Cowichan Bay, taking it even off the mouth of the Campbell in a dry year.

Salt-water coho fishing is good fun. One uses a big fly, usually of dyed polar-bear fur, tied on a 2/0 hook but tied to about twice the length of the hook so that it wets down into the long, slender shape of a launce fish. Much of the fishing is trolling, and a serious fisherman takes two rods and a guide to row him steadily about among the fish. When fish are taking well, that is exciting enough; great waves surge up behind the flies, there is a bulging swirl and the first reel runs, then another and both rods have fish. That is a double-header, a lively piece of business because a good fall coho thinks nothing of tearing off a hundred yards of line and throwing in three or four beau-tiful jumps with his run. But it is taking the fishing too seri-ously. It is better to have two fishermen to a boat, each with a rod, and several boats in a party, each with two fishermen. Let there be fisherwomen as well as fishermen, the two sexes about equally mixed, and a good lunch aboard the boats, not too dry a lunch, the wet part of it available at all times. Double-headers under these conditions are really something, and the quieter moments, when the fish are not taking freely, pass quickly and cheerfully.

It is still possible, even in the busy places like Cowichan Bay and Campbell River, to find occasionally cohos feeding so well and so near the surface that casting for them is a paying proposition. It is best to be alone then or with a good guide at the oars and to use just one rod. Fish slash the surface with their feeding, gulls hover and scream, whole schools of launce fish jump out ahead of the smooth, swift feeding waves. Sometimes a cast into the movement brings an instant pull, and the reel sings and sings through the length of that glorious first run. More often the cohos are moving fast, intent upon their launce fish, and it is hard to get their attention with bear fur on a hook, even bright, lustrous, polar-bear fur dyed many beautiful colors. You cast and cast, dropping the fly among the leaping launce fish or just beyond them, drawing it back in highest hope; the launce fish are all alive, quick and vigorous, full of escape—surely the stumbling, halting thing that is your fly trying to look like one of them will seem to the fish an easier prize and one more worth pursuit if only for its difference. Then suddenly you see that wave behind the fly. You keep it coming, praying for the take and the pull. If you have a guide, he can keep the boat moving until the fish makes up his mind to take the fly or turn away. You can try tricks then, paying out line to let the fly fall back to him, jerking it ahead to make him more eager, you hope; but if you do and he turns away, you'll curse your tricks, and if you don't and he turns away, you'll wish you had tried tricks. Perhaps it is better to be alone; then you bring in line, and the wave follows and follows, perhaps ending in the boil and the pull that you want or ending within two or three feet of the boat as a frightened fish sheers off to chase launce fish again instead of bear fur. And you cast again, angrily, and the pull comes instantly this time, from unbroken water.

The late cohos are the biggest because cohos grow right through the summer from their blueback stage almost until they enter the rivers. A big male of eighteen or twenty pounds, even if his sides are a little red and his nose is a little hooked, is a fine bold creature to deal with if your only means of persuasion is a singlehanded fly rod. Ungratefully, I sometimes regret that in British Columbia we have no fish like the grayling or the pike to take over when the trout season is finished. But the cohos carry fishing over until the end of October, and in December it is time to think of steelhead again. Even in November you can catch cutthroat trout in tidal waters if you have the heart for it; the game laws allow it and the fish are there. The Pacific coast is generous to anglers, perhaps too generous, but at least this generosity demands of them that they see and know the waters in all their moods and all their months.

FIRST FALL FRESHET

I HAVE written a little of the orthodox forms of fly-fishing for cohos at the more popular places—off Campbell River and in Cowichan Bay. But the coho is the most obliging of Pacific salmon from the angler's point of view; none of the others feeds so recklessly or keeps feeding so late in the spawning migration, and none of them puts up such a swift and intensely spectacular fight when hooked. There are many opportunities for catching cohos and almost as many methods of fishing for them.

My first chance of catching cohos came in 1927. I was shooting ducks one day in October along the shore of Johnstone

Strait just south of the mouth of the Nimpkish when I noticed salmon swimming and occasionally jumping in the shallow water of the tide flats. I came round the point from Smith Cove to the mouth of Theimar Creek and found more fish, some of them jumping at the falls. As the tide flooded, fish began to slip over the falls in considerable number, and I realized that the creek, for all its small size, must have a fairly important run of cohos. The next Sunday I was down there with a rod, and after trying for a long while, I hooked one fish, a very red and very vicious old cock who took hold of a small silver doctor and very nearly broke the trout rod I had no right to be fishing with.

I had meant to take two full weeks out of September in 1928 to work on the Nimpkish tyees; but the crew I was working with needed me, and I did not get away until October. And by that time the tyees had felt the draw of the first freshet and traveled far beyond my reach. I meant to give my holiday to ducks and grouse, and to some extent I did so; but I remembered the old red cock at Theimar Creek, and it wasn't long before Ed and I found cohos on the tide flats again. We began to carry a rod with us, as well as the shotguns.

At first we caught only grilse, precocious males that weighed between one and two pounds but were invariably bright silver and full of fight. Then, one evening, as we were passing between the Fishing Island and the shore in the canoe on our way home from duck shooting, I cast a devon minnow into a school of fish and hooked another old red cock. He wasn't such a very dark fish and he was in beautiful shape, but I felt a little discouraged because it seemed that only an occasional red male, in his spawning anger, would slash at what we had to offer.

Three or four days later we discarded that theory. It was a dull day, too calm for ducks and with a slow tide flooding over the flats through the whole afternoon. We were near an old deserted logging camp, halfway between the mouth of the Nimpkish and Theimar Falls. Hair seals were hunting salmon two or three hundred yards offshore, and many schools of fish showed in the smooth water over the flats. "We may as well go out and try for them," I told Ed. "We can't do any worse than we're doing here."

The first school I cast to gave us a fish at the second or third try, a beautiful fourteen-pound female, perfectly shaped and perfectly silver. A few casts later we caught her mate, an eighteen-pound male, as beautiful as she was and as little marked by spawning color or shape. After that we seemed to lose this lot, but it must have been a freshly arrived school, just turning in toward the creek.

During the afternoon we found many other schools and hooked many other fish—fish not so bright as those first two, which had the fresh clean gloss of deep salt water still on them, but clean and good fish and strong fighters. All this we did with a three-inch blue and silver devon minnow, and we went home happily at dark with a canoe load of fish for Mrs. Lansdowne to salt down for the winter.

During the rest of the month we caught a hundred or more fine cohos, nearly all of them along the flats near Theimar Falls, and hooked and lost many others. In the shallow water it was very fine fishing because we could watch the movements of the schools easily and often pick individual fish and try to draw them; but it was not always easy. Often we would fish hard for hours, covering schools at almost every cast, and catch nothing at all, though fish after fish would lightly touch the minnow; then we would hook one, or perhaps half a dozen in quick succession, and decide we had learned something, only to have the same thing happen again the next day.

The blue and silver minnow gave us all our best fishing, though we caught fish on other minnows, on phantoms, wagtails, small plugs, spoons and spinners of all kinds. Unfortunately we knew nothing then of bucktail or polar-bear-hair flies, but I often used regular full-dressed English and Scottish salmon flies and caught several fish with them.

A River Never Sleeps

We noticed that year that we could seldom catch a coho
in or near the Nimpkish, though plenty of fish were running.
We didn't worry much because the Theimar Creek fishing was
so good. But in other years, when the Theimar run had been
seriously reduced by illegal purse seining, I worked hard on
the Nimpkish cohos. There was one year in particular when a
huge run came to the river and thousands of fish passed
straight in almost daily from the north. They cut in rather
sharply from Johnstone Strait, across the shallow point above
the river and into the channel, where they worked slowly up
toward the Blue Clay Pool. I fished for them a great deal because there was little else around, but I rarely hooked one. I
remember catching three or four in Lansdowne Pool, another
opposite Sachem Island and another near the point of the Fishing Island, but that was about all.

The problem bothered me so much that I made up my mind
to work at it. I went down in the boat one day and anchored
in the channel, opposite the Fishing Island. There were fish
everywhere in the water, passing under the boat, along either
side of it, all across the deep part of the channel and in the
shoal water near the north bank of the river. I had brought
with me every variety of minnow and spoon and spinner and
fly I possessed and I laid them all out on the seat of the boat
and began to fish. I gave each lure a fair trial, casting it and
fishing it until I was sure that not one but a hundred fish had
seen it, and I kept that up all day long. At dark I had two fish,
one hooked on a small silver minnow, the other on a trout fly,
a No. 6 parmachene belle.

The next day I went down to Theimar Creek, found a single
school there and hooked two fish in two successive casts.

I can think now of a few more things I should have liked to
try on the Nimpkish fish—better flies, especially—but I have
never been able to account for the difference between the two
runs in any satisfactory way at all; Theimar Creek and the
Nimpkish River are not more than a mile apart, the fish are

284

exactly the same species, of exactly the same age and at the same stage of maturity, and the water is almost the same. Something a little like it happens in the Campbell. In some years, when there is a good coho run, one may go up the river to try for an October trout, and every cast of the fly will hook a coho. In another year, with an equally good run of cohos in the river, one may go up especially to try for them and catch nothing at all or perhaps one or two fish with great difficulty.

But in spite of such uncertainties, I would rather catch cohos in the Campbell—right in the fresh-water pools of the river, not in the estuary or out off the mouth—during October than in any other place or at any other time that I know. I watch eagerly for the first good spell of rain and southeast gale to bring the river up in a good rise, two feet or more above its summer level, in late September or early October. Then, generally with Reg, I go up to the Sandy Pool. Reg takes his minnow rod and I take a fly rod and we really want fish, cohos and coho grilse, to smoke and put away for the early part of the winter. In a good year we have all we want in an hour or two. In a bad year Reg gets discouraged after a little while and leaves me to do what I can with my fly. Toward dark I come up out of the tail of the pool and go on home myself, usually with one or two fish, which is always enough to get Reg out again the next day.

Fishing on one's own two feet instead of from a boat and hooking them on the fly in a good strong river current gives the cohos a chance to show what they can really do. And even when they are dark and full of spawn, the fight they put up is in no way inferior to the best fight of a steelhead; a run of a hundred yards, with half a dozen great, free jumps, is not at all unusual. And the fish are not always dark. I have caught October fish in the Sandy Pool as bright as any I ever caught in salt water, with sea lice still clinging to them and launce fish only partly digested in their stomachs.

In 1942, the last wartime season I was within reach of the

Campbell, I went out on the river not more than half a dozen times. But September had been a good month; I had finished a book early in the month, and through the rest of it I had smoothed out a mass of civil defense problems, done a good deal of long-promised carpentering about the house, planned a new book and settled some worrying cases in court. I knew I had a day's fishing coming.

The river had been high for a week or more, so high that we had seen the children's bear twice. We call him the children's bear, because the children always see him first, and for that reason they love him with all the pride of possession. Valerie saw him the very first time, three or four years ago now, one evening in September when we were all eating supper on the porch. He wasn't such a big bear then, but he was big enough and very black and he was already fond of fish, because he was walking carefully along the rocks and logs of the river bank, examining every little pool, though he must have known his chances weren't very good because there was nothing in the river but the earliest humpbacks and perhaps a few tyees, all of them strong and vigorous and devoted to water that gives bears little chance. Mary saw him first in 1942, also at evening time. Mary was four years old and had cried quite bitterly only the week before when she had seen, all on her own, a fine big buck swimming the river. Now she was wide-eyed and breathless, and I could see that her heart was beating very fast, but she knew it was a bear and she was proud and pleased that she had seen him first.

We all went down as close as we could get to our own bank of the river and watched him. He was a very big bear, with a beautiful black coat, long and shaggy, and he moved with all the liquid grace bears have. He was looking for fish and not finding them because the river was too high. We saw him look hard down into the water, peering down with his head thrust forward over the surface, then lift his forepaws and swing smoothly and softly away. He raised his head on stretched

neck, lowered it again and thrust it forward. He lifted his forepaws again briefly, lowered them again and slid on in his slow
soft walking, head, shoulders, short back and long legs all sliding on the soft padding of black paws. He went down almost to
the highway bridge, deeply concerned with his own interests,
lost in the deliberateness of his search, yet calm and thorough.
He came back a little way and then turned up into the bush,
and we saw him only in the agitation of the little alders and
maples and firs.

I went up the river next morning. It was a day of moderate
storm, windy but with little rain. The river raced by, strangely
dark and swift after the sparkling, broken current of summer;
there were dead leaves in it now and other little, scarcely
seen debris that dimmed the outlines of the round rocks on
the bottom. The maples were green-gold, not yet really golden,
but it was fall all right—almost winter.

I went in at the head of the pool, and the river seemed
strange to me; it was so long since I had fished it. I felt myself
wondering whether I had started in high enough, whether I
had missed the cast that leads almost out of the rapid into
the slow water that tapers into the eddy. I was fishing Preston
Jennings's Lord Iris, the fly I had lazily or hurriedly left on
a heavy leader after my last day's steelhead fishing back in
February; but no fish took me under the foot of the rapids,
where they often do. I told myself that was natural enough;
it wasn't a good coho year, and there weren't nearly so many
fish in the river as usual. But it added to the feeling that I had
lost touch with the river, that I wasn't working it right and
it wouldn't work for me.

Then I realized that the river was very much higher than
usual, high and difficult, and that whether the fish were there
or not, I should be lucky to get one. I felt more comfortable
and worked well out until the water was over the belt loops of
my waders and I could reach the fly into any part of the swift
water. But I fished down past the spruce tree and past the wil-

low bush at the end of the sand beach and found nothing at all. From there on alders and willows grow thickly down to the water's edge, and one has to roll cast, still reaching across the eddy to the edge of the current on the far side. I hooked a grilse and lost him almost at once—too large a fly. Then nothing again until I was almost down to the little spruce just above the rocks. That wasn't so strange; I always fish that reach faithfully and honestly because it looks good, but I haven't moved half a dozen fish there in my life. Something else hit the fly opposite the little spruce, and I had time to see he was a golden cutthroat of three or four pounds before the hook came away.

I promised myself a fish below the rocks—perhaps two or three. It is a good place for fish to lie on during high river, half protected but with good, broken current drawing over it and several holes that are a little deeper than the general level of the river bed. Cohos always lie there and steelhead generally do not, for some strange reason. But my first coho took in a steelhead lie, well above the rocks, two or three casts below the cutthroat. He took line as he wanted, and I didn't see him at all until he was right out in the leaping current opposite the big rocks; then he jumped twice, just to show me he was a good fish, and kept going. I followed as fast as I could in water that was always within three or four inches of the tops of my waders, over an uneven bottom of round rocks that were always pushing my feet over into some place that threatened to have just the necessary extra depth to fill the waders. I came to the rocks still dry and still with the fish on. Then I really fought him; only the tip of the largest rock was showing above water, but the current was fairly slack below them, and anyway I wasn't going on down to disturb the good water below. The fish checked with sixty or seventy yards of line out and came slowly back against the current. He ran again when he was opposite me, straight across, and jumped four or five times in the run. But I held him then and brought him into the shelter

of the rocks a few minutes later; it made me feel right with the river and myself again.

It was hard going below the rocks, but I killed another fish of ten or twelve pounds about halfway down, then fished through and came out at the boat landing without another touch. Lancer was waiting for me there, a little bored with fishing in the grouse season, but he wagged his tail contentedly enough and flopped down in the sand as I began to clean the fish. Then suddenly he was on his feet again, neck hairs standing straight up, ears pricked, eyes glaring across the river, an angry growl churning deep in his throat. I looked across and the bear was there, far out on a raft of logs and drift, looking into the water. Lancer barked once, sharply, and the bear looked up. He peered across at us with his little eyes, lifted his nose and tried to find us on the wind, swayed his big head from side to side and looked down into the river again. I felt sorry for him—we had fish and he hadn't. I left one of the fish uncleaned and sat down to watch him. He looked sad and lonely and defeated, the more so because he was so big. I was grateful to him for being the children's bear and hoped he would find the body of a dead tyee under the drift.

But the bear found nothing, and Lancer and I watched him turn away and go on down the far bank, looking under every log, behind every rock and grassy point. Lancer wanted to swim across and run him, but I scolded him back to heel, and we followed the bear down. He hunted as methodically and carefully as he had the night before and found nothing at all. About halfway between the tail of the pool and the house he turned up and went over the hill. Lancer and I went home and left the cleaned fish there, then we took the other one around by the highway bridge, packed it up along the opposite bank and dumped it a few feet from the edge of the water. It wasn't right that the children's bear shouldn't have a fish.

TOP, BOTTOM AND MIDDLE

CHARLES COTTON, the true father of fly-fishing, told his friend and pupil Viator: "I shall divide Angling for Trout or Grayling, into these three ways: At the Top; at the Bottom; and in the Middle. . . . That which we call Angling at the Top, is with a fly: at the Bottom, with a ground-bait; in the Middle, with a minnow, or ground-bait."

A fully competent fly-fisher of the present day would say the same thing, but with this difference: the fly can be used profitably at all three depths, top, bottom and middle. This difference is due to several important developments since Cotton's time—to greater knowledge of entomology, improved technique in the making of flies, increased knowledge of the ways of fish and mechanically new methods of controlling a fly in the water. It means that the fly-fisherman is now a complete fisher, able to catch fish in any weather or at any season, able to deal with any mood or vagary of the fish, able, as a matter of fact, to catch many species of fish besides trout and salmon and grayling without resorting, as Viator puts it, to ways of fishing that are "not so easy, not so cleanly, nor as 'tis said, so genteel."

Cotton subdivides his three main headings. He says, for instance: "Angling at the Top is of two sorts: with a quick-fly or with an artificial-fly." In terms of today that means dapping with a live fly on the hook or fishing an artificial fly, usually downstream and usually wet. Dapping is a method not much used nowadays on English streams, and I have never seen it used on the North American continent, unless fishing with a live grasshopper be reckoned dapping. But Cotton's subdivisions are important and have their modern counterparts in dry-fly fishing, nymph fishing and greased-line fishing—not exact counterparts by any means, but interestingly comparable. If the early fly-fishers were, as most authorities argue, primarily and almost exclusively wet-fly fishers, then dapping with the natural fly is surely the forerunner of dry-fly fishing.

Personally, I am not altogether sure that the arguments of the authorities are quite sound on this point. They usually argue (1) that early fly-fishers did not waterproof their flies with oil or other floatant and did not dry them between casts by false casting; (2) that the early fly-fishers always, or nearly always, fished downstream, and this, the authorities say, precludes the possibility of their having fished dry because drag would instantly occur and scare every fish in sight. I am fully prepared to concede that all fly-fishers, from Dame Juliana in the fifteenth century up to but not including George Pulman in the nineteenth, did usually fish their flies wet and sunk. But I suspect they caught many fish on dry flies. Most trout flies, unless wetted before use, will float through two or three casts. And it is not impossible to fish a dry fly downstream. One does not normally fish that way on a chalk stream, partly because of drag and partly because one's own offensive motions are too obvious; but I have caught quite a few difficult chalk-stream trout by making a cast downstream with a slack line and floating the fly over them before the line could tighten and produce drag. And here in the rough water of western streams, where drag does not matter so much, the dry fly fished down is often one of the deadliest methods. What I feel is that the early fly-fisher would often, in making his first few casts with a new fly, find his fly floating. Then, having a long rod and a light line which he always held well up, he would be likely to walk down a little with his fly, thus delaying drag, or even let the wind (he fished with it always behind him) belly his line, lift his fly and drop it again in the most natural way imaginable. On a day of upstream wind he could cover fish with their tails toward him, as the modern dry-fly fisherman does, and must often have let his fly drift back over a rise.

It seems certain that something of this sort must have happened quite often even to anglers who had no other idea than to fish wet, and it must have happened at least occasionally in such a way that the fly was presented perfectly to the trout and was taken firmly and well. From there it is a simple step to suppose that many anglers consciously took advantage of the floating qualities of a new fly for as long as these lasted; and in doing so they were undoubtedly laying the foundations of the dry-fly art which Pulman was the first to reveal in writing.

Pulman wrote first in 1841 and completed his contribution in 1851. Forty years later Halford was writing and dry-fly fishing was coming into the full flower of its development. Dry-fly fishing became an extremely effective method on many of the richest streams in England; it became a delicate, complicated and altogether attractive art; it became fashionable—and, I am sorry to say, many dry-fly fishermen became arrogantly convinced that the dry fly was the one and only sporting and respectable method of catching trout.

Anglers, for all their contemplative reputation, are often contentious individuals. That is as it should be; any worthwhile occupation will develop its rigorous partisans, and any art grows mainly through violent contentions. Fly-fishermen have fought their share of word battles among themselves, supporters of upstream fishing against downstream practitioners, believers in exact imitation against users of fancy flies, dry-fly fishermen against wet-fly fishermen. We who sit on the side lines reap entertainment continually and material benefit eventually, when the smoke of battle has died down and we find the issue clear before us. Really, the dry fly–wet fly battle is all over and has been for sometime—Mr. Skues cleared it up for everyone with *Minor Tactics* and *The Way of a Trout with a Fly*—but there are still a certain number of dry-fly fishermen who feel that the wet fly is a lesser, if not actually a contemptible, form of a great sport.

My own early training directed me to this unattractive view, and I was, for a year or two, a very arrogant dry-fly fisherman. Wet-fly fishing, I felt, was a crude and unattractive chuck-and-chance-it method, and wet flies themselves were deadly caricatures of nature that took a wholly unfair advantage of unsuspecting trout raised in the decent confines of a chalk stream.

I began to shift a little, but only a little, from this position when I caught a number of fish one day with a waterlogged dry fly. It seemed to me that the difference between what I was doing and ordinary dry-fly fishing was very slight: my fly was below the surface, but I was drifting it over feeding fish without drag, casting upstream, striking to the rise and using the same rod, reel, line, gut, even the same fly. I was catching fish that had not seemed any too willing to come up to the dry fly and I was enjoying myself thoroughly. Something in the calm, quiet way the fish took the fly, opening their mouths to intercept it rather than moving for it; in the way the surface humped over them as they took, seldom breaking; in the way they shook their heads when they felt the hook; something in all this seemed to me at least as exciting and fascinating as dry-fly fishing and certainly as difficult.

I fished that way quite often and soon discovered Mr. Skues's *Minor Tactics* and realized that what I was doing was not only sensible and orthodox, but was recognized as a proper chalk-stream method by many people and as a well-developed art with far more attractions than I had discovered for myself. I bought lightly dressed tups and greenwells and followed Mr. Skues to the letter whenever conditions seemed right. Then Major Greenhill, training me through trout for salmon fishing, taught me that the ordinary downstream wet fly was not the clumsy and murderous thing I had supposed it, and I became for the first time something like a fly-fisherman.

To return to Cotton's top, bottom and middle. We must reckon today that fly-fishing "at the top" is dry-fly fishing. And dry-fly fishing is of at least two kinds—the orthodox dry fly of the chalk streams, cast upstream and usually over fish that have been seen rising or are in position to rise; and the fast-water dry fly of LaBranche and others. The fast-water dry fly is primarily a North American method, and it has two fairly separate forms, eastern and western. The eastern fishermen work with flies not entirely different from those of the chalk streams, and Jennings gives importance to American dressings of such flies as the Iron Blue, the Red Quill, the Green Drake and some sedges, as well as Royal Coachman, Bi-visible, Quill Gordon. Hendrickson and many peculiarly American patterns. La Branche fishes upstream, searching the water and making not just one or two, but very many, casts over each likely spot to persuade a reluctant fish to come up, and he describes his method as "creating a whole family of flies instead of imitating an individual member thereof." In other words, he doesn't wait for a hatch of flies, but tries to persuade the fish that the hatch has started, counting on his own river knowledge to show him where the fish will be lying.

The western method is a still sharper departure from the orthodox. Western dry-fly men are often fishing very fast and broken water, and their patterns must be very good floaters; so for wing material they frequently use deer hair, which is hollow. These flies float so well that they can be fished freely, upstream or down in the most broken water, and this gives the fisherman a chance to search water almost as thoroughly and quickly with them as with the wet fly. Drag is often of slight importance and sometimes is actually an advantage; many fishermen use two or more flies on a leader, working either upstream or down, covering water from all angles, down and across, up and across, straight across, straight up or straight down.

I have had wonderful sport with big fish in very heavy,

broken water by this method, letting a deer hair pattern down the big runs on a slack line, bringing it back to me by holding the rod high so that the fly bounces from wave to wave, then slacking away or making a new cast and letting it drift down again. Big cutthroats and sometimes summer steelhead are particularly susceptible to this method. Time and again I have had a big cutthroat come right out of the water over the top of the bouncing fly, not touching it, trying to drown it perhaps. I slack away then, letting the fly drift, and nine times out of ten he turns and takes it nobly. That is exciting and beautiful to watch, if not so subtle and delicate as a more orthodox dry-fly method.

The proved usefulness of the dry fly in fast water has tremendously increased its popularity and it has, unfortunately, led again to a tendency to discount the wet fly. This is a pity and a mistake because there are many times when the wet fly is not only more effective, but actually more interesting, more comfortable and more satisfying to fish. It is nearly always more difficult.

There are at least four separate methods of wet-fly fishing, and if we match the dry fly to Cotton's "At the Top," it is necessary to describe a new depth—"in the surface." The greased-line method of wet-fly fishing, developed by A. H. E. Wood for Atlantic salmon in low water and described by "Jock Scott," uses this depth, fishing a lightly dressed fly on a long, slim hook just under the surface film; the fly is held to its depth by a well-greased line and is fully controlled throughout its swim by mending the cast—that is, lifting the belly of the line upstream each time the current threatens to pull on it and drag the fly into artificial motion across the stream. The greased-line wet fly not only catches Atlantic salmon and steelhead when nothing else will, but is at times very deadly for feeding trout of all three species. And the simple mechanical feature of the method, the mending of the line, is the most useful single improvement in the history of wet-fly technique.

It is intensely useful not only in greased-line fishing but in all forms of wet-fly fishing and even in dry-fly fishing, because it means that a skillful fisherman can control the depth and speed of his fly almost at will when he is fishing downstream or across, and to some extent even when he is fishing up and across.

This mending of the line is a large part of the story in fishing the deep-sunk fly—Cotton's "At the Bottom." One may at times need to get down deep for feeding trout, but the principal use of the deep-sunk fly is for salmon and steelhead in cold winter weather. One casts fairly well across the stream, letting the ungreased line fall slack, and makes an instant upstream mend to the full extent of the slack line. The rest of the cast is fished out as slowly as possible; with a sinking line there is seldom a chance for a second mend, but one can delay drag by using the length of one's rod to steer the line clear of the fierce currents. I have many times been able to touch bottom in six or eight feet of really fast water with no other weight than the hook of a 2/o fly by this means; and the method has made fly-fishing for winter steelheads as profitable for me as the minnow or prawn.

There are two remaining forms of wet-fly fishing, nymph fishing and the orthodox wet fly, and these fit Cotton's "In the Middle." One may vary depth as conditions and water suggest all the way from "in the surface" to "At the Bottom," but such extremes are not what I am thinking of now.

Nymph fishing is Mr. Skues's development, and the best description that comes to me is to call it the "orthodox upstream dry fly sunk." All the aquatic flies that make good dry-fly fishing spend a long period of their lives in nymphal or larval shape under water. For every hatch of May flies that floats on the surface of a stream there must first have been a progression of nymphs up through the water, and this progression is perfectly exposed to the attacks of feeding trout. A good movement of nymphs, even if there are flies on the surface of the water at the same time, may hold the whole attention of the trout, and Mr. Skues rightly points out that it is senseless to plug floating flies at the head of a trout who is wholly concerned, for the time being at least, with underwater food.

Emerging nymphs are little, if at all, resistant to the current. So in nymph fishing one casts a lightly dressed fly (first wetting it to make sure it sinks instantly) upstream to a bulging fish or over a likely place. The fly drifts back without artificial movement, exactly as the dry fly does, except that it sinks instead of floating. The trout intercepts it, and at this point is the angler's highest test—he must strike as to a rise for the dry fly but often without seeing anything more than a slight bulge on the surface of the water, a brief, barely visible flash as the fish turns, or an infinitesimal draw on his floating gut or line. Often and often one strikes into a good fish with the nymph and it is utterly impossible to remember afterward just what was seen or sensed to cause the lifting of the rod. In this respect nymph fishing is more difficult than dry-fly fishing; in that slight drag will probably not scare a feeding fish, it is sometimes less difficult. In all other respects it is essentially the same, a perfect complement to the dry fly, in no way a competitor.

Ordinary wet-fly fishing is the most flexible of all fly-fishing methods. The orthodox method is to cast one or more flies downstream and across and bring them round on the current with plenty of artificial movement, sweeping the river in a succession of curves, each one a yard or two farther downstream than the last. But no competent fly-fisher is content with anything so simple; the good wet-fly fisherman puts into his work useful points from all the other methods of fly-fishing.

On occasion the wet-fly fisherman may fish upstream, covering rising fish as the nymph fisher or the dry-fly man does, but working his fly, and this is perhaps the most difficult, mechan-

ıcally, of all types of fly-fishing. But even the simplest form
of the wet fly, downstream in fairly rough water, should
never be what the disaffected call "chuck-and-chance-it," an
unimaginative series of casts all fished out the same way. One
covers the water rhythmically, mathematically, to some limited
extent mechanically, but never without controlling the fly to
a pace and motion of one's own choosing, imitating perhaps
the drift of a drowned creature, perhaps the more buoyant
movement of a rising nymph, perhaps the struggles of an
aquatic insect washed from its protecting rock, perhaps the
halting flight of sick or injured salmon fry, perhaps the darting
jerks of bullhead or stickleback. And every water, however
full it may be of fish, has its special, likely holding places.
Through each of these the good wet-fly fisherman will bring
his fly with all the care and accuracy of a dry-fly man covering
a rising fish, and he will feel the same eager suspense, the same
quickening to the moment that the dry-fly fisherman feels as
he shoots line to let the fly fall, for better or for worse, in the
spot he has chosen.

On occasion one may need to cast more delicately and accurately with dry fly than with wet and perhaps to imitate
more closely the natural flies that the fish are taking. These
things are important too in wet-fly fishing, even the difference
between, say, humpback fry and coho fry or the smaller difference between coho and Chinook fry, in spite of the fact
that fish take nothing so recklessly as they take fry. In dry-fly
fishing one must control the fly closely, be always on guard
against drag—but that is negative control rather than posi-
tive, exerted in the cast rather than during the drift of the fly.
One controls a wet fly right through its fishing, from the
moment it touches the water until it is lifted again; one repro-
duces all types and speeds of movement, from simple drift to
an accelerated swing that uses the full speed of the current
and rapid manipulation of the line; and one may make half
a dozen adjustments of speed in the course of a single cast.

October

All methods of fly-fishing are good; each is superior in its own place and time, under its own ideal conditions, to the others; not only superior in effectiveness, but in the pleasure and satisfaction that one derives from fishing it. None is invariably more difficult, more subtle, more artistic or more worth while than the others. The really good fly-fisherman is he who can meet all conditions of fishing by working his fly with equal competence at the Top, at the Bottom, in the Middle, and, let us add, three centuries after Cotton, in the Surface.

NOVEMBER

Iɴ Nᴏᴠᴇᴍʙᴇʀ the salmon die.
The winter has varying ways of repairing summer drought—
sometimes by heavy September rains that fill the soil against
delayed Indian summer in October, sometimes by intermittent
October rains, sometimes by heavy snows and sudden thaws

during December and January. Nearly always by November the earth is wet and the swamps are full so that all rain that falls runs off to the rivers and the rivers are high. The death of the salmon is a strange and wonderful thing, a great gesture of abundance. Two or three short months ago they were vigorous creatures, bright and strong, full of drive and power. Eggs and milt were heavy and rich in them, their bodies were built to performance by two or three or four, perhaps five or six years of fierce, active feeding. Stemming the ocean currents as maturity grew in them, they found their rivers; still in strength against the current they found their spawning beds and in them buried and fertilized the eggs of a new generation that would return in time to the same purpose, the same death. And now in November they are dying; not just the weak ones or the old ones, the injured or diseased ones, but all of them, all the vigorous flashing host that came in surging life through salt water and fresh only yesterday.

It is strange that they should all die, not one escape, strange that the design should be so exact, so closely functional, strangest of all that the change should be so abrupt, from fullest life to rotting death, without intermission of gradual senility or growing weakness. It is, of course, the spawning; the growth of eggs and milt draws heavily from the make-up of the body, leaving only the strength necessary for the digging of the nest, for the fighting on the beds, for the violent shedding of spawn and milt. The eggs of the female draw more from her body than the milt draws from the male, so the male pours his surplus into the bony growth of hooked jaw and humped shoulder, and the two end their spawning rite at matching stages of exhaustion. For a little while longer they have a decayed strength that lets them hold in fast water, even swim against it and jump clear of it as they jumped out over the ocean banks, but death grows on them more swiftly than ever their strength grew on them in the ocean years.

Atlantic salmon and steelhead, which come through the

same process of life to the same spawning, do not all die. They return to the sea and in due time perhaps one in ten returns to spawn again. Apparently there is the same pouring of strength into eggs and milt and body changes, there is the same darkening of color, the same fraying of fins, the same exhaustion; yet these things are not exactly the same, and their bodies retain some germ of recovery that Pacific salmon cast from them. A spawning steelhead often seems in worse physical condition than a spawning Pacific salmon: the body is actually exhausted to the point where the flesh is dirty gray instead of pink, and the muscles move sluggishly and lazily. But once spawning is completed, the restoration begins; within a few short weeks the exhausted fish may be bright silver again, with firm pink flesh, great strength and quickness and all the appearances of health and survival, though the body will still seem abnormally slender and close observation will show that fins and tail are frayed or torn.

This restoration comes from within. There is nothing in the streams to build it, and the spawned-out fish do not feed very actively during their recovery. One may find in their stomachs little samples of food, perhaps a dragonfly or stone-fly nymph, May-fly or caddis larvae in small quantities, or even a small bullhead or two or three humpback fry; but a one-pound cutthroat lying alongside a ten-pound steelhead will have by far the greater weight and mass of feed in his stomach. Pacific salmon have none of this passive power of convalescence; in their spawning life itself goes out of them even though they seem to live for a short while longer. I have seen dead Chinook and coho females, recently spawned, whose bodies were firm and clean, almost bright, seemingly stronger and better fish in every way than the best of mended steelhead kelts, but some little thing, without which all their strength is useless, has gone from them.

The will to live continues after spawning. It would be reasonable to expect a resignation to the inevitable, but there is none. A spawned-out fish, almost dead, will turn away from danger in a surge of fear-built strength. I once watched two spawned-out Chinooks, huge fish, in the shallow water of a long, broken rapid. They showed at first just over the lip of the pool above, dorsal and caudal fins breaking as the current forced them down. They drifted a little way, weakly and awkwardly, and then, as though suddenly afraid of death, one threshed its way with furious strength for ten or a dozen yards upstream. The other followed instantly, and for a while they held, side by side again, weaving back and forth until at last the current caught their sides and swept them down. This happened many times; and each time they were swept down, they fought back again, keeping always together but never winning quite back to the place they had left. They swung over at last into an eddy on the far side and seemed to rest there, because I could not see them again. There was a painful sadness in watching, a bleakness in the struggle against death that could gain nothing.

Yet the dying salmon are not wasted. A whole natural economy is built on their bodies. Bald eagles wait in the trees, bears hunt in the shallows and along the banks, mink and marten and coons come nightly to the feast. All through the winter mallards and mergansers feed in the eddies, and in freshet time the herring gulls come in to plunge down on the swift water and pick up the rotting drift. Caddis larvae and other carnivorous insects crawl over the carcasses that are caught in the bottoms of the pools or against the rocks in the eddies. The stream builds its fertility on this death and readies itself to support a new generation of salmon.

It is still strange that they should all die, that life should go out with the spawn; for it does go out with the spawn. Age has little to do with it, except in the case of the humpbacks, for even the grilse die, and the Chinooks and sockeyes spawn and die at several different ages. It would be natural to suppose that at least the grilse might live. They have come back after only a single year in salt water, instead of two or three or four, as fully developed males, able to shed milt and fertilize the eggs of the largest females. They are only little fish, weighing a pound or two, still close to their fresh-water life, and there would be food in the streams to build them back to a measure of strength. But their spawned-out bodies litter the shallows, and none escape. They have served a purpose, one supposes, as insurance against any shortage of full-grown males: so long as the superfluity of grilse is there no female will bury unfertilized eggs.

The whole of salmon spawning is a strange mixture of waste and insurance against waste. Salmon of the same species run to spawn at different ages, and for that reason no early cataclysm in fresh water can wipe out the run of any single year—there will always be at least a few fish to run up and spawn in the corresponding year. This seems a wise provision, yet it is not made for the humpbacks. All humpbacks have the same life history, all spawn at two years so that a cycle can be utterly wiped out, though it may be built back very gradually by fish straying from other rivers or by artificial replanting. There is no waste in the fertilization of the eggs because the design of the nest building sets up a flow of current that holds the milt close down on the eggs as they are shed. There is no waste under the gravel because the eggs are deeply buried, perfectly protected from everything except the washing or silting of heavy flood. Each stage of development and hatching is in itself a multiplication of protection, and the alevins, as they come from the gravel, are still protected in large measure by the remains of the yolk sac and can rest for several days among the rocks of the bottom with but little movement. Then all protection is suddenly swept away. As free-swimming fry they must feed, and to feed they must move; soon, for most of them, the seaward migration starts. Within a few weeks ninety per cent of them are in the bellies of predators, and all the safety of the long winter in the gravel is wasted.

None of it is really waste—not the dead bodies of the spawned-out fish nor the tiny lives of the fry; both are used to build other life. It is rather a part of a broad design of plenty. Salmon are an abundant resource that thrives on abundance. One hears occasionally that spawning beds are overcrowded, that the late-running fish are digging out the nests and scattering the eggs of the earlier spawners. Strictly from man's point of view there may be economic waste in this; it is just possible that a greater catch of fish might have been made without seriously affecting the total number of eggs to reach full development in the following season. But there is nothing in the history of the runs to prove that crowded spawning beds are anything but beneficial to the salmon themselves. The mighty runs of sockeyes that crowded the spawning grounds of the Fraser in the great years up to 1913 always yielded runs of matching size in the following cycle year, and the lesser runs of the years between yielded lesser runs in their cycles.

It is useless to pretend that even nearly everything about the salmon runs is yet comprehensible. Man's intervention has made so many changes and erected such a variety of artificial circumstances that one scarcely can know the original design, much less understand it. Why should there have been, on the Fraser, one year in every four that brought a run of sockeyes five or six times greater than the abundance of the intermediate years? Why should the Fraser's great run be sockeyes while the Columbia's great run is Chinooks? Perhaps because the Fraser is a watershed of good lakes, which the sockeyes need for their fresh-water development; but even so, what in the first place turned the young sockeyes to the specialized feeding they can find only in lakes? How long has it lasted, this crowding wealth of salmon in every stream and river from Alaska to northern California? How did the runs change in the years before the white man came?

There is only the mighty, general picture of the northwest

Pacific coast in one's mind: a mountainous coast of huge inlets, scattered islands and fiercely tidal channels; clean, generous streams sparkling and leaping down from summer snow on the mountaintops and great rivers grandly flowing between dark-timbered banks; and always timber, evergreen timber from water line to snow line, Douglas fir and red cedar and hemlock, spruce and true fir and yellow cedar, white pine sometimes, alder and willow and maple along the creek beds. Each year the salmon come to climb the streams into the timber where the Indians waited their coming and the eagles waited and the furbearers and fish ducks. The land had given itself to the support of great trees, and these drew its fertility and its moisture, soaked up its sunshine until there was little left for the support of other life. So the salmon carried the life of the sea along the rivers and back into the timber for land dwellers that might not otherwise have found living.

THE RIDDLE OF THE OXHORN

A GOOD many years ago, probably in 1928, I became interested in a controversy over the exact use of the oxhorn that Homer mentions as a part of ancient fishing gear. The battle, which waxed quite hot at times in spite of its scholarly aspect, was waged in the correspondence columns of *The Fishing Gazette*, and the principals were Herr Rauser, a German professor, and the late William Radcliffe, author of the most learned fishing book I know, *Fishing from the Earliest Times*. Other readers joined in and added fuel to the fire, and I found before long that I had myself become a strong Radcliffe partisan. Herr Rauser was a very disagreeable correspondent, angry and violent and quite without the respect I felt he should have had for the author of *Fishing from the Earliest Times*.

I don't remember the exact point of difference, and in any case it doesn't matter very much to this story. Mr. Radcliffe treats the oxhorn question quite gently in his book and with a great deal of scholarly detachment. He lists six or seven theories as to the use of the horn, adding only mild comments of his own: oxhorn may have been used as a collar to protect the line from the teeth of a big fish, as a container for a lead plummet, as a means of concealing the shape of hook and plummet, as part of a spear, as the hook itself, or as a lure, perhaps not entirely unlike a devon minnow. Herr Rauser had some other idea or else took strong exception to one of these.

Somewhere about the time the argument was reaching its height, I was taking a skiffload of trapping gear up the Nimpkish River during the November dog-salmon run. In those years the Nimpkish dogs ran as I have never seen salmon run anywhere else, as I imagine all salmon ran to all rivers in the northwest before commercial fishing cut their numbers. Often a whole length of the river, as far as we could see, was white with their jumping. Often, passing over a quiet reach in the canoe, we saw the whole bottom moving and swaying and knew it was dog salmon packed flank to flank. As we worked the big skiff round the bad places, wading the shallows, we tripped over dog salmon, felt them strike against our legs, saw them darting away to deep water or threshing against the bank inside us in frantic fear. At no time of day or night was the river quiet of their splashing and leaping.

Taking the skiff up was slow work and not too easy on the full-flowing river—generally we called it a day and went home when we had passed two or three rapids. So we were moving a good deal up and down the river all through the run. We saw the fish as they came in on the tides in the lower reaches, moving up in schools, crowding through the Blue Clay Pool, between Sachem Island and the Indian Island, between the In-

dian Island and the south bank. Only a few of them jumped—
a single jumping fish marked the position of a whole school—
but there were twenty or thirty in the air or splashing back
wherever one looked. In amongst the white breaks the round
dark heads of seals streaked the smooth water or lifted on
stretched necks to search about them. Seals love the Nimpkish
River and constantly swim the full length of it to the lake;
on any day during the run we would see fifteen or twenty of
them fishing the tidal reaches and half a dozen more in each
of the long quiet pools above tidewater.

Everything came to prey on the dog salmon. Bald eagles in
hundreds—we counted two hundred in two miles one day—
perched in tall trees along the river or quarreled and fed at
the edge of the water. Always at dusk we saw black bears,
standing on sweepers to peer down into the water, wading
the shallow bars to fish or dragging the carcasses of salmon
away from the water. Coons and mink picked up the leavings
of the bigger animals, and we saw them too, and ducks of many
kinds flighted in from salt water. There seemed to be more
otters than usual in Wright's Canyon and Ned's Canyon.
Everything except the deer came down for the fish. We fished
ourselves, and the Indians moved into their fishing camps to
smoke all the fish they could for the winter.

The day we brought the skiff past the biggest of the Indian
fishing camps and I thought I had found a new clew to the
riddle of the oxhorn was the first clear day in two or three
weeks. We felt good about it and were making time until I
picked up the spinning rod and made a cast in the middle of
a rapid. Something took hold, and the line went out as no tyee
had ever taken it. I braked all I dared and began to run back
down the river; but he was still taking line, and Ed swung the
skiff out and hollered to me to jump in as he came past. I
jumped and scrambled aboard somehow, and in a moment we
were back at the foot of the rapid. But the fish was still traveling.

A River Never Sleeps

"For God's sake hold him," Ed told me, "or we'll lose another rapid."

But I couldn't hold him, and we saw him jump, big and bright silver, against the white water of the next rapid. Eagles screamed above us, and the sunlight was good and we were young.

"We've got to get him," I said.

"You're darn right." Ed pushed the big skiff into the current again. "But hold him at the end of this one."

We rode out half of that rapid, then worked the fish into an eddy and I jumped out and tailed him in water up to my chest—a fifteen-pound dog salmon hooked just above the dorsal fin. We had caught lots with the hook securely in their mouths, but I think that was an unlucky fish. And he certainly behaved like a surprised fish.

We climbed the two rapids again, passed the pool above them, and then were in the long easy rapid by the Indian smokehouses. From the foot of it we could see the canoes out on the rippled sunlit water, and I told Ed that I wanted to watch them, so we went on up. On the bank squaws were filleting the fish, working swiftly and easily to cut the good thick flesh from ribs and backbone. Three canoes were fishing, and in each one man was holding the canoe with a pole in the stern while another stood poised in the bow with the spear. We saw Jimmy and Stanley in one canoe and watched them because we knew they were good. Jimmy held the canoe, swung it across and pushed it up a little way, then held it again. Stanley stood straight up in the bow, the sixteen-foot pole of his spear balanced in both hands. He drove it suddenly, sliding the pole through his hands to the end, held it there and pulled back. Two dog salmon struggled on barbed spear points that had pulled free of the pole and were held to it now only by short lengths of cod line. Stanley recovered the pole hand over hand, flopped the fish into the canoe, set his spear points back in place and almost immediately threw again and speared another fish.

310

Soon after that they came into the bank with a full canoe load.

I examined the spear curiously. The pole was very slender and light, not tapered at all except at the very tip where one point slipped on. A foot or two from the end a tapered trigger was whipped to the pole and the second point was on that; a third point was on a third trigger equally spaced from the second one.

"You like to try?" Stanley asked me.

"Sure would," I said, and I did, and I speared fish, but that's not part of the story. There was horn in the spear points; the barbs were horn, fitted and whipped to steel points; the two horn barbs made the cup that fitted over the tapered end of the pole, and when the head came free, they held the point from drawing back through the fish. I recognized deerhorn and mountain goathorn on two different heads.

"Which is best?" I asked Stanley.

"Goathorn," Stanley said. "We always use goathorn when we can get it. Sometimes we make the point out of bone instead of steel—not often now; too much work. Steel is better anyway."

I remembered the riddle of the oxhorn. If goathorn and deerhorn, why not oxhorn? For the moment I felt myself scholar, explorer, scientist and half a dozen other wise and estimable types of person.

"You sell me one?"

Stanley smiled and shook his head. "No. Too much work to make 'em."

Jimmy wouldn't sell me one, nor would any of the other Indians.

"Why not?" I asked Ed when we were on the way home.

"I don't know. You can't tell about Indians. Maybe you asked them too suddenly. Maybe they're afraid we'll catch too many fish with them. What do you want them for anyway? We can get lots of fish other ways."

A River Never Sleeps

I wrote William Radcliffe about the spearheads and told him I hoped to send specimens later. Mr. Radcliffe was delighted with the information, not because he felt that the riddle of the oxhorn was solved at last, but because the Nimpkish spearheads might have some bearing on the discovery of small points of reindeerhorn in the caves of paleolithic man in France. That, I felt, made it very definitely my business to get hold of specimen spearheads to send back to him.

I cultivated Jimmy's acquaintance during the next few months, watched his fishing quite often, gave him gold and silver coins to hammer out for me (at a price) into shapes of thunderbirds and fish. Every once in a while I mentioned spearheads, but Jimmy always made difficulties—too much trouble to make, nobody had any to spare and other excuses of that sort. There was something dark and mysterious about the difficulty, and I couldn't possibly guess what it was. It partook somehow of the Indian's sensible suspicion of a white man's motives, and I classed it with the impenetrable mystery of the native copper ceremonial vessels that the Nimpkish Indians have. They scarcely ever speak of these vessels or show them because they feel that white men will go where the copper is and that will be the end of native copper for the Nimpkish Indians. Undoubtedly they are right; but whether any Indian now alive knows where the copper came from is another question and one that probably doesn't matter a great deal, since the tradition of silence is established.

Nearly a year later I was fishing tyees in Lansdowne Pool when I saw Jimmy come up with his canoe to the shallow bar about a hundred yards below the pool. I knew he was going to spear tyees—sachems, he called them—but I didn't pay much attention because I was in high hopes of hooking a fish myself. A few minutes later I did so, a bright thirty-five-pounder that took complete charge. I fought hard to keep him in the pool, but he kept going in spite of me, and I had to follow him down. I gaffed him on the bar twenty or thirty feet from where

Jimmy was fighting a fish of his own. Jimmy got his and smiled
at me.

"Good sport, eh?" he said. He looked closely at my rod,
touched the reel and fingered the line. "You catch 'em on that
pole all the time? Trolling?"

I explained about casting, and he nodded slowly.

"No boat going over them. Better maybe."

I examined his own gear with a good deal of interest. He
had a short spear, four or five feet long, with a barbed steel
point bound on. A length of heavy cod line was attached to
the spear and he had played the fish out on that.

"Good for sachems," Jimmy said. "Long pole break all the
time. Fish too strong."

We said nothing of spearheads that day and nothing on the
several other days that I saw him down at the mouth of the
river. I had pretty well given up hope, even though I knew
I was going away in a little while and wanted them more than
ever. Jimmy was a good troller, probably the best rowboat
troller among the Indians, and he seemed to like fishing at the
mouth of the river. We fished alongside each other many evenings, and he saw me hook fish by casting and play them out
on the rod. Once I saw him kill a fifty-eight-pounder on his
hand line. The fish was really strong and towed Jimmy's canoe
pretty much as it pleased, but Jimmy tired him at last and
slipped him neatly over the gunwale and into the canoe. I was
impressed and a little jealous when I saw the huge wide body
lying there. I judged the fish to be at least a sixty-pounder, and
if the devil had ever made me the offer, I would probably have
sold my soul quite cheerfully for the privilege of hooking one
like him. I think Jimmy sensed something of this, and my admiration pleased him, because he grinned like a schoolgirl and
said, "Big fish, eh? You catch one like that soon. Lots of sport
then."

The boat was late on the night I was to leave Alert Bay, and
I walked up to the Chinese café for a piece of pie and a cup

of coffee. Jimmy was in there and I went over to say good-by to him.

"You go away?" he asked. "For a long time?"

I nodded. "I guess so, Jimmy. Got to go back to the Old Country."

"You see that man? The man writes books about fishing the way you tell me?"

"Sure," I said.

"You still want spearheads?"

"You're darn right I do."

"I got some. Bring 'em down to boat. You wait."

The boat was ready to pull out at any moment and I was still waiting in the rain on the dark wharf. Then Jimmy came around the end of the cannery. He held out a clumsy package wrapped in newspaper.

"Swell, Jimmy," I said. "How much do you want for them?"

"Nothing," he said. "We fish together. You catch lots of fish your way—good sport."

"Nonsense," I said. "You had lots of trouble to make these. You let me pay you."

But he wouldn't take anything. "Old ones," he said. "Not much good."

Then the boat whistled. We shook hands quickly and I went aboard. As soon as I could, I opened the package and looked at the spearheads. One was newly made, with a steel point and deerhorn barbs whipped to cod line. The other three had been used but were in perfect shape, bone pointed, whipped to plaited rawhide with fiber or sinews of some kind. One had barbs of goathorn, black and polished, one of deerhorn and the third had one barb of deerhorn and the other of goathorn. The smell of smoke was in the rawhide, and as I looked down at them I was back on the Nimpkish, on the long rapid near the fishing camp, with dog salmon showing all about me in the November river.

BEFORE I DIE

IF ONE has to die, I should think November would be the best month for it. It is a gray, stormy month; the salmon are dying, and the year is done. I should think there is nothing very bad about dying except for the people one has to leave and the things one hasn't had time to do. When the time comes, if I know what it's all about, I suppose I shall think, among other things, of the fish I haven't caught and the places I haven't fished.

I shall, of course, do my best to meet such regrets ahead of time and I keep in my mind, as I suppose most fishermen do, an often-changing list of the places I should like to fish and of the fish I should like to catch. My first desire is a pious one and constant. I should like to fish Charles Cotton's Dove in Derbyshire, where he fished it. I should like to see whatever is left of the famous Fishing House; I should like to come down to the river from Ashbourne, as Cotton and his friend did, and see the grand scenery of the descent that worried Viator; most of all, I should like to go down to the river from Beresford Hall and follow it to Pike Pool and beyond on a good day in May. Then I should turn round and fish up, all the way to the Fishing House again, because I suspect that the Dove runs as clear as it ever did and that the fish would not be so accommodating to the downstream fisher as they were in Cotton's day.

Such a visit to Dovedale would be a pilgrimage, and I should expect from it a pilgrim's reward. I should hope to come away with a little of the free generosity that was Cotton's, so that I might be able to ask a traveler to my house and my fishing with the same grace he used and treat him, once there, with the same easy and courteous hospitality. Above all, I should hope to come away with a little of the gentleness of spirit and humble loyalty that made Cotton write:

I shall freely and bluntly tell you, that I am a Brother of the Angle too; and, peradventure, can give you some instructions How to Angle for a Trout in a Clear River, that my Father Walton himself will not disapprove; though he did either purposely omit, or did not remember, them, when you and he sat discoursing under the sycamore tree.

That was the perfect fisherman speaking, and almost the perfect man; for Cotton surely knew that his Father Walton had no knowledge or practice that would permit him to discourse on fly fishing as Cotton could. Charles Cotton was a rare soul, and I like him the better because the books sometimes call him a rake. One little biographical note I have seen says of him: "He was apparently always in difficulties, always happy and always a favorite." It would be hard to write "lovable" so clearly in any other sentence of the same number of words.

I am afraid the fishing might not be so good in the Dove as it was in Cotton's day. But there is at least one place in England where it is better than it ever was—in the Test at Stockbridge. I should like to fish the Test not just once, but once or twice a week through a whole season, because there is so much in the changing months on a. chalk stream and so much in getting to know the favorite corners and even the individual fish, the public characters of high education. Such fishing is the touchstone of a fly-fisher's skill, and I should like to measure myself against it and learn what I am good for. And those southern rivers, Test, Itchen and Kennet, like the Dove, have a host of literary associations; they are a part of fly-fishing tradition, the authentic cradle of the dry fly.

For Atlantic salmon I should like to fish the Tay in Scotland, in January, and I should hope that the river would grant me a forty-pounder, hooked in a snowstorm for preference, on a doublehanded fly rod and a 3/0 Jock Scott; the wind should be hurling the snow upstream, the sound of the storm should be all about and the fish should have the strength of his weight with the speed and jumping heart of a grilse. In another season, I should like to fish the Dee at Cairnton with the greased line, as Wood fished it; rather even than fish it myself, I would, if Mr. Wood were still living, watch him on a day when the river was low and the fish were hard to move. It would always be better to watch than fish if one could watch the masters on their favorite streams—Cotton on Dove, Halford on Test or Itchen, Scrope on Tay, Stewart on Tweed, Wood on Dee. But a master of fly-fishing, like any great artist, must nearly always die before we ordinary mortals quit arguing with him and recognize his stature, so we can seldom hope to watch one and know him for what he is; I have been lucky enough to watch some good men in the twenty years I have fished—my Uncle Decie, Major Greenhill on the Frome, General Money on the Stamp, Tommy Brayshaw at Little River—and I'm grateful for it. Watching any man who really likes to fish is a happy business and watching a good man is pure joy.

Still thinking of Atlantic salmon, I should like to fish a big Norwegian river, one where the hope of a fifty- or sixty-pounder is not altogether unreasonable. I should not really expect to get such a fish, but I should like to put out a big fly in the heavy water and try my luck. Every cast would have in it the fisherman's lasting hope that this time, this time he will be there, he will see it, he will come up and take hold; one would be fishing "loaded" water in the fullest and strongest possible sense. And I should like to fish a New Brunswick salmon river, with the dry fly for preference, certainly from a canoe handled by a wise, quiet guide. Fishing from a boat or a canoe is nearly always less good than fishing from one's own two feet; half the challenge of difficult water is gone because the whole river is within easy reach and the strongest and wildest fish can be followed with ease. But eastern Canadian rivers and canoes seem to go together, and I suspect that some of the guides are very good, so good that fishing with them would be like watching a master. Lastly, I should like to fish one of the famous pools on the Wye, a deep slow pool such as I imagine the Cow Pond to be, fish it not with fly but with prawn, a prawn hung and hovered over a known lie, far down in the black water. I should hope for a forty-pounder, but I would settle for anything over twenty-five so long as he took deep down with a slow quiet stop that burst, a moment later, into a tearing run that rapped the reel handles on my knuckles.

Many places in the eastern states and eastern Canada have built a strong curiosity in me. The dry-fly streams in New York state are surely a part of an angler's education; just the name of the Beaverkill is enough—and the Neversink is another name that calls. Eastern fishermen have told me that I should be disappointed, that there is nothing there to compare with what we have in the west. But that is one of the beauties of fly-fishing—everything is proportionate to the river one is fishing. A pound trout from a difficult stream on a four-ounce rod is a triumph fully as great as a four-pounder on a six-ounce rod from the Campbell or a fifteen-pound steelhead on a twelve-ounce rod, or a tuna in the hundreds of pounds on a big-game rod. Much of American fly-fishing tradition is being built on those eastern streams, and the influence of the men who fish them has long ago spread clear across the continent and daily works to new developments in Oregon, Washington, California, even British Columbia.

There are brook trout in the Nipigon that I should like to catch just to have fished the river and seen the fish. And small-mouthed bass. We have smallmouthed bass even here on Vancouver Island, but I do not want them here; I want them among the frogs and lily pads in the slow water of their native streams, coming fiercely up to the big awkward flies in the way that has stopped the hearts of so many fishermen. Bass are not trout or salmon, and I do not think I could ever like them so well; but they are fine fish and good fighters. I used to fish for largemouthed bass in Lake Cavanaugh in Washington when I worked there years ago and I still think of them very often. I used to go down to the foot of the lake at week ends really to fish for trout. But there I would meet Mike, the blacksmith from Camp Eleven. For some reason I have run across half a dozen logging-camp blacksmiths since then, all Central Europeans named Mike and all great fishermen, quiet and persistent and skillful; but this was the first Mike and the best of them all. We used to meet without saying much, and through Sunday morning Mike would fish with a worm, and I would fish with the fly. At lunchtime we would meet and talk a little and compare our catches, and Mike would always have some fine, big, green-colored bass as well as his trout. He taught me at last to fish for them, fifteen or twenty feet down, with a cork bobber at the surface, a good worm on a No. 8 hook and two little thumbnail spinners just above to flash as the bobber bounced on the waves. Once I had learned, we would fish side by side through the afternoon, and the little wizened old man who seldom spoke at all gave me such a full feeling of comradeship as I have seldom known. Almost all blacksmiths and almost all Mikes are good men; but he was the best of them all.

Here in the west I have been lucky and have seen many rivers and caught many fish; but the list I hope for is still a long one. I should like to find the best summer steelhead stream in British Columbia or Alaska. For some reason winter runs of steelhead are commoner than summer runs, but the summer-run fish are almost incomparably better, at least when they first come in. But there are streams along the coast, tucked away at the heads of the inlets, that have great summer runs and have hardly ever been fished. There is one in Ramsay Arm that I mean to go to now that the war is over and another, I think, in Gardner Canal, and there must be many in Alaska. It would be possible to find one so good and so full of fish that one could use the greased-line method with a barbless hook and still have to turn fish back.

In Oregon I should like to fish the Rogue and the Deschutes. In California, Owens River, because it flows through clear-banked meadows and looks like a fine dry-fly stream. In Yellowstone Park there are many streams, strangely good and strangely little fished, full of things to be learned. Ernie Antle has told me of mountain rivers like chalk streams, with clear water flowing over gold gravel beds and trailing banks of weed and big brown trout rising steadily to fabulous hatches of flies. The roads, Ernie says, run close along the streams, the cars go past, but hardly anyone bothers to stop and fish. I think Yellowstone would be worth looking into.

Back in British Columbia again, I should like to find and fish a really great Kamloops trout lake, such as Knouff Lake used to be, with a strong hatch of traveling sedges and ten- and fifteen-pounders coming up to the dry fly.

I have tried to make the list short, picking high spots here and there, and I can do so fairly easily because in fishing I would generally prefer to learn more about the known than to discover the unknown. There are still two Alaskan rivers I should like to visit, not to fish, but to watch. I should like to see the Yukon and watch something of its great run of Chinooks. And I should like to watch a sockeye run to the Karluk River and Karluk Lake.

All this says nothing of the distant places. Every trout fisherman must dream sometimes of New Zealand, where the great rainbow trout come up on the shallow bars in the big lakes, and everyone who knows and loves Pacific salmon must sometimes wish to see what Chinooks look like down there, so many thousands of miles from home in a country where winter is summer and summer winter and the coastal currents do nothing to help the migration. It is hard not to wonder about the Pacific salmon that run to Japanese and Siberian rivers; it seems strange to think of them there, and there must be differences and comparisons that would reward the journey. Russia has one last salmonoid, too, that I should like to see, the huchen. Not a big fish nor a very remarkable one so far as I can learn, but the name is *Salmo hucho* and that is call enough to anyone who has known only *gairdneri, clarkii, trutta* and *salar*.

With the whole world to choose from and no limit set upon the imagination, one could go on almost without end. So far I have thought at least as much in terms of places as in terms of fish, and perhaps reasonably enough, because the river one is fishing is almost always as important as the fish one catches. There is little similarity between, say, a cutthroat trout caught in the Campbell and a brown trout caught in the Test, little enough between hooking a winter salmon in the Tay and a summer fish in the Dee. But it is easy to think of fish one would like to catch anywhere at all, provided only that they took well and fought their full weight and strength. Big fish, for instance. I should like to catch a forty-pound Atlantic salmon on the fly in any river, a brown trout of five pounds or over in any chalk stream, a thirty-pound pike from any eddy in any dark, slow river, a steelhead somewhere between twenty-five and thirty pounds, again on the fly, but in any river where steelhead are native. I should like to hook a ten-pound cutthroat on a dry fly at the mouth of a stream running into any big Pacific coast lake—preferably one of the deep, narrow lakes between high mountains, but any lake would do.

For the beauty of his color I should like to catch *Coryphaena*, the false dolphin. I have never seen one, and all who write about them say that the colors are indescribably beautiful when the fish is fresh from the water. That is a challenge. I should like to see for myself and, having seen, to describe.

I should like to hook and release a sailfish, perhaps two, and one big marlin. Big-game fishing has little in common with trout and salmon fishing; it is a separate sport of its own. But it deals with windy blue and white water, with rods and reels and lines and hooks, with intense excitement and physical effort. Decie, my fly-fishing uncle, once told me of breaking a rod in the first tunny he hooked, and the picture is clear as the moment when his words first brought it to my mind: the tremendous strike to the drifting herring, his own reaction, the straining rod so suddenly shattered in three or four places that it seemed to hold its curve, marked by the breaks, for an appreciable moment of time before it fell apart and the line broke too. Decie went back for another rod, white-faced and shaken.

I think I have just claim to one or two big fish—the steelhead bigger than twenty-five pounds, for instance, and a tyee salmon over sixty. No man has a right to come suddenly to such fish, though it happens that some men do; but the chance piles up as time goes on and one catches more and more fish of the species. Mathematically, perhaps, it does not, since no single chance is better than any other that went before it; but the mind accepts the accumulation, and it is easy to feel that some law of averages is bound to work for one sooner or later. I hope I shall catch my sixty-pound tyee by casting, not trolling; because of that and because I feel that only one such fish will come in a lifetime, I seldom troll for tyees—I will hold my chance for a place where I can cast a spoon across the leaders of a school.

Lastly, there are places I should like to revisit. There are not so very many of them, and two of them, paradoxically, I have never fished, but any visit to them would be a return because description has made them so vivid in my mind that I feel I have been there. In the hallway at home there was a stuffed mahseer of forty or fifty pounds which Decie caught in India at the junction of the Poonch and the Jhelum rivers, and I should like to go to that junction and catch my first mahseer. A man whose name I have long ago forgotten described to me his fishing for bright silver bonefish over the tide flats of Florida: the fish moving in on the tide to the waiting dead bait, the take and the swift tremendous run of a light little fish through water only three or four feet deep. I should like to catch my first bonefish as he did and where he did.

If the fates are kind at all, I shall someday get back to the Frome and fish it again for both trout and salmon. I have been back once, and the return was very good, better than I had dared to hope. The interval has been much longer this time and the change in myself much greater. I have new skills and perhaps have lost old skills and knowledge of the water. But I should like to try it out.

One day I shall get back to the Nimpkish again and wait as the arrowhead ripples come up on the evening tide ahead of the moving tyees. One day I shall get back to Deer Creek in Washington and learn just how good that stream can be for summer steelhead. And now, because I'm away from her, I must hope one day to get back to my own Campbell River on Vancouver Island. Of all my hopes, that is the one most sure of realization, yet of them all it is the only one that really counts. For it I would let all the others stay in the distant dreamland to which they really belong.

DECEMBER

Fᴏʀ the fly-fisherman on the Pacific coast, December is the beginning rather than the end of the year. In November even the most enthusiastic fly-fisherman may decide to lay his rods aside, dry off his lines and tie up some flies against a new season. Then in December, with the running of the first winter steelheads, the new season starts.

In November the salmon die by hundreds and by thousands on the shallow bars, in the eddies, under the sweepers along the banks. In December salmon are living again, millions upon millions where only thousands died, growing and stirring and developing within the chorions of orange eggs deep under the gravel. The eggs are settled in safety, some singly, more in groups, all held by the protecting gravel, hidden far below the reach of enemies and predators. One used to suppose that the eggs themselves were hunted and destroyed in unresisting immobility by crawling stone-fly nymphs and fierce dragon nymphs, by caddises and the other creatures that live on the gravel and among the rocks of the stream beds. But these creatures have their life within the upper two or three inches of the stream bed, and the eggs are buried far deeper, twelve inches or more below. It seemed once that, huddled there in darkness through the long winter months, many would die and spread rottenness and disease among the others. But it is clean down in the gravel; pure water filters down, and a crust of silt forms at the surface of the gravel to make the filter screen finer still and the hidden cradles of the salmon aseptic as the operating room of a hospital.

So the salmon live, and there is stirring and growth in the eggs under the gravel. For a brief while the land holds the whole essence of the tons upon tons of silver strength that will come back from the sea in three or four or five years' time. The rivers look the same; one passes along them, fishes down them, almost without thinking of all the wealth that is buried out of sight, all the power of development that is left to fend for itself and fends so well.

A December river is dark and cold, though not so cold as it will be, and full running before the frosts of January and February cut down the flow from the hills. December on the coast has dark, wet days when it is easy to be up at dawn and almost natural to be out at dusk. Perhaps December is not a good fishing month and December weather not good fishing weather, but I like December fishing. I do not know when the first winter steelhead run to the Campbell. Some fish run, I think, in every month of the year. I caught a sixteen-pounder once in the Canyon Pool in September and I saw another there in August, lying in the sunlight in shallow water. But I go out to look for fish as soon as the river comes to the right height in December, and the earliest I have ever found the winter run was in 1935, when I caught two fresh fish and a kelt on November thirtieth. Why the kelt I do not know—it can only be that he was one of the few that run to the river in summer or early fall; but the other two were true fish of the winter run, and in that year the run held right on from then. Some years it is impossible to fish early in the month; often the river holds high in flood almost until Christmas time. And when the water is right the dying cohos are sometimes troublesome, the old red cocks taking hold of fly or minnow at every cast until one gives up and goes home in disgust, knowing well that even the most eager of steelhead cannot get in ahead of them. But in some years everything is right, and it is well to go out then because December steelhead are the brightest and cleanest and hardest fighters of all the winter run.

However the river is, I always go out on December twenty-third or twenty-fourth, because Christmas Eve is a fast day and the time is so good that only a fresh steelhead seems to fit it. Generally we find one, and it is good to bring him back to the house and think on the way of where to take the children to hunt for a Christmas tree this year—even in this country of Christmas trees it is a problem that needs thought, because the abundance sets a high standard—the tree must be of exact height, symmetrical, thick and bushy. So one thinks of that and of Christmas Eve and the great day itself, and often the first steelhead of a new fishing year becomes a part of Christmas.

A few years ago a friend who had a short leave went up the

river on Christmas Day. He had never caught a steelhead and
he came back, late at night, through wet snow, tired and fishless. We gave him a drink and asked about his day. Yes, he had
caught a fish, a good big fish, but red—a spawned-out spring
salmon he thought, and he had left it on the bank. He described
the fish, and I read steelhead into every word of the description, so we went out next day, plowing through knee-deep
snow with more snow falling round us, clambering over saplings and brush weighted by the white wetness, wet ourselves
and fairly miserable until we found his fish. It was his first
steelhead, a big cock, just a little red along the sides but in perfect condition and not yet near spawning.

That fish—why he should have been red I don't know—was
the first of one of the finest winter runs I have ever seen in the
Campbell. Another friend, also on a short leave, came up on
December thirtieth. The river was high from snow that had
melted, but the weather had turned suddenly to a hard gray
coldness that drew the rise down almost as one watched. On
the last day of the old year we went out to the Sandy Pool because it seemed that the water would still be too high at the
Island Pools. The head of the pool was blank, though we tried
it with minnow and prawn as well as the fly. Then Tommy
caught a good, bright fish just above the big rocks. Following
him down, I picked up a second one, and we decided to have
lunch. It was cold, and the fish had been very good, quick and
strong and full of fight, so we almost decided that we had
had all we deserved. But there was good Canadian rye in
Tommy's flask, and the river looked promising again when
we had finished it, so we went to look for more fish.

I turned away to the head of the pool and left Tommy at the
rocks. I saw his rod bend as I made my first cast and knew
from the way he held that a strong fish was going away from
him clear across the river. The fish jumped, big and silver, right
out against the face of the far bank, and I started down. When
I got there, Tommy was still holding, standing in water that

touched the very tops of his wading stockings, and with the
fish a full hundred yards downstream. Through long minutes
Tommy strained and lifted to recover line (it was impossible
to follow farther), and at last I went down in my high waders
to look for a chance to set the gaff. But the fish would not
come in, and the fight had to be fought out; so Tommy fought
it, and slowly the fish came back, making run after run, but
checked shorter each time. Once or twice he came in sight,
and I got the gaff ready, but each time he fought away again.
Then suddenly he was straight upstream from me, still head
down and strong, but in water I could almost reach. I saw
Tommy's rod jump back and the line come away. The fish
was four or five feet away from me, holding quite still against
the current, not yet aware of his freedom. I reached forward,
brought the little gaff across in a backhand stroke, felt it set
solidly and lifted him out. The hook had broken cleanly away
from the wire of the flight; the eye of one of the swivels, we
found later, had pulled out until it was held by only a single
turn of soft brass wire. He was a very unlucky fish; but he
weighed fourteen pounds, and the sharp lines of sea color were
silver and steel gray against the snow when we laid him down
to look at him.

By January second the cold weather had brought the river
well down, and we went up to try the Island Pools. I was
hopeful of the lower pool because it holds so surely when a
new run is in, but we found another fisherman there. He had,
he told us, already lost three fish. As we watched he hooked
a fourth and killed him. The main pool was too high for
Tommy's short waders, but I knew the man who was in the
pool ahead of us and knew that he always missed the head of
the lower pool. So I told Tommy to start in well up, and he
came into a good fish on the first cast and killed it. That made
five fish hooked in an hour or two in one little pool not more
than thirty yards long. I went up to the main pool and began
to fish it down with a fly. A big cutthroat took hold, and I

saw Tommy hook another fish in the lower pool. I turned my cutthroat back and fished on. About halfway down the pool and well across, a good fish came to me. He took well up in the water, at the start of the fly's swing, and broke heavily without jumping. For thirty or forty seconds he seemed slow and quiet, then he began to run. I checked him hard, but he had his head downstream and all his strength still with him, so I had to follow, stumbling over big round boulders in deep water. Just beyond the tail of the pool, in the fastest water of the rapid below, he checked and held.

I went down to him and waded out into the strong water. He was a clean fish, bluish and shadowy under the smooth surface tension of the heavy water, and he seemed to hold there without effort. I worked slowly out to him, but the gaff was too short to reach him; and when I tried to draw him to it, the current caught his side and swept him down. Three times I tried; three times I watched him there, and the shape and color of him under the water were so beautiful that I knew I wouldn't want to set the gaff, even if I could reach him. After the third failure he was in deeper and stronger water than ever, so I lifted hard and tumbled him on down, steering him among the big rocks and white water toward the lower pool. He tumbled beautifully, jumping twice to show he was still strong, and as he reached the quiet water of the lower pool, the fly came away.

Tommy had come up to me while I was still reaching with the gaff. He had lost two good fish in the lower pool, and the other fisherman had lost a third—eight fish in all.

"We should have let you take the fly down before we spoiled it with the minnow and prawn," Tommy said.

But I took the fly down anyway and hooked my fish at the tail—a thirteen-pounder. So the old year ended and the new year began with winter steelhead, the fish that brings life back to the rivers after the salmon have died in November and left their eggs to develop under the gravel.

FISHING BOOKS

I HAVE written this book simply to define and pass on some of the pleasure I have had from fishing. It was the idea of the many friends and acquaintances who have repeatedly asked me, "Why don't you tell about things that have happened when you've been fishing? Forget all the scientific angle for once and give us screaming reels and fighting monsters and all that stuff." I should fall down badly on the job and prove myself mighty ungrateful if I said nothing of the hours and hours of strongest pleasure I have had from other men's writing about fish and fishing.

There are fishing books almost without number, and more books about fly-fishing than about any other branch of the sport. Angling, we have it on the best of all authorities, is the contemplative man's recreation, and contemplative men are naturally inclined to recollect emotion in tranquillity. From there to writing of the emotions and their causes is a short step. Anglers of all kinds, good, bad and indifferent, jump to the pen and slam down their recollections. Rather more often than one would expect, the books turn out well; and over the centuries anglers have written a fair number of books about their sport that are properly classed as good literature.

These books—Juliana's *Treatise*, *The Compleat Angler* of Walton and Cotton, Scrope's *Days and Nights of Salmon Fishing*, Grey's *Flyfishing*, to name only a few of the more widely recognized—stand far out from the general run of fishing books and have their place in every angler's library. But there is a lot of good writing in lesser books than these, and there is a tremendous amount of good technical writing which, though without literary pretensions, has done much to develop the sport and so has its place on the shelves.

At first thought it seems easy to separate fishing books into two groups, technical and nontechnical; then, perhaps, to separate them again into two more groups, those that deal mainly with fishing and those that deal mainly with fish or entomology or some other subject directly related to fishing. None of these divisions is really satisfactory because there is a great deal of overlapping: any discussion of the subject that is at all thorough necessarily includes some natural history; any technical discussion includes a generous number of descriptive examples; and the nontechnical writers are always drawn into technical detail somewhere along the line.

There is one division, possibly even harder to make, that appeals strongly to me. It applies better to books on fly-fishing than to the literature of general angling; but fly-fishing books are the vast majority, and much of the best writing is in them. This is the division between books that have made definite and permanent contribution to the development of fly-fishing technique and the great mass of others that have no such intention or else have not made the grade. For my own purposes I call books of this first group "the framework," and copies of them, I think, should form the base of any fly-fisherman's library. Not to read them and own them is to miss much of the meaning of fly-fishing.

Dame Juliana Berners's *Treatise of Fishing with an Angle* is the first book on fishing in the English language and also the first book on fly-fishing. According to the experts, it was probably not written by Dame Juliana and it was probably in being for nearly a hundred years before 1496, the date of the first printing. Certainly it is a vastly more extensive, thorough and accurate treatise than one has a right to expect of a first effort to deal with any subject. Whoever wrote the book was writing of a sport already well developed and had access to the collective experience of many other men. The book, as

Hills points out in his *History of Flyfishing*, also follows the pattern set for British sporting books by Edward Duke of York in *The Master of Game*, and in its own turn has influenced the shape of almost all subsequent fishing books: Juliana compares her sport to other similar sports, much to its own advantage, develops its delights and the virtues it breeds in men, moves from there to her technical information, then turns again at the end to redefine and emphasize her first point in the light of her readers' grown knowledge of the subject. Any reader of fishing books will recognize the sequence.

The *Treatise* is an important book to own and is an easy book to own, for there are several reasonably priced editions. My own is a facsimile of the 1496 edition, published in 1880, a pretty book and not at all an expensive one. I find it fairly difficult to read the black letter and my mind solves the archaic spelling slowly, but these delays give me a greater love of the book and force its sparing and beautiful descriptive words hard upon me; each seems only the richer for its unfamiliar shape.

From Juliana, passing Leonard Mascall in 1590, and Gervase Markham in 1614, one comes to Walton in 1653 and Cotton in 1676. Of the two, Cotton is vastly more important to fly-fishermen and I prefer his book, the second part of the *Complete Angler*. It is a warmer, neater book than Walton's, and the love of a single country and the knowledge of a single river flow all through it. Cotton seems less didactic than Walton, and his relationship with his pupil is somehow happier. I love Cotton's book with a deep love and I love it in the favorite of several editions I own, Major's fourth, a polished and pretty book with engravings and cuts that fit the text as the text itself fits the Derbyshire Dove.

Cotton wrote so thoroughly and so well that it is a long step to the next joint in the framework. There are books between that I own and value—Gay's *Rural Sports*, Bowlker's *Art of Angling*, with the first good plate of flies, Humphry Davy's

Salmonia, but it was Pulman in 1841 who advanced the sport to a point far beyond anything Cotton knew. Pulman's *Vade Mecum of Flyfishing* is a tiny volume, slim and not too well printed on indifferent paper for a list of West Country subscribers, but it is the first book that sets forth clearly and unequivocally the basis of modern dry-fly technique, an upstream cast and the drift of a floating fly to a rising trout. I have a copy of the 1841 Pulman and I treasure it as a great responsibility. It came to me rather strangely while I was still in my teens. My grandfather called me into his study one evening and, after a lengthy and grandfatherly lecture on some quite unrelated subject, drew the little, brown, dusty Pulman from a bookcase and gave it to me. To him it was just a fishing book that he happened to have come across, and to me it was not very important alongside the showier modern books I had. But I kept it carefully because I was somehow proud that the old man had chosen me for the gift instead of one of his many fishing sons and friends; and now that I have learned its value, I read it and handle it with reverence both for the man who wrote it and for the man who gave it.

To complete Pulman in the framework it is necessary to own also the 1851 edition, which I do not. In this third edition of his book, Pulman gives an account of false casting to dry the fly and so discovers all the simple mechanics of the method. It seems a little strange that a Devonshire man, fishing Devonshire streams, should have been the first to put down on paper the fishing method that reached the flower of its development and use on the very different streams of Hampshire. Even now, when its use has spread round the world, the dry fly is probably less commonly used in Devonshire than in the west. But there is no possible doubt as to Pulman's claim, and there is little or nothing to show exactly how or where he first learned or developed for himself the technique he describes.

Juliana and Cotton were their own entomologists, but in 1836, just before Pulman, Ronalds wrote a real angler's entomology which held its place for nearly a hundred years. *The Flyfisher's Entomology* is still a good book on the subject, and again it is an easy book to own, having passed through many editions. My copy is the fourth edition, 1849, and the plates in it, of flies both natural and artificial, are more beautiful than any others I know, except possibly those in Preston Jennings's *Book of Trout Flies*, which was published by the Derrydale Press in New York a few years ago. Ronalds put all fly-fishermen deeply in his debt, for he gave them a truer and better understanding of their subject and he laid the foundation of all the great development that came within the two or three decades around the turn of the nineteenth century. His entomology is supplanted now by others more modern, but no fly-fisherman's library can ever be really complete without it.

Through the middle of the nineteenth century there were great stirrings. Charles Kingsley wrote then, and William Scrope and Francis Francis and Stoddart and Theackston and Stewart. Of all these, Stewart is greatly important for his insistence on upstream technique and his exact description of it. But one works inevitably forward to Halford in 1886 and the start of the golden age of technique. Halford, far more than any other man, developed and established the dry fly. He was a pedestrian writer, but his books are complete and clear and unbelievably thorough. Halford left nothing to chance, and one cannot escape him. I own only *The Dryfly Man's Handbook*, which I think is the most useful of the three or four I know, and mine is a worn copy, for it is the one that my Uncle Decie sent me in the same package with my first double-tapered line. I would almost as soon lose Pulman as lose that copy of the *Handbook*. While Halford was still writing, winning the world of fly-fishermen from wet fly to dry, Skues boldly produced *Minor Tactics of the Chalkstream* to win them back to proper use of the wet fly as well as the dry. *Minor Tactics* and *The Way of a Trout with a Fly* are both great books. It is impossible for a keen fly-fisherman not to be won by Skues. For several years before I discovered *Minor Tactics* I had fished the halfstone and tup's indispensable, lightly dressed and well wetted, upstream to bulging trout with deadliest effect. I called it to myself, defensively, "fishing the drowned dry fly." Then I read *Minor Tactics* and saw that Skues had set down all the attractive delicacy of the method, establishing the art with a wealth of beautiful argument. Nymph-fishing has a place anywhere, if only for the intensity of pleasure there is in tightening surely upon the fish's unseen move to the submerged fly.

Beyond Skues the framework has one more beam that I can clearly recognize as belonging—the greased-line method developed by the late A. H. E. Wood and recorded by Jock Scott in *Greased Line Fishing for Salmon.* Jock Scott's book is good, and the usefulness of the method goes far beyond the catching of Atlantic salmon; it is deadly for our western steelhead in low water and often deadly for difficult trout in almost any water. The principle of the mend is even useful in fishing the deep-sunk wet fly, since one can always make at least one mend as the line goes out on the water and so get the fly well down before the current begins to lift the line.

In North America Hewitt has given us dry-fly fishing for salmon in *Secrets of the Salmon*, and La Branche has written *The Dry Fly and Fast Water*, a title that explains itself. La Branche's book has done great things for the Pacific west, where most streams are fast and the dry fly was once but little used. And the west has contributed its own share in the bravely floating deer-hair flies of the Mackenzie and other rivers. I often fish dry now over water that I considered only fit for the wet fly a few years ago—strong, broken, leaping waves of heavy current that can only be reached from an upstream stance. I throw out my deer-hair pattern on a slack line, drift it down, draw it back in a dance from wave top to wave top, laugh for joy as a three-pound cutthroat leaps clear out over

it, draw it up a yard more, then slack it down to him and
strike to the solid rise. It is great fishing.

This, then, is the framework of technique. There is more
to it, much more—fly tying, for instance. Nearly all the books
of the framework give fly dressings, and several of them,
notably Charles Cotton's, describe exactly how one must go
about building a fly on a bare hook. Skues describes the dressing of his nymphs and other sunken flies. Jock Scott gives the
dressings of the favorite greased-line patterns. J. W. Dunne, in
Sunshine and the Dry Fly, has thoroughly explored the eternal
problem of a complete series for the English chalk streams and
has gone far toward imitating by illusion the translucency of
a May fly's body. But of all books that deal solely or princi-
pally with fly tying, three stand out: H. C. McLelland on the
dry fly, J. H. Hale on the salmon fly and Pryce Tannat's *How
to Dress Salmon Flies*. Of the three, the last is my favorite;
from it the clumsiest fingers can learn to tie a neat and handsome fly, and the least imaginative mind can realize the high
joys of craftsmanship that are to be found in the traditional
and complicated dressings of favorite salmon patterns. In
North America there is a whole new field for the fly dresser,
and Preston Jennings has started work in the east. His *Book
of Trout Flies* sets a high standard, and his constant encouragement to fly-fishermen all over the continent must surely bring
forth another book—I hope a western book—to match it before
very long.

The technical books, all the books in the framework, are
good and important. One loves many of them—some because
they are truly fine books, some for what they teach, some for
the achievement they represent. But there is a vast body of
books that have no place in the framework and which are not
exclusively, if at all, concerned with the technique of fly-fishing. I like to divide these into two classes, scientific and literary.
To the scientific books, those dealing with ichthyology, entomology and all the manifold phases of aquatic life, I owe

a deep debt. Through them I have explored a thousand mysteries and known many pleasures that would otherwise have been shut off from me or far less keenly felt.

One of the earliest of the scientific books, which I have never seen but mean to own one day, is John Taverner's *Certaine Experiments concerning Fish and Fruite*. Taverner, writing in 1600, used the lovely English of his time, clear and graceful and telling, and he knew the natural history of both fish and aquatic insects in a way that no other writer seemed to know them until two or more centuries later. He wrote his observations unpretentiously and they stand out vividly from the page in accuracy that seems prophetic, so little does it fit with the knowledge and thought of his time.

I like Cotton's natural history. He is often wrong, but he is reaching for something, setting down what he has seen as accurately as his brain can interpret the record his eyes have made on it. Knowledge of aquatic life grew slowly after him. Ronalds, a century and a half later, made the first great advance, and after Ronalds and Pictet, the great Swiss entomologist, angling writers did well by the insect life on which their sport depends. But the twentieth century is the time of true development, not only in entomology, but in all underwater knowledge. In the first forty years of it scientists have disclosed a pattern of underwater living that was scarcely even guessed at before.

It is hard to pick from among the great names. I think of Hutton in England and still bitterly regret that my copy of his beautiful *Life History of the Salmon* disappeared so many years ago. I think of Calderwood and Menzies, of Herbert Maxwell and Malloch and Tate Regan. Malloch's *Salmon, Sea Trout and Other Freshwater Fish*, published in 1910, is a collection of photographs clearer and more revealing than any other I know. It would be well if someone would use the improved technique and improved cameras of today to make another such collection. Francis Ward also used the camera well in his *Marvels of Fish Life* and *Animal Life under Water*, and he rendered untold service to all of us by showing more clearly than anyone else what a fish probably sees and how he sees it.

The list of Canadian and American scientists to whom I—and other fishermen with me—owe deep gratitude is almost without end: to Jordan and Evermann perhaps first of all, because they have set out in a clear reference book the identification and life histories of so many North American fish. The Needhams, father and son, have done much for anglers. I value my copy of J. R. Needham's *Life of Inland Waters* for its ready information on such matters as diatoms and algae and plankton of all kinds, and for its simple treatment of all types of stream and pond life. Paul Needham's *Trout Streams* is more directly for the angler and sets forth many principles of conservation that all fishermen should know.

But the greatest wealth of information is in scientific papers, numberless papers that are often dull and difficult, but whose sum is astounding revelation. I have a filing cabinet full of them, some scarcely opened, others thumbed and tattered with use. Many of those that I know well I love deeply, and the sight of them lying on my desk or about the room brings a glow of satisfaction into me, almost as warm as that which comes from handling Major's *Complete Angler* or J. W. Hills's beautiful *A Summer on the Test*. The names of the writers are legion: our own Canadians, Clemens and Foerster and Pritchard, Mottley, Tester, Tully, Huntsman and Belding; many great Americans, Gilbert, Rich, Davidson, Craig, Holmes, Cobb, the Needhams again. Any paper by such men as these is a promise of revelation, perhaps only some little step forward toward truer and fuller knowledge, perhaps a giant step, such as that made by Foerster in his studies of the sockeye salmon at Cultus Lake or that by Hobbs in his work on salmon and trout in New Zealand. Scientific papers are the bare bones of natural history, but it is the prerogative of an angler's imagination to cover them with the flesh of his experience and so give them life.

I have said that the fishing books do not separate easily into groups. Some teach and are full of good, even great, writing; others teach awkwardly and painfully, but importantly; many do not teach at all, yet make hard reading, and others which do not aim to teach may have in them a clear expression of some point that one can apply directly by the waterside at a later time. Most fishing books try to tell something that is new, try to share easily some knowledge that has come only slowly to their authors. But one reads fishing books mainly for pleasure, for their touching of the mind that brings the life of the rivers and lakes and seas and meadows into a quiet, warm, lamplit room.

It is good to read the old writers and to feel with them across the centuries the community of interest that is true friendship. If the copy one has is an early edition, well read, one feels the minds and hands of the others who have read it linking one with the original time, and it is good to wonder about their thoughts as they read. Anglers read and write as no other sportsmen do; they are contemplative, as Master Walton has said, yet perhaps more aggressively intellectual than that simple statement would argue. They probe into their sport, all angles and implications of it, mechanical, natural, aesthetic and sensual. And in their probings they become argumentative, at times downright contentious.

I like David Webster for his individuality and his contentiousness. He published *The Angler and the Loop Rod* in 1885, just a year before Halford's first book, and he was still using, and violently arguing for, the tapered horsehair line that Charles Cotton used. Webster is a really fine example of a contentious writer. He tears Pennell mercilessly apart for recommending the downstream wet fly, for denying exact imitation, for disregarding the size of flies, for half a dozen different reasons. He leaves Captain Dick battered and bruised and even handles roughly such names as Francis Francis and Ronalds because they dare to write of the merits and beauty of the grayling. But one is bound to like his book because he is such a formidable fisherman and usually so right in his observations. He recognized the nymphal stage of aquatic flies and was one of the first to feel for imitation of it. It would have been an experience to have fished with Webster, perhaps a trying one at times, but always a rich one.

There are many gentle fishing writers one must love. Walton perhaps first of all, but William Senior, H. T. Sheringham of *The Field*, R. B. Marston of *The Fishing Gazette*, Lord Grey, Chaytor and Buckland were all lovable men who wrote well in quiet and satisfying prose of what they had seen and known. Henry Williamson's *Salar* and *Tarka* are great books of purest entertainment for any man who loves rivers. Patrick Chalmers writes easily and lovingly of all English waters and fishing ways. Eugene Connett's *Any Luck?* is one of the happiest fishing books there is.

One could draw the list on and on; it is almost endless, for fishing books number far up in the thousands, and few are without pages to fit an evening mood. Think of two contrasting Americans, Ray Bergman and John Taintor Foote, the one at pains to describe and explain and instruct, the other determined only to entertain. Match these to the scholarly Radcliffe's *Fishing from the Earliest Times* and Buchan's thrilling *John McNab*. It is a tremendous range within a single subject, and one has to call favorites at last. Good men have written good books on fishing here, there and everywhere; but for some reason the chalk streams of England, of Hampshire particularly, seem to have inspired the finest fishing writing.

Charles Kingsley wrote of the chalk streams aggressively, yet lovingly and well. Lord Grey's book is as smooth and rich and beautiful as the Hampshire meadows themselves. Plunket Greene, the singer, thought of the beautiful title *Where the Bright Waters Meet* and wrote a laughing, happy book to match it, a strangely simple and unspoiled book through which a calm, free voice sings of the little Bourne and of greater rivers as well.

J. W. Hills I came upon almost by chance. I bought his handsomely produced *Summer on the Test* for the twelve Norman Wilkinson etchings, sat down with it one evening and knew that I had bought myself a book as well as a series of etchings. I read through it almost grudgingly, turning the big, thick pages slowly, loving the heavy black print against the white paper, loving the words that grew up from it to me. It was a rich and luxurious experience, passed over for the first time all too quickly in spite of my caution.

Hills, I found, had written other books: the *Golden River*, which tells of fishing in Paraguay; *River Keeper*, which tells the story of Alfred Lunn, the great self-taught scientist who was keeper on the Houghton Club water at Stockbridge. One of his best and most useful books, *A History of Fly Fishing for Trout*, I have already quoted in this chapter; in fact, without having read it, I should never have written a chapter just like this. I have explored fishing books from childhood, gathered a library of them about me, marked special desires in secondhand catalogues, poked about among dusty shelves in the dim light of secondhand bookshops in a dozen or more cities; but until I came upon Hills's *History*, I had no really clear picture in my mind of the steady thread of development that runs through fishing literature.

Hills had every quality a fishing writer should have. He was, quite evidently, a fine practical fisherman. He was very well read, and not only in fishing literature. He had a deep appreciation of everything that goes with fishing—rivers and weed, meadows and trees and sunlight, natural flies and their imitations; all the life of the waterside, bird or wild beast or tame beast. He took all of these things as they came and wrote of them as they are, and he wrote beautifully, in simple words that clearly reveal how much a highly civilized man can find in the sport.

It has often been said that too many books have been written about fishing. Undoubtedly there are fishing books in print that might better have been left in manuscript or, better still, tucked away in the secret minds of their authors. But that is equally true of all branches of literature. North American fishing literature, I am quite sure, is altogether inadequate. I remember coming out west some twenty years ago to all this wonderful coast country of rivers and lakes and salt water. I knew nothing of the fishing, except that there was plenty of it and it was good, so I hunted the bookstores for something that would guide me. I found Cobb's excellent *Pacific Salmon Fisheries*, one or two eastern books, dated in the distant past, and an inept guide to the waters of Washington, prepared for the casual tourist fisherman. In the same bookstores now one will normally find a dozen or more recent titles, at least some of them dealing with western fish and fishing. But I feel sure that the many millions of American and Canadian fishermen would welcome far more than this, and I think that in time North America is bound to build for itself a fishing literature in every way comparable to that of the British Isles. I hope I shall live to read and recognize a good solid part of it.

TO KNOW A RIVER ...

I HAVE written in this book nearly always of rivers—occasionally of lakes or the salt water, but nearly always of rivers and river fishing. A river is water in its loveliest form; rivers have life and sound and movement and infinity of variation, rivers are veins of the earth through which the life blood returns to the heart. Rivers can attain

overwhelming grandeur, as the Columbia does in the reaches
all the way from Pasco to the sea; they may slide softly through
flat meadows or batter their way down mountain slopes and
through narrow canyons; they may be heavy, almost dark,
with history, as the Thames is from its mouth at least up to
Richmond; or they may be sparkling fresh on mountain slopes
through virgin forest and alpine meadows.

Lakes and the sea have great secret depths quite hidden from
man and often almost barren of life. A river too may have its
deep and secret places, may be so large that one can never
know it properly; but most rivers that give sport to fly-fishermen are comparatively small, and one feels that it is within the
range of the mind to know them intimately—intimately as to
their changes through the seasons, as to the shifts and quirks of
current, the sharp runs, the slow glides, the eddies and bars
and crossing places, the very rocks of the bottom. And in
knowing a river intimately is a very large part of the joy of fly-
fishing.

One may love a river as soon as one sets eyes upon it; it may
have certain features that fit instantly with one's conception
of beauty, or it may recall the qualities of some other river,
well known and deeply loved. One may feel in the same way
an instant affinity for a man or a woman and know that here
is pleasure and warmth and the foundation of deep friendship.
In either case the full riches of the discovery are not immediately released—they cannot be; only knowledge and close experience can release them. Rivers, I suppose, are not at all like
human beings, but it is still possible to make apt comparisons;
and this is one: understanding, whether instinctive and immediate or developing naturally through time or grown by
conscious effort, is a necessary preliminary to love. Under-
standing of another human being can never be complete, but
as it grows toward completeness, it becomes love almost inevitably. One cannot know intimately all the ways and movements of a river without growing into love of it. And there

December

is no exhaustion to the growth of love through knowledge, whether the love be for a person or a river, because the knowledge can never become complete. One can come to feel in time that the whole is within one's compass, not yet wholly and intimately known, but there for the knowing, within the last little move of reaching; but there will always be something ahead, something more to know.

I have known very few rivers thoroughly and intimately. There is not time to know many, and one can know only certain chosen lengths of the few. I know some miles of the Dorsetshire Frome and of the little river Wrackle that cuts away from the Frome by Stratton Mill and rejoins it farther down, because I grew up with them and had all the quick instinctive learning power of the very young when I fished there. It was a happy and proud thing to know those streams, and the knowing paid great dividends in fish; it paid even greater dividends in something that I can still recapture—sheer happiness in remembering a bend or a run or the spread below a bridge as I saw them best, perhaps open in sunlight with the green weeds trailing and a good fish rising steadily, or perhaps pitted by rain under a gray sky, or white and black and golden, opaque in the long slant of the twilight. I knew those streams through fishing them, through cutting the weeds in them, through shooting ducks and snipe all along them, through setting night lines in them, through exploring them when the hatches were down and the water was very low. I carry them with me wherever I go and can fish them almost as well sitting here as I could were I walking the meadow grass along their banks six thousand miles from here.

I learned other waters almost as easily, though more superficially, when I was very young. The lower reaches of the Frome, between Wool and Wareham, where we used to fish for salmon, were harder to know than the best of the trout water because the river was deeper and darker and slower down there, more secret within itself. But I fished with a man who knew all the secrets, and we used the prawn a lot, fishing it deep down and slow, close to bottom and close under the banks. Fish lay where he said they should lie and took hold as he said they would take, and one remembered and fished it that way for oneself until the knowledge was properly one's own. I think I could still start at Bindon Mill and work on all the way down to the Salmon Water without missing so very many of the good places. And then, perhaps, I could walk back along the railroad track toward evening with a decent weight of salmon on my back.

I knew the little length of narrow carrier in Lewington's field by the bakery at Headbourne Worthy; it was so small and clear that one couldn't help knowing it and so difficult that one had to know it. I knew where each fish lay and why, how he would rise and when, what chance of ground would hide me during the cast, what tuft of grass would probably catch my fly on each attempted recovery. And Denis and I knew the narrow part of Avington Lake where the great pike lay under the shadow of the rank weeds; we knew the schools of roach and rudd and the few solitary trout; we had seen the big carp and the slow black tench; we knew, almost, where each little one- or two-pound pike had his hunting ground.

The winter days at Avington, under the tall bare beeches and ashes and sycamores, were very good. There were always mallard to be seen in hundreds, always herons, sometimes a peregrine falcon chasing the mallards; the cock pheasants were richer, burnished gold against the gold of fallen beech leaves, and rabbits sometimes rustled the leaves softly, unaware that we were fishing near them. The rank thick weed banks of the bottom showed clearly, green through the shallow water of the narrow part of the lake. We cast our big spoons and phantoms and wagtails far out, letting them into the unrippled water as gently as we could, then brought them twinkling back over the dark mystery of the weed beds. Sometimes a big pike was lying out over the weeds, and we tried and tried to tempt him. Sometimes one appeared suddenly behind the spoon, followed it and took or turned away. Sometimes—and this was best and surest of all—there was a heavy flash and a swirl as the spoon passed over a known lie, then the pull and the lunging fight.

The first western river I learned was the Nimpkish, the seven twisting miles of it that lie between the lake and the sea. I learned the best of the trout pools first, wading the round and slippery rocks in an old pair of calked shoes, letting the swift water climb up to the pockets of my shirt and sometimes letting it knock me down and carry me half the length of a pool before I could find a way out of it. Then I learned the tyee pools and the cutthroat trout runs of the tidal reaches. Taking the canoe up to go over the traps, lining the big skiff through to the lake, fishing for steelhead, watching the salmon runs, I learned more of it and felt it my own. But I never really knew the river as one can know a river. I don't know, even today, just how and when the steelhead run there, nor more than a fraction of their lying places. And I never could solve the secrets of Ned's Canyon and Wright's Canyon or that third one of the long, slow, deep pools on the river; they were so big, and I knew so many other places to catch fish that it was hard to give them time. But I once wrote a book that had the Nimpkish for a heroine and I saw and learned so much of her for myself through five or six years that I feel my faulty knowledge has given me a full love of her. Whenever I think of a western fishing river, one typical of all the best things that western fishing can offer, I think of the Nimpkish; and I expect I always shall.

The Campbell I know almost as a man should know a river. I don't know the whole story, or anything like the whole story; but the outlines of plot and characterization are clear and definite, much of the detail is filled in and each new detail fits neatly into an appointed place as I learn it. The Campbell is a little like the Nimpkish, yet most unlike it. Both rivers are broad and clear and swift, with broken, white water, rare,

smooth pools and rocky beds. But the Campbell runs only
three or four miles to salt water from the foot of its great Elk
Falls, beyond which salmon and steelhead and cutthroat trout
from the sea cannot pass. The Nimpkish is a highway to all the
miles of Nimpkish Lake and the Kla-anche River and Woss
Lake, to the Hustan River and the chain of lakes beyond that,
and to all the tributary streams of the watershed. The Campbell draws to itself a noble run of winter steelhead, a run of
fine cutthroats, a queer little run of small summer steelheads;
it has its great tyees, its dying run of humpbacks, a fair run of
cohos and dogs in some years, but no more than an occasional
sockeye, probably a stray from some other parent stream. The
Nimpkish has all the runs that the Campbell has in fullest
strength and adds to them a fine run of true summer steelheads,
a wonderful sockeye run and a fabulous dog-salmon run. The
Campbell is the simpler river of the two, easier to know and
understand for all those reasons. Nimpkish is more wonderful,
more impressive, more beautiful; but Campbell—and not simply
because I live within sight and sound of her—is the better of
the two to love.

I can mark the months on the Campbell and tell myself, at
least to my own satisfaction, what will be happening in the
river during each one of them: In January the steelhead are
running well; in February the cutthroats are spawning; in
March and April the winter steelheads spawn; in May the little
summer steelhead should be in the Island Pools, most of the
humpback fry will already have found their way to the sea and
the flying ants will hatch out; in August it is time to go to the
Canyon Pool and look for the big cutthroats; in September the
tyees are in the river; during October the cohos will come; in
December the steelhead again. I know the May-fly and stone-
fly nymphs that I will find under the rocks and the caddises
that will crawl over the bottom in the different months; I know
the rocks that the net-winged midges will blacken with their
tiny cases, the places where the bright-green cladophora will

grow richly, and where and when the rocks will be slippery with brown diatom growth. Some of these things, perhaps, are not important to know if one only wishes to catch fish; but they have their part in the pleasure of fishing.

I find I am quite often wrong about the Campbell even now. I may say that it is too early for the fish to be in, then go up and find them there. I can't always judge when the freshets are coming, but that, perhaps, is no more than saying I'm not an infallible weather prophet. Perhaps it is truer to say that I often find new things about the river than that I am often wrong about her; and sometimes I suddenly realize things that I have known for quite a long time almost unconsciously. It is years, for instance, since I first knew that I could kill fish well in August with the fly I call the "Silver Brown." I tied the fly to imitate coho fry, which are the only numerous salmon fry in that month. In spring, when the river is full of many kinds of fry, the Silver Brown does not do so well for me, and I use the Silver Lady, which has a paler wing and a more complicated tying. I changed over with comparatively little thought, and the true inference of the change only came to me this year —trout may at times feed rather selectively on fry of different species.

Apart from bullheads and sticklebacks, one can expect some five or six different species of fry in the Campbell. Cutthroat fry and coho fry are so much alike that no sensible fish would bother to distinguish between them; it is reasonable to use the Silver Brown as an imitation of both. But humpback fry are like no other fry, trout or salmon; they are, for instance, quite without parr marks, their bellies are brightest silver, their backs generally bluish. I remember that I have fished a fly with long blue hackles for wings and often killed well with it during the humpback run. From there it is only a step to the making of a special humpback imitation; I think I shall start with something of this sort: tail—green swan, body—flat silver tinsel, hackle—scarlet and quite small, wing—blue hackles, back to back, enclosing a white strip and perhaps a strand or two of blue herl, cheeks—pale-blue chatterer. When I fish the river again in springtime, I shall use that fly.

If a coho-cutthroat imitation and a humpback imitation, why not imitations of the others in their days and seasons? The Silver Lady, perhaps, is sufficiently like spring salmon and steelhead fry. Yet the spring salmon fry has a light brown in his back and an impression of palest pink about him which the steelhead fry has not. It might make all the difference one day. So I shall build a fly with a tail of pink swan, a silver body and wings of barred summer duck enclosing yellow swan; and if that isn't good, I shall try grizzled hackles, preferably from a Plymouth cock with a touch of Red Game in him, set back to back with light-red hackles between them.

None of that is desperately important or highly significant, and I suppose I should feel ashamed of having waited ten or fifteen years to think of it. What I really feel is a good measure of gratitude to the Campbell for having at last brought home to me the rather obvious point that, if it is worth trying for exact imitation of sedges and May flies, it is worth trying for reasonably exact imitations of salmon and trout fry. In time I shall think of dressings for the green color that is dominant in the backs of dog-salmon fry and the olive–grass green of the young sockeye's back. I may catch very few more fish through my efforts than I should have caught without them, but it's going to be fun.

I fish the Campbell with a sense of ownership fully as strong as that of any legitimate owner of fishing rights in the world, not because I do own any part of the river, nor even because I should like to or should like to keep other people away from it; I should not care to do either of these things. The sense of ownership grows simply from knowing the river. I know the easiest ways along the banks and the best ways down to the pools. I know where to start in at a pool, where to look for the fish in it, how and where I can wade, what point I can reach with an easy cast, what lie I can barely cover with my strongest effort. This is comfortable and pleasant and might well begin to seem monotonous sooner or later were it not something of an illusion. I have a fair idea of what to expect from the river, and usually, because I fish it that way, the river gives me approximately what I expect of it. But sooner or later something always comes up to change the set of my ways. Perhaps one day, waiting for a friend to fish down a pool, I start in a little farther up than usual and immediately hook a fish where I had never been able to hook one before. A little more of the river becomes mine, alive and productive to me. Or perhaps I notice in some unusual slant of light what looks to be a glide of water along the edge of a rapid; I go down to it and work my fly through, and whether or not a fish comes to it, more of the river is known and mine.

For years I have promised myself to fish through the sort of half pool below the Sandy Pool. It starts almost opposite my own line fence and is little more than a smoothing off of the long rapid that runs right down to the Highway Bridge; but there are many big rocks in it and—I can say this now—some obvious holding water. I fished it twice this spring. On the first evening I caught two or three fair-sized cutthroats, and once a really good fish broke water at the fly. I went down earlier on the second evening. A three-pound cutthroat came to my first cast. There was a slow silver gleam as the fly came around on the second cast, a solid heavy pull and the 2X gut was broken. I put up heavier gut and hooked a clean steelhead that ran me almost to the end of the backing. I hooked two others along the pool that evening, both of them too close to their spawning; but the pool is the Line Fence Pool now, something so close to home and so obvious that I took ten years to learn about it, a discovery as well worth while as any I have ever made.

One discovers other things than new pools and new fish lies in old pools. One learns to mark one's casts by such things as the kidney stones and the flat rock in General Money's Pool in the Stamp, one learns to hope for the sight of a pileated wood-pecker crossing the river in swooping flight at this place, a flock of mergansers at that place, a dipper against black rocks and rippled water somewhere else, deer coming down to eat the moss on the rocks at the water's edge in hard weather. All these things are precious in repetition and, repeated or no, they build the river for one. They are part of the background of knowing and loving it, as is every fish hooked, every cast fished through, every rock trodden. And men and women come strongly into it. Here, I can remind myself, was where Ann sat that first day we came up the river together, and here it was that she loved the September sun the year before Valerie was born. Here we stopped and Letcher made us an old-fashioned before we went on to the Canyon Pool that day. Here Buckie brought his first fish to the bank, here I gaffed Sandy's first steelhead for him, here Tommy hooked one last winter, there it was that the big fish took Reg's line across the roots of the cedar tree. . . .

I still don't know why I fish or why other men fish, except that we like it and it makes us think and feel. But I do know that if it were not for the strong, quick life of rivers, for their sparkle in the sunshine, for the cold grayness of them under rain and the feel of them about my legs as I set my feet hard down on rocks or sand or gravel, I should fish less often. A river is never quite silent; it can never, of its very nature, be quite still; it is never quite the same from one day to the next. It has its own life and its own beauty, and the creatures it nourishes are alive and beautiful also. Perhaps fishing is, for me, only an excuse to be near rivers. If so, I'm glad I thought of it.